The Grads Are Playing Tonight!

THE GRADS ARE
PLAYING

COMMERCIAL GRADUATES BASKETBALL CLUB
OF EDMONTON ALBERTA
AT TORONTO ONTARIO APRIL 1926
CANADIAN CHAMPIONS

PHOTO RIGGS
PANORAMIC CAMERA CO
251 VICTORIA ST TORONTO

TONIGHT!

The Story of the Edmonton Commercial Graduates Basketball Club

M. ANN HALL

THE UNIVERSITY OF ALBERTA PRESS

Published by

The University of Alberta Press
Ring House 2
Edmonton, Alberta, Canada   T6G 2E1
www.uap.ualberta.ca

LIBRARY AND ARCHIVES CANADA CATALOGUING IN PUBLICATION

Hall, M. Ann (Margaret Ann), 1942–
    The Grads are playing tonight! : the story of the Edmonton Commercial Graduates Basketball Club / M. Ann Hall.

Includes bibliographical references and index.
Also issued in electronic format.
ISBN 978-0-88864-602-6

    1. Edmonton Commercial Graduates (Basketball team)—History. 2. Basketball for women—Alberta—Edmonton—History. 3. Women basketball players—Canada—Biography. 4. Basketball—Alberta—Edmonton—History. I. Title.

GV885.42.E3H34 2011   796.323097123'34   C2011-907213-0

First edition, first printing, 2011.
Printed and bound in Canada by Houghton Boston Printers, Saskatoon, Saskatchewan.
Copyediting and Proofreading by Joanne Muzak.
Indexing by Judy Dunlop.

The University of Alberta Press is committed to protecting our natural environment. As part of our efforts, this book is printed on Enviro Paper: it contains 100% post-consumer recycled fibres and is acid- and chlorine-free.

The University of Alberta Press gratefully acknowledges the support received for its publishing program from The Canada Council for the Arts. The University of Alberta Press also gratefully acknowledges the financial support of the Government of Canada through the Canada Book Fund (CBF) and the Government of Alberta through the Alberta Multimedia Development Fund (AMDF) for its publishing activities.

This book was funded in part by the Alberta Historical Resources Foundation.

Tribute to the "Grads"

They brought their city more than fame,
They brought their nation more than pride;
The strongest foe, the toughest game
Were things they simply took in stride.
For first they faced the inward jars—
The jealousy, the selfish dreams;
Those things which make outstanding stars
But wreck consistent, winning teams.
The pass that meant another's score,
The faith that fed another's drive
Were constant, on and off the floor,
For every year of twenty-five.

—FREDERICK B. WATT

Contents

Foreword

TODAY IT SEEMS UTTERLY INCOMPREHENSIBLE to several generations of Canadian sports fans, but once upon a time, a long time ago, there was an Edmonton team that could claim greatness to equal the almost mythical glory gangs of Oilers and Eskimos. Greatness to match that of Wayne Gretzky and the group coached by Glen Sather, including Hockey Hall of Famers Mark Messier, Jari Kurri, Grant Fuhr, Paul Coffey, and Glenn Anderson, who won five Stanley Cups over a span of seven seasons? Success to compare to the five-in-a-row Grey Cup champion Eskimos coached by Hugh Campbell, featuring the likes of Warren Moon, Tom Wilkinson, Dan Kepley, Dave Fennell, Brian Kelly, and Dave Cutler? Could such a team have existed?

Before this sports columnist would go on to cover those great Eskimos and Oilers teams, it seemed like pure fiction to listen to the tales of Jack Deakin, my old *Edmonton Journal* sports editor, over drinks, invariably at 4 A.M., about J. Percy Page and the Edmonton Grads. Deakin colourfully told about a team that in its time brought glory to Edmonton on a scale that would not be outdone by Jackie Parker, Normie Kwong, Johnny Bright, and

Rollie Miles and the three-in-a-row Grey Cup Eskimos of 1954–55–56. In the wee hours of many a morning after the paper was put to bed, Deakin related tales of the first team to own the town that became known as the City of Champions, the first team to put Edmonton on the map in sports, and not just nationally but internationally. A basketball team. A *girls'* basketball team!

Deakin explained that the Edmonton Grads were a team of graduates of McDougall Commercial High School coached by J. Percy Page, who may be familiar to readers now as the former Lieutenant Governor of the province of Alberta. The Edmonton Grads drew capacity crowds of more than 6,000 people, 10 per cent of the population when Edmonton was little more than a pimple on the prairie. The Grads even outdrew hockey teams of the time. Deakin told of how the Grads took three tours to Europe and won what were effectively demonstration sport versions of the Olympics in Paris in 1924, Amsterdam in 1928, and Berlin in 1936. He spoke of how they played 522 games and won 502. And he spun stories of how a third of the population welcomed them home on return from some of their many conquests. He told the young scribes on his staff how James A. Naismith, the inventor of basketball, declared the Grads to be, in many ways, the greatest team ever to play the game he had invented. One night, Deakin produced a report from the newspaper morgue in which Naismith called the team "the finest basketball team that ever stepped out on a floor."

As it happened, sports editor Deakin assigned me to cover a reunion of the team, which gave me the opportunity to meet many of the Grads and J. Percy Page. All those years later, the women spoke of Page with a reverence I've heard few players have for a former coach, no matter the success involved. They explained how he coached them not just to be the glory of their times playing international basketball, but also in life, by coaching them how to represent themselves and their city, at all times as ladies first.

Covering the Oilers in the World Hockey Association one year as a young sportswriter, I found myself in Springfield, Massachusetts, the town where hockey legend Eddie Shore, a.k.a. the Edmonton Express, who married Edmonton Grad star Kate Macrae, ran his minor league Springfield Indians. It's in Springfield where Canadian Naismith invented the game of basketball, and where the Basketball Hall of Fame and Museum are located. On display at the time was the uniform of Noel MacDonald, the greatest of the Grads, but recognition for the team was token and infuriating if you knew their story. In a recent visit, there was no evidence whatsoever of their existence in a new Hall of Fame building in Springfield. In Toronto, the massive Underwood International Trophy, bigger than the Stanley Cup, sat at a display in Canada's Sports Hall of Fame, but it ended up in boxes when the place was closed in recent years. Hopefully visitors to Canada's fabulous new Sports Hall of Fame in Calgary are able to see this trophy.

One by one the members of the team died, many without notice. It was as if the Edmonton Grads had faded into history, forgotten by time. Then one day in 2010 I was invited to the 100th birthday party for Grad Edith Stone Sutton. And it all became real for me again with the spunky old gal who proclaimed it great to be alive and an Edmonton Grad. She used the occasion to declare herself the "last living member of the Edmonton Grads," despite the fact her twin sister and teammate Helen Stone Stewart was still alive in Vancouver and teammate Kay MacRitchie MacBeth was living in Comox. Edith was, however, the last Grad still living in Edmonton. "Look at me. I'm the last one. All by myself," she said. Then she paused for a moment. "It's lonely at the top," she laughed. This was a happy occasion. Posing for a picture with me, she hooted, "Imagine, at my age, being interviewed by a sportswriter!"

There were greater honours at the open house birthday party held at Queen Alexandra Community Hall on University Avenue,

a block from the house where Edith still lives a "fiercely independent" life, as she always has according to her grandson Michael
Sutton. MP Linda Duncan presented her with a plaque proclaiming
the day a "national historic occasion." There were also proclama-
tions from Queen Elizabeth, the Governor General, the Lieutenant
Governor, Prime Minister, Premier, and several other officials, including Edmonton Mayor Stephen Mandel, who held up a 1932 team
picture of her and said, "You were a good looking broad back then
and a better looking broad now. You're an angel." There were birthday cakes in the forms of a basketball, a court, and a basketball shoe.
The walls were decorated with pictures of the team. And there was
the National Film Board movie about the team that James Naismith
called "the finest basketball team that ever stepped out on a floor."

The gal who played on the team from 1930 through 1934 said the
best part of her 100th birthday was being able to have an occasion
to keep the memory of the Grads alive. "People today haven't heard
of the Edmonton Grads. It was a long time ago. And for a lot of it,
you had to be there," she said, speaking of filling buildings for wom-
en's basketball games and being the toast of the town. "I remember
Toronto. Oh, my, they were jealous of Edmonton. I can't possibly
explain the way it was then. You don't know unless you were there.
It was a special team and a special time. It will never happen again.
It's amazing it happened then."

Now this book comes along to take you there. Remarkably, what
you are about to read is the first ever book written about this team.
To me, this wonderful work by author M. Ann Hall is like opening
a time capsule. What makes this book exceptional, I think, is the
scholarly research approach, which was required at this time if for
no other reason than to make this now so difficult-to-believe story
believable. At the same time, you will discover that the meticulous
documentation takes little away from the terrific tales described by

my old sports editor Jack Deakin with what seemed to me to be great hyperbole.

Thank you, Ann Hall, for *The Grads Are Playing Tonight!* It's game time...

TERRY JONES
Edmonton Sun Sports Columnist
January 2011

Abbreviations

ASHFM	Alberta Sports Hall of Fame and Museum
CEA	City of Edmonton Archives
CSHF	Canada's Sports Hall of Fame
GA	Glenbow Archives
LAC	Library and Archives Canada
PAA	Provincial Archives of Alberta
SCA	Smith College Archives
UAL	University of Alberta Libraries

Acknowledgements

HISTORICAL PROJECTS like this one could not be completed without the assistance of skilled reference librarians and archivists, and
I have benefitted from the enthusiasm and patience of many, especially in locating long hidden documents, artifacts, and images. In
particular, I wish to thank Paula Aurini-Onderwater and Sharon Bell
at the City of Edmonton Archives; Sandy Williams and Tanya Read at
the Alberta Sports Hall of Fame and Museum; Susan Kooyman at the
Glenbow Archives; Heather Kerr at the Edmonton Artifact Centre;
and Robert Cole in Peel's Prairie Provinces, University of Alberta
Libraries. Many others, unfortunately anonymous, assisted me at the
Provincial Archives of Alberta and in the Rutherford Library at the
University of Alberta.

By the time I began my research, most of the Edmonton Grads
had passed away or were too elderly to be interviewed. Fortunately,
I was able to interview Helen Northup Alexander and Betty Bawden
Bowen before they died. I was also able to interview Kay MacRitchie
MacBeth and Edith Stone Sutton several times, both of whom are
still alive as this book goes to press. Others interviewed include
Patricia Page Hollingsworth, J. Percy Page's daughter, and June
Causgrove Cox, a former Grad Cub. I am also very grateful to the

following relatives of the Grads, who took the time to answer my many questions: Diane Anderson, Alex Cromarty, Kay Deedrick, Myrt Ferrier, Penny Gartner, Don Hollingsworth, Verna McIlveen, Ronnie Mills, Edward (Ted) W. Shore, Jr., Judith Silvertsen, Jennifer Spriddle, Logan Tait, and Jane Webb.

Working with the University of Alberta Press has been a pleasure, and especially with the fine team of individuals who worked on this project: Alan Brownoff, Linda Cameron, Cathie Crooks, Peter Midgley, and Mary Lou Roy. Special thanks to Joanne Muzak for improving my prose and pointing out inconsistencies. The reader has certainly benefitted from all your hard work.

Finally, three people deserve a special mention. David Dorward, the driving force behind Edmonton's new GO Community Centre, has been a keen supporter of this project from its early beginnings. His generosity allowed me to acquire the very best images to illustrate this book. Nancy Mitchell, my sister, used her superb genealogical research skills to find important details about the lives of several Grads. Jane Haslett, my partner, not only endured this project longer than anyone else, she also listened patiently to my endless stories and commented upon the many drafts.

Introduction

THE GRADS ARE PLAYING TONIGHT! For twenty-five years, from
1915 to 1940, this refrain brought thousands of excited fans out to
watch the Edmonton Commercial Graduates play basketball. Almost
all members of the team were graduates of McDougall Commercial
High School, and from the time they entered the school as young
students, they came under the tutelage of J. Percy Page, their teacher,
coach, and mentor. They played over 400 official games, losing only
twenty for a winning average of 95 per cent. They travelled more
than 125,000 miles in Canada, the United States, and Europe. They
crossed the Atlantic three times to defend their world title at exhibition games held in conjunction with the Summer Olympics in Paris,
Amsterdam, and Berlin. They disbanded in 1940, long before wom-
en's basketball became an Olympic sport.

Only seven teams ever scored 50 or more points against the Grads
in a single game, whereas the Grads turned the 50-point corner in no
less than 162 games. Their highest score was 136 in an official game
against the University of Alberta in 1934. They held the Underwood
International Trophy (USA versus Canada) for seventeen years, and
it was presented to them permanently on their twenty-fifth anniversary. They won their games on outdoor and indoor courts of all sizes,

on courts with glass backboards and no backboards, in low ceiling halls allowing little loft to the ball, in all kinds of weather, and under all conditions. Their records were established with only two evening practices a week, since every Grad held a full-time job, usually in an Edmonton business. The consistent training of replacements went on through a sophisticated feeder system of school teams and the Gradettes. The most talented players slipped smoothly into openings on the Grads with a sound knowledge of the Page system of play. Despite this, Coach Page never took very much credit for a playing system. No scouting was maintained; no plays were charted or films of other teams studied. From the beginning, Page recognized the important fundamentals of success: great stress on teamwork and the value of repetition. He also had another tremendous asset, which was the ability to inspire teams to play harder for him than they did for the crowds.

Despite the Edmonton Grads' amazing record, a book about the team has never been written before now. Many articles have been published, most repeating the essence of their story, although the best pieces are by sportswriters of the day who watched them play. The team has left behind a full record of their many games in both the *Edmonton Journal* and the *Edmonton Bulletin*, which published play-by-play descriptions of their most important matches. Sports reporters from both papers followed the team assiduously throughout their twenty-five-year history, reporting every announcement and detail, even in the off season, in much the same way today's media follow men's professional sport. When the team travelled, reports were sent back to the local papers via Canadian Press, or sometimes an Edmonton sportswriter went with them and filed his own accounts. Beginning in 1935, Percy Page's daughter Patricia wrote a twice-weekly column called "Feminine Flashes" for the *Edmonton Journal*, which was often full of interesting details about the team and its members.

This is the story of the Edmonton Commercial Graduates Basketball Club, which was much more than just a basketball team called the Edmonton Grads. It was a hugely successful athletic organization, managed primarily by J. Percy Page with assistance from other coaches at McDougall High School, local businessmen and prominent citizens, and the players themselves. The Grads, and their younger sisters the Gradettes, were only two teams in this remarkable organization. There were also the junior and senior high school basketball teams, where young players could one day dream about becoming a Gradette and perhaps even a Grad. Another important cog in this remarkable organization was the Boy Grads, who spent many an evening playing—and often being beaten by—the Grads. Damage to their pride aside, they knew their role was to provide the toughest possible competition to prepare the Grads for bigger and stronger women's teams from the United States.

This story would be dull and boring if it were presented chronologically because, with only a few exceptions, the Grads were a winning team. There would be no drama and very little suspense. Although it does start at the beginning, this book is written thematically to explain the reasons for the Grads' perpetual success. For those wishing a year-by-year account of the team's opponents, scores, travels, and important events, they will find this in Appendix 1 at the back of the book. Chapter 1 explains how the Grads emerged in 1915 from a single Edmonton school—McDougall Commercial High School. It also provides insight into the early days of basketball in Alberta when girls and women took up the relatively new sport because it was vigorous, competitive, and allowed them to sweat. The game expanded considerably as it moved off the outdoor dirt or grass courts and into the indoor gymnasiums in the new schools that were built to accommodate a growing population.

Chapter 2 examines the Grads as unusual civic boosters. They were the first sports team to bring valuable attention and publicity to our city. Wherever they travelled and played, people learned about Edmonton and Alberta and Canada through the Grads. They were superb ambassadors for a city, which in those days was called the "Edmonton of the Grads." The team travelled abroad several times to defend their world title and to lobby for the inclusion of basketball into the Summer Olympic Games. These journeys, discussed in Chapter 3, were far more than simply a team travelling afar to compete. They were also an opportunity for young working women to see the world, something they would not have been able to do on their own. For most Grads these trips were an unforgettable highlight in their lives.

From 1922, when they won their first Canadian championship, to 1940, when the team disbanded, the Grads used only thirty-eight players. Almost all are gone now, although as this book goes to press, there are still two alive, one of whom is over 100 years old. Unfortunately, I started this project too late to interview many of these elderly Grads, but I was able to talk with a few before they passed away, and these were memorable occasions. I have also sought out recorded interviews done by others over the years, and a few have turned up, all very useful. Yet, in all the available material published about the Grads, the voices of the individual players are rarely heard, and we know little about these women. Mainly through newspaper accounts, I was able to piece together their playing careers as Grads, but it was also important to know something about their family history, and more importantly, what became of them after they ceased being a Grad. It has taken considerable effort to learn about these women's lives. For a few of the women, I found little biographical information. In other cases, I was able to contact a relative, usually a son or daughter, who was more than willing to provide details about their mother's life. Although collectively known as the Edmonton Grads, they were as different a group of women as one would find anywhere, and they need to be recognized and honoured as individuals. Chapters 4, 6, and 8 contain their individual biographies arranged in the order in which each Grad joined the team.

Although Coach Page often attributed the Grads' success to teamwork, shooting accuracy, and the simplicity of their plays, there were many factors that contributed to their remarkable record. These factors are discussed in Chapter 5; they include the highly efficient feeder system at McDougall School, game preparation and style of play, the role played by Percy Page as business manager and coach, and perhaps most important of all, his belief in a cohesive team rather than a collection of individual stars.

For much of its history, and even in some areas today, the game of basketball was played under two sets of rules—one set for men and the other for women. These gender-based rules developed because of differing ideas about the physical capacities of males and females. The original rules for women were more restrictive and allowed less movement on the basketball court, in keeping with the belief in women's physical inferiority. From 1923 onwards, the Grads played only men's rules, which meant that Coach Page looked to the United States rather than eastern Canada, where women's rules dominated, for competition to challenge his team. Chapter 7 discusses the implications of these gender-based rules, especially for the Grads, and examines in some detail who and where they played throughout Canada and the United States.

The Grads resembled a large extended family with Percy Page, supported by his wife Maude, as its head. He and his wife set the standards for how each Grad should behave and comport herself, and if she was not willing to be a lady first and a basketball player second, then, quite simply, she would never be a Grad. Chapter 9 explores the notion of the Grads as a family. Mr. and Mrs. Page had considerable influence on these young women, especially when they played on the team, and their influence extended to long after they had retired. As a team, the Grads have been remembered for their remarkable record and appropriately honoured throughout the years since their last game in June 1940. Their legacy and why they are important to Edmonton's history is the theme of Chapter 10.

Through this book, the Grads are playing again tonight!

1 How It Began

JUST AFTER SEVEN O'CLOCK on the morning of May 23, 1922, six young women and their coach arrived at the Canadian Pacific Railway train station in downtown Edmonton. Hundreds of high school students, family, and friends descended on the station that chilly morning to congratulate the new Dominion women's basketball champions. As the women stepped off the train, they were met with the loudest possible cheers. Winnie Martin, captain of the team, was jubilantly hoisted onto someone's shoulders and carried to a waiting car. So were the other team members. Led by the Edmonton Newsboys Band, the parade headed up Jasper Avenue, turned south, then stopped at the Hotel Macdonald.

His Worship, Mayor David M. Duggan, along with more than 100 guests, feted the victorious team over breakfast. "You have achieved a higher point in sport than any other organization which has left the city."[1] Duggan was clearly pleased at the attention his city had received, especially in the eastern press. The president of the Alberta Basketball Association, Cecil Race, declared Alberta to be a great basketball province. The local school board presented each player and their coach with medals commemorating the victory. The Edmonton Commercial Graduates Basketball team, known simply as the Grads and then eight years old, was the toast of the town.

Players Connie Smith, Nellie Perry, Eleanor Mountifield, Winnie Martin, sisters Dorothy and Daisy Johnson, and their coach J. Percy Page had travelled over 2,000 miles by train to Ontario to play the London Shamrocks, eastern Canadian titleholders. Among the players were two teachers, a bookkeeper, and three stenographers, all of whom needed time off from their jobs, as did Percy Page, principal of McDougall Commercial High School. Although they won the first game handily by a score of 41–8, they lost the second 8–21. But, they still won the series by 20 points. Women's basketball in those days was governed by two sets of rules. Before 1923, the Grads played the restrictive, six-player Spalding ladies' rules, which were used in the first game of the series with the Shamrocks. The Shamrocks, however, favoured the five-player men's rules used in the second game, which they won. No matter. The Grads were declared the first Dominion champions, a title they did not surrender until 1940 when they disbanded.

Basketball at McDougall Commercial School

Basketball was a relatively new sport for girls, especially in Alberta schools. It had been introduced by a progressive school inspector, and in 1904, Lacombe claimed the honour of having the first

Early women's basketball in Alberta, c. 1910. [PAA A12005]

girls' high school basketball team in the province.[2] As the game
spread, the Lacombe girls played teams in Wetaskiwin, Red Deer,
Stettler, Ponoka, and Edmonton for a high school championship.
Girls loved the new game because it was vigorous, competitive,
and made them sweat. It was also an improvement over the boring military drill, formal gymnastics, and club swinging usually
endured by girls. Even better, they often played outside on dirt and
grass courts because not many schools had indoor gymnasiums.
Such was the case at the new John A. McDougall Public School,
which opened in 1913 just north of 109 Avenue on 107 Street on the
Hudson's Bay Reserve. A year after its opening, McDougall became
the site of commercial classes for business and secretarial students to ease overcrowding at the nearby Victoria High School.

The McDougall Commercial classes were taught by Percy Page and
assisted by Ernest Hyde. Because there were no other teachers, both
had to take over the physical education classes. Hyde chose the boys
and left Page with the girls. Legend suggests that this decision was
made by a coin toss, but it was more likely because Percy was married

and Ernest was not that Percy became the girls' teacher. Even more pragmatically, the boys' class was smaller. Page agreed the girls could play basketball, but with no indoor gymnasium they practised on a hastily constructed rough outdoor court at the south end of the school grounds. Although there was a spacious, basketball-equipped gymnasium at Victoria High School, just a few blocks south, the Commercial girls were refused permission to practise there because Victoria wanted Commercial's best players to play for them.

By 1914, a city high school basketball league for girls had been established. The Commercial girls requested entry, and along with Victoria High, Strathcona High, and Edmonton Technical, they played their first season. The Commercial team won the league. Later that fall they travelled to Camrose and won the Alberta provincial championship, beating the future teachers attending Camrose Normal School. The girls on that first team, all students at Commercial, were forwards Nellie Batson—who was also their captain—and Ella Osborne, guards Geraldine Reid and Iola Mitchell, and centers Mary Bremner and Ethel Anderson.

Early in 1915 an intercollegiate basketball league was started with Strathcona High, Victoria High, University of Alberta, City Teachers, and of course, Commercial High. With snow on the ground, the Commercial girls were now allowed to practise in the Victoria gymnasium. Players, coaches, and fans alike predicted that the Commercial team would be hard to beat as they were excellent individual players with their success due mainly to "accurate throwing."[3] Teamwork was not yet a significant feature of their play. Nevertheless, they won the intercollegiate championship in March as well as the provincial championship against Camrose Normal. "The Camrose girls were much heavier than the local team," reported the *Edmonton Journal*, "but hardly as speedy or as clever in handling the ball."[4] Scores were not high in those days; Commercial won 12–7.

Commercial again entered the high school championship in

the fall of 1915 for the Richardson trophy, but this time Strathcona High beat them by 2 points in a playoff game.[5] They also added a new player, Winnie Martin, whose defensive play in a previous game, along with her typing skills, brought this comment: "The girl who can write 100 words on the typewriter in nothing is just as speedy on the court. Her checking and long and accurate passing for the full length of the court was a big factor in the victory."[6] By the winter of 1916, there were enough players in the Girls' City Basketball League to warrant two divisions—a junior and senior. Commercial entered teams and won both divisions. This was the beginning of a feeder system, which would eventually provide the Grads with a continuous supply of talented players.

Another first took place at a provincial championship game between Commercial High and Camrose Normal School on March 31, 1916 when an admission fee of twenty-five cents was charged to help defray the travelling expenses of the visiting team. Before a large crowd at the Victoria High School gym, Commercial won their second provincial championship with a score of 13–2, still low by any standards, but remarkable in that the opposing team scored only one basket.

Commercial Graduates Basketball Club

The lives of the original team members were changing. Ethel Anderson had to quit school at Christmas in 1915 because her mother was ill.[7] Nellie Batson left school to take up a job with the Grand Trunk Railway. Several others—Ella Osborne, Geraldine Reid, Iola Mitchell, and Mary Bremner—graduated from Commercial High in the summer of 1916 to seek jobs in Edmonton. Winnie Martin went back to Victoria High to gain her senior matriculation because she wished to go to university. But most still wanted to play basketball and at the same time retain their affiliation with Commercial.

*Original 1915 Edmonton Grads team. Back row: Ethel Anderson, Geraldine Reid,
Ella Osborne, and Winnie Martin; centre row: Dr. W.G. Carpenter (superintendent
of Edmonton Schools), Nellie Batson (captain), and Coach Percy Page; front row:
Iola Mitchell and Mary Bremner.* [CEA 80-16-87]

They formed the Commercial Athletic Society, where any student or
graduate of the school, as well as those who attended another business school and were pursuing a business career, was eligible for
membership.[8] The media called them the "Commercial Graduates,"
shortened later to just the "Grads," and the famous team was born.

At the same time, the Harold A. Wilson Company donated a trophy in the shape of a shield for the women's provincial basketball

championship. The rules allowed that the trophy could be competed for at any time, but no team could challenge more than once every three months. The team holding the trophy could be called upon to defend it at any time.[9] For the Commercial Graduates, barred from competing in any of the high school leagues because they were ex-students, this was their only opportunity for competition and the highlight of the year. In the spring of 1917, after a year's absence and playing under their new name, forwards Nellie Batson and Ella Osborne, centers Ethel Anderson and Elena Todd, and guards Winnie Martin and Geraldine Reid defeated a challenge team from Wetaskiwin by 30–14 to win the provincial title. Newcomer Elena Todd, a slim 5'7" sharpshooter and star player with the senior high school team, easily moved up to play with the Commercial Graduates. Players came and went in those early years, and some of them have long since been forgotten, but their names appear in the newspaper accounts. In every way, they were as much a part of the Grads' early history as the thirty-eight women who are officially recognized as the "real" Edmonton Grads.[10] Aside from those mentioned previously, other Commercial Graduates who played on the team before 1922 were Connie Lamont, Dorothy Shaw, Mona Karran, Kathleen Hall, and Alfretta Dickson.

By 1919, a team from Commercial had successfully defended the provincial title for five consecutive years, beating at least one challenger a year. This winning run came to a halt in April of the same year when the Commercial Graduates were challenged by the University of Alberta (also known simply as Varsity) for the Wilson trophy and went down to defeat by just two points. The Graduates wanted an immediate rematch, but the rules required that they must wait at least two months. In November they got their revenge and narrowly defeated Varsity 21–18 to regain the provincial title.

The availability of indoor gymnasiums in Edmonton made it easier for teams to practise and play in the winter months. One of

Champion basketball teams of McDougall Commercial High School and its graduates, 1919–1920. [PAA A11427]

the first gymnasiums opened in 1908 in the downtown Edmonton YMCA. The first high schools built in Edmonton also included gymnasiums. Strathcona Collegiate Institute opened on the south side in 1909, and Victoria High School, originally called Edmonton High School, opened in 1911 on the Hudson's Bay Reserve. In 1914, an addition built behind Athabasca Hall on the University of Alberta campus provided a larger dining hall and new gymnasium. With no suitable gymnasium at McDougall High School, Percy Page was forced to look elsewhere for his teams to practise. He wrote to the school board requesting permission for the Commercial girls to practise in the Victoria High School gymnasium one night a week from eight to nine-thirty: "Either Mrs. Page or myself, or both of us, would always be present, and the girls would be glad to pay a small fee to re-imburse the Board for lighting charges. I would personally guarantee to see that no damage of any kind was done."[11] Luckily his request was granted.

As World War I approached, the federal government built local armouries to store military equipment and serve as training centers and "homes" for soldiers who were recruited to fight in the war. One was completed in 1915 in Edmonton on the Hudson's Bay Reserve near Victoria High School. The inside dimensions of the hall were 100 by 200 feet, certainly large enough to accommodate a basketball court, which is exactly what happened in peacetime. The military authorities in Ottawa consented, a floor was marked out, hoops and stands installed, and by mid-January 1920, the Edmonton Drill Hall (later renamed the Prince of Wales Armouries) was available to basketball leagues in the city. A ladies' mercantile league, comprised of teams from local businesses such as the Hudson's Bay Company and government offices such as Alberta Government Telephones, began in the city in 1921. By 1922, there were ten teams in the league, but the Commercial Graduates were ineligible because team members had to be employed by the sponsoring business or company, even though teams were allowed to play two "outside" players.[12]

By 1920, the Commercial Graduates' main opposition was the University of Alberta's Varsity team, coached by Cecil Race, who was also registrar of the university. During the 1919–1920 season, Varsity played thirteen games either in the Edmonton city league, against the University of Saskatchewan, or in challenge matches for the provincial title, winning all but one game. The so-called provincial title went back and forth between the north and south sides of the Saskatchewan River. Varsity lost the Wilson trophy to the Commercial Graduates in November 1919 and challenged them again the following April. The game was played under protest because one of the Commercial Graduates' players, Connie Smith, was still a student at Commercial High. Varsity's objections were upheld and the game was ordered replayed without the contentious

Miss Smith. This time they beat the Commercial Graduates 30–22 and retained the provincial title. The Commercial Graduates were obviously lacking a pair of scoring forwards because in both games against Varsity, forward Elena Todd single-handedly scored *all* their points. A few days later, Varsity also defeated the Commercial High School team, which this time rightfully included Connie Smith.

The rivalry between Commercial and Varsity came to a head the next season. Following a 25–3 rout whereby the Commercial Graduates regained the Wilson trophy, the University of Alberta student paper, *The Gateway*, published an account of the game accusing Commercial of "decidedly unfair methods" and likened their play more to rugby than to basketball.[13] These accusations brought a lengthy reply from the executive committee of the Commercial Graduates' Club, which *The Gateway* refused to publish because it was too long. This incensed the Commercial Graduates even more and prompted them to send all correspondence to the *Edmonton Journal*, where it was published.[14] They carefully refuted all charges, certainly those of roughness, claiming that of the 167 games played by Commercial teams—junior, senior, and graduate—over the previous seven years, only one player had ever been expelled from a game for too many fouls. They also offered to waive the two-month waiting period before a team could challenge for the Wilson trophy again, meet the Varsity team on any neutral floor—Victoria High, YMCA, or the Armouries—at any time, and let them choose the referees. Varsity ignored the offer.

The Commercial Graduates was not just a basketball team. They were already building a formidable organization through the Commercial Graduates Basketball Club, which included the junior and senior high school teams, the Commercial Graduates team, and most important of all, a formal administrative organization with an honorary president, president, secretary, business manager, executive committee, and patronesses. In 1920, for example, the honorary president was J. Victor (Vic) Horner, a twenty-three-year-old flyer and war veteran; the president was Winnie Martin; Martin's teammate Geraldine Reid was secretary; the business manager was, of course, Percy Page; and the executive committee included Mrs. Marjorie McGregor, Edith Greenlees, and Pearl Simonson. Chosen as patronesses were Mrs. David McIntosh, Mrs. Percy Page, and Mrs. James Horner, Vic Horner's mother. The overall responsibility of this group was to look after the affairs of the club, promote the teams, and, as upstanding citizens of Edmonton, provide the club with a degree of decorum and respectability. The newly elected 1920 executive immediately got to work organizing a combined dance and concert at the Hotel Macdonald to recognize the "brilliant success" of the teams.[15]

Undisputed Champions of Alberta

By the end of the 1920 season, the highly successful record of the McDougall Commercial High School basketball teams was probably unequalled by any other school in the country.[16] They were the undisputed champions in three leagues. During the previous seven years, the junior Commercial teams had won consecutive high school championships. In all that time, they had lost only one game, and in the previous year, their record was 243 points with only 6 points scored against them. The senior high school teams had won the high school championship (Richardson trophy) four times, tied twice, and once lost out by a single basket. The provincial title (Wilson trophy) had been contested six times; the Commercial Graduates won it four times and the University of Alberta won it twice. In less than a decade, Percy Page and his teams had built a solid foundation for success, something not fully understood by most teams, who thought it would be easy to challenge the Grads.

In December 1920, the Commercial Graduates ventured outside the province to Saskatoon, further than they ever had before, to play teams from the local YWCA and the University of Saskatchewan. They won both games by respectable basketball scores of 50–8 and 47–15. Supported by her teammates Kathleen Hall and Daisy Johnson, Elena Todd on the forward line was sensational. On defence were stalwarts Winnie Martin and Connie Smith, with Eleanor Mountifield and Elizabeth Elrick sharing the center position. Local newspaper accounts stressed the team's sportsmanship and clean play. One Saskatoon paper observed that it would be difficult to select the stars in the Commercial organization because they appeared to be so well-balanced and "exhibited such vast superiority that their stars were probably prevented from showing their real ability."[17] This was an early observation of a characteristic that would define the Grads over the years to come. They always played as a team and no one player was ever to outshine the others.

There is no evidence the Commercial Grads played any official games in the 1921 season, primarily because there was no one for them to play. The University of Alberta, along with teams from eight other educational institutions, played in a newly formed girls' intercollegiate league. Both McDougall and Commercial High School entered their senior teams in this league. Because Varsity easily won the south side championship and Commercial won the north, the two teams met in a two-game playoff. Commercial beat the university team 17–13 in the first game but lost the second game 29–23, which meant they lost the championship by only 2 points—quite a feat for a team of high school students. By now, McDougall High School had equipped its gymnasium— small as it was—for basketball and the Commercial teams could all practise there, which probably contributed to their success.

Women's basketball was booming in Alberta. It was well-established in Edmonton, with teams also in Calgary and further south

1920–1921 Edmonton Commercial Graduates. Standing: Eleanor Mountifield, Connie Smith, Elena Todd, and Winnie Martin; sitting: Elizabeth Elrick, Percy Page, and Nellie Perry. [PAA A11435]

all wishing to take part in a properly organized provincial championship. Edna Bakewell, originally from Seattle, was a superb basketball player and energetic student leader at the University of Alberta. As President of the Women's Athletic Association, she helped further the development of women's athletics on the campus. In 1922, she joined the university staff as an instructor in physical education and coach of the women's basketball team. The Bakewell cup, which she donated in 1921, provided a better basis for the senior women's provincial championship. It was to be played for once a year and only by teams who had played in an organized league during the basketball season.[18] Spalding's official basketball rules for women would be used.

The six women on the Commercial Graduates team of 1922 were graduates of McDougall, already having played basketball for several years as they made their way through the junior and senior high school teams. The most senior player was Winnie Martin, one of the original players, who, after graduation from Commercial, attained her high school matriculation and went to university. By 1922 she was a teacher at Commercial. Eleanor Mountifield, an all-round athlete who was now working in an Edmonton business, had been playing on Commercial teams since 1917. Daisy Johnson, a schoolteacher in Jarrow, a rural community south and east of Edmonton, had little time to practise with the team. Her younger sister, Dorothy (Dot) was playing her first year in senior company. The two remaining players, Nellie Perry and Connie Smith, were both working as stenographers in Edmonton businesses.

Eight teams entered the first provincial competition in 1922: four in Edmonton (Varsity, Victoria High, Normal School, and the Commercial Grads), one from the Calgary area (Okotoks), and three from the Lethbridge district (Lethbridge High School, Cardston, and Barons). Medicine Hat was also supposed to have a team but it did not materialize. The Commercial Grads, decked out in new black and gold uniforms—the colours of the tiger—won the Edmonton district league, although they were beaten once by Victoria High. Coach Page continually experimented with his lineup to find just the right combination. The local newspapers covered the games, providing readers with firsthand accounts and insights into the abilities of individual players. "Miss Perry," noted the *Edmonton Journal*, "does not shoot an overhead ball such as characterizes the average lady player but snares the ball on the run and shoots with deadly precision that might well be the envy of many of the male players around the city."[19]

In southern Alberta competition, the team in Barons was victorious and destined to play the Grads for the provincial championship. Home-and-home games in Barons and Edmonton were not possible because of the expense. Confident of victory, the Grads offered to travel south, with a stop in Lethbridge to play an exhibition game, before heading to Barons for a sudden death match. Taller, heavier, and far more skilled, the Grads beat the Lethbridge team by a score of 46–11 and demolished the team in Barons by 56–14. As one reporter noted, "For all-round grace of movement, rapidity in passing and accuracy of shooting, there is nothing in this part of the province to touch them."[20] A new player accompanied them on this trip— Mary Dunn, a short and sturdy guard, also a graduate of McDougall and now working as a stenographer in Edmonton. She did not see much action in this series, but her time to shine would come soon enough. The Commercial Graduates, clearly an exciting team to watch, were beginning to develop a devoted fan base. With no way to find out how their team did on road trips, except to read about it in the newspaper the next day, the *Edmonton Journal* provided a phone number where interested readers could obtain an immediate score.

First Dominion Championships

Teams representing the Commercial Graduates Club had now won the Alberta title more than any other team; they also claimed the western Canadian title since having beaten the University of Saskatchewan a year ago, and in 1922 defeated the University of Alberta, who in turn had beaten the University of Manitoba. Women's basketball had not yet developed in British Columbia to the extent that teams were willing to travel and challenge teams on the Prairies. It was now time for the Commercial Graduates to play a team from eastern Canada (meaning Ontario) for the first "Dominion" championship to be sanctioned by the Amateur Athletic Union of Canada. Page sent a telegram to Carrie Blackwell, president of the Ontario Ladies' Basketball Association and manager of the London Shamrocks, the Ontario champions, suggesting

First Dominion champions, 1922: Daisy Johnson, Percy Page, Nellie Perry, Eleanor Mountifield (captain), Dorothy Johnson, Winnie Martin, and Connie Smith.
[PAA A11428]

a two-game series in Winnipeg. He also proposed that one game be played under the Spalding women's rules familiar to the Grads, and that the men's rules used by the Shamrocks govern the second game, with total points to count. Miss Blackwell responded enthusiastically. The only obstacle was funding for her team's trip to Winnipeg.

After several weeks of negotiation, the Commercial Graduates decided to travel to London to meet the Shamrocks in a two-game series. An exhibition game would also be staged against a team in St. Thomas, who had almost beaten the Shamrocks, in addition to a game with an all-star team in Toronto. All that was needed was to raise the necessary capital to finance the trip. Page estimated that they needed at least $1,500. The eastern teams guaranteed $600, plus a share of the gate receipts at London and St. Thomas, which meant that the remainder had to be raised by the Commercial Graduates Basketball Club. The team first contacted J.J. Seitz, president of the Underwood Typewriter Company of Canada, offering to play under the sponsorship of his company, if he cared to advance the money. Mr. Seitz wrote back saying that he didn't think it wise to accept sponsorship of the team, but if they could raise half of the amount, he would personally contribute the other half.[21] At this point, the club decided against a public drive for funds, instead relying on the generosity of friends and local businesses "who are interested in clean amateur sport to see that the trip is made possible."[22] Some eighty named donors, as well as several anonymous ones, contributed about $500, while the members of the team and Page himself put up the rest of the money. This enabled Coach Page, Mrs. Page as chaperone, and only six players to make the trip. They were all set, except for one important matter.

The journey would occur in mid-May while school was still in session, which required Percy Page, now principal of McDougall Commercial High School, along with team captain Winnie Martin, who was now a teacher at Commercial, to obtain permission from the Edmonton Public School Board for a short leave of absence. Page appeared before the board himself and on behalf of Winnie and promised to be back in Edmonton in eight days. Board minutes indicate a spirited discussion with one trustee noting favourably that Mr. Page had turned down several offers to leave Edmonton, and that he and the team had brought much honour to the school system and the city. Those against the leave argued that it didn't really "mean anything" to win a Dominion championship, and thus could not see the point. In the end, the board voted four to two that they be granted the leave.[23]

The "prairie queens," as one newspaper called them, left Edmonton by a CPR train on a Friday evening and were in London, Ontario, by noon the following Tuesday.[24] Passengers on the train were entertained by the daily mimeographed "Commercial Chronicle," a tongue-in-cheek and humorous newsletter written by Page and stencilled by one of the Grads en route. As the team approached their destination, the London and Toronto papers were rife with basketball gossip in anticipation of the games. Tickets were hard to come by and the London organizers were forced to secure a larger space to accommodate more and more eager fans. The *Toronto Daily Star*, not always sympathetic to the growth of women's sport, commented, "The importance amateur sport has attained in Canada is amply evidenced by the fact that the Edmonton ladies' basketball team, champions of Western Canada, will arrive in London tomorrow to play for the Dominion title. It is 2,049 miles from Edmonton to Toronto. Think of it, 4,098 miles [of] travelling by a ladies team in search of a championship emblem. That is real sport."[25]

Upon arriving in London, the Commercial Graduates went straight to the basketball court to warm up and practise. Their first game against the Shamrocks would use the Spalding ladies' rules requiring all six players, so there would be no substitutions if a player became tired or, worse still, fouled out. As the game started before a crowd of 1,500 spectators, it became clear that the London team was never a serious contender. The Grads put on a dazzling display of basketball with remarkable shooting, exceptional guarding, and individual stamina. They swamped the Shamrocks by 41–8. The next day they played an exhibition game against the St. Thomas Collegiate Institute team. Even by conceding to score only one point for a basket instead of the usual two, and with the first period under ladies' rules and the second under men's, the Grads still beat them by a score of 19–16. However, that same evening, probably due to fatigue and the fact that the game was played using the less familiar men's rules, they lost to the Shamrocks 8–21. It didn't matter because the combined score for both games with the Shamrocks was 49–29, and the Grads had won the first Dominion championship. They capped it off the following day by defeating an all-star team from Toronto 29–11; the Toronto team included well-known sprinters Rosa Grosse and Grace Conacher. Tired, happy, and with their heads held high, the six Grads, along with Coach Page and his chaperone wife Maude, got back on the train for the long journey home and the ecstatic reception awaiting them in Edmonton.

Coach J. Percy Page

Who was this methodical and determined Percy Page and where had he come from? The young teacher was not originally from Alberta. His family had settled for many years in Halton County, at the western edge of Lake Ontario, although Page was born in 1887 in Rochester, New York. His father, Absalom Page, and his uncle, John Mitchell, operated a grist mill in Trafalgar Township in Halton County. In 1886 Absalom moved with his wife Elizabeth and two daughters to Rochester to work as a miller. A third child, George Roy, was born in 1886, and John Percy, the youngest of four children, was born the following year. Sadly, their mother died three years later, and Percy, along with his sister Ella May, went to live with their aunt and uncle, Mary (Absalom's sister) and John Mitchell, back in Ontario. Absalom Page remarried a few years later and continued to live in New York State with his daughter Laura and his second wife Mary Howell. By 1901, Percy and his siblings Ella May and George Roy were living in the Ontario village of Bronte (now part of Oakville) with their widowed Aunt Mary and grandmother Johanna Page.[26]

An excellent student, Page attended public school in Bronte and then went to high school in Oakville and Hamilton. A keen athlete, he played on school teams, but his favourite sport was long distance running. During the summers he worked in the family business, the Page & Mitchell's Bronte Steam Mills.[27] After graduating from high school, he attended the Ontario Normal College in Hamilton to qualify as a teacher. In those days, teachers were often not much older than their students, so in 1906, at only nineteen years old, Page began his teaching career at Rothesay Collegiate School for Boys in Rothesay, New Brunswick. He continued his sports activities by playing for the Saint John Marathons, the Maritimes senior ice hockey champions.[28] Returning to Ontario after a year, he took up a position at the Collegiate Institute in St. Thomas, where his coaching career began. The girls' basketball team needed a coach and Page volunteered his services. Familiar with basketball fundamentals and not much else, he bought a book about the game, and from that point onwards, he became a student of the game by reading everything he could about it.[29]

In 1910, Page completed his commercial teaching credentials and married a fellow teacher from St. Thomas, Maude Roche. With her usual wry sense of humour, his wife would joke that they had met at skating rink and she "has had him on ice ever since."[30] The young couple arrived in Edmonton in the fall of 1912 and set up home on the north side, not far from McDougall High School. Page had been hired by the Edmonton Public School Board to introduce commercial training to the city's high schools. His job was to establish a course of study to teach students the essentials of bookkeeping, stenography, typing, rapid calculation, accounting, and anything else they needed to know to work in a business. Always looking to improve his education, Page was awarded a bachelor of arts degree in 1913 from Queen's University in Kingston, making him one of the few high school teachers with a university degree to be hired in Edmonton at the time.[31]

Coach J. Percy Page.

[CEA EB-27-43]

McDougall High School, 1914. [GA NC-6-765]

When Percy Page and his wife Maude arrived in Edmonton, they found a city on the verge of a frantic boom period. In 1911, the citizens of Strathcona, an independent community on the south side of the North Saskatchewan River, had voted to amalgamate with north-side Edmonton, bringing their combined population to just over 30,000, which ballooned to more than 50,000 by the end of 1912. Newcomers, mostly from the United States and Europe, were drawn to Edmonton and surrounding area by the prospect of cheap land and a vibrant city spread along both sides of the river. The boom was short-lived due to over-speculation and collapsing money markets, but Edmonton continued to prosper and grow, so much so that by the eve of World War I in 1914 its population had reached 72,000.

Early Women's Sport in Edmonton

Like many Canadian cities before the Great War, Edmonton offered a wide variety of sports, but these sports were played mainly in voluntary clubs such as the YMCA, where mostly individual men and boys participated. As the city grew, unfulfilled spectators demanded more sport entertainment, which was envisioned as men's-only sport. Edmonton's citizens could choose from senior men's ice hockey in the winter, soccer and football in the fall, and most popular of all, professional baseball in the summer. Built in 1913, the indoor Edmonton Stock Pavilion was the pride and joy of local sports boosters; it was the largest of its kind in Canada—an arena floor larger than Madison Square Garden in New York with a capacity of 6,000 spectators. Later on, the Edmonton Grads benefitted significantly from this facility because they could guarantee a large venue to attract visiting teams.[32]

Working-class women, who flocked to the cities before and during World War I seeking employment in the factories, stores, and businesses, had little hope of attending college or university, where women's sport was well-established and flourishing. Neither could they afford to belong to the elite tennis, golf, and curling clubs, which long ago had welcomed women, albeit on the basis of restricted times to play. Instead, working-class women sought to expand their sporting opportunities and athletic presence through a grassroots movement that established women's athletic clubs, organizations, and leagues in an increasing variety of sports, especially basketball, ice hockey, softball, and track and field. Individual sponsors, businesses, factories, municipalities, and sometimes women themselves provided the necessary equipment, uniforms, and facilities to allow them to play and compete. The Hudson's Bay Company in western Canada, for example, was active in providing recreational sport opportunities for its employees, many of whom were young women.

An athletic facility was often built near the store. In Edmonton, the Fur Trappers, who played in a ladies' mercantile basketball league were frequently the best "100% mercantile" team in the province.[33]

The period immediately following the war and throughout the 1920s was tremendously exciting for Canadian sportswomen and their fans. Nothing seemed to hold them back. Often called the "golden age" of women's sport, it was a time when popular team sports like basketball, ice hockey, and softball became sufficiently organized to hold provincial and Dominion championships, and the best athletes, especially in track and field, began to compete internationally and eventually at the Olympic Games. There was a growing public enchantment with these new stars of the athletic world and the sports press obliged by reporting their exploits and, for the most part, treating them seriously. "Canadian women are not just knocking at the door of the world of sport," observed a male sportswriter, "they have crashed the gate, swarmed the field and, in some cases, have driven mere man to the sidelines."[34] The Edmonton Grads were very much a part of this exciting era, and they helped fashion a new model of athletic womanhood, characterized by the masculine qualities of skill, strength, speed, agility, and energy, while at the same time retaining their femininity. Their very presence helped to redefine the earlier contested notions of womanhood.

2 Unlikely Civic Boosters

WILLIAM F. "DEACON" WHITE, Edmonton's first promoter of big-league sport, had little interest in promoting women's sport, and certainly not women's basketball. Originally from Chicago, he arrived in Edmonton in 1906 as the playing manager of a touring baseball team from Washington. He enjoyed the city so much he decided to stay. The prospect of starting a professional baseball team in Edmonton was a big attraction. White played a major role in the formation of the Western Canada Baseball League and coached the Edmonton team as well as the Eskimos Rugby Club. When war broke out, he signed up with the Canadian Over-Seas Expeditionary Force. After being wounded in France, he rejoined his unit and was put in charge of organizing recreational baseball for

William F. "Deacon" White. [PAA A7286]

the troops; discharged in 1919, he returned to Edmonton to continue his sporting ventures especially in baseball, football, and hockey.[1]

One day in the spring of 1923, Joseph Driscoll, owner of a sporting goods store in Edmonton, coaxed Deacon White to watch the Grads in action at McDougall Commercial. That day, the Grads were practising against a boys' team from McDougall and playing men's rules. "Having come to scoff," Page remembered years later, "he remained to praise."[2] White was stunned. "It was really amazing," he commented in the *Edmonton Bulletin* the next day, "to see them crash into their men opponents and in turn get crashed into unavoidably, without, to use a rough expression, a squawk."[3] As a sports promoter, he immediately saw the possibilities of big-time basketball in Edmonton, even if it was played by women.

The Grads wanted to bring the London Shamrocks to Edmonton in 1923 for a rematch, but they lacked the funds to do it themselves. If they could pull it off, this would be a first for Edmonton—no other sport, men's or women's, had ever brought a Dominion championship series to the city. Deacon White offered to underwrite the games himself, agreeing to protect the Commercial Graduates Club against any loss, and to a 50–50 split if there were any profits. After much negotiation between Percy Page and Carrie Blackwell, manager of the London Shamrocks, the terms were settled. The visitors were guaranteed $700 in expense money, more than the Grads had received the previous year in London. Since the only venue able to accommodate a large crowd was the Edmonton Arena, a basketball court would be erected in the centre of the dirt oval on a specially built wood floor at considerable expense. Finally, and much to the disadvantage of the Grads, both games would be played using the Spalding men's rules, with the total score determining the champion.

Advance ticket sales—sold at Joe Driscoll's store—were brisk with a capacity crowd of 5,000 expected on both nights. The city promised to run an extra streetcar service to the Arena, and the popular Edmonton Newsboys Band would entertain the crowd between halves. The Commercial Graduates—now an expanded team of eight players—were not overly familiar to Edmonton fans, but the local papers ran one or more articles a day in the lead-up to the series. They also provided useful information about the players and their Shamrock opposition. Grads captain Eleanor Mountifield, a "tall, graceful, willowy blond" at right guard, excelled at setting up the play and passing to her teammates. Eleanor would be responsible for guarding an outstanding Shamrock forward, Pearl Blackwell, the tallest member of the team and sister of Carrie Blackwell, their playing manager. Beside Eleanor at left guard would be Mary Dunn, short and sturdy, "who likes the rough and tumble going." Her check would be Isabel Duncan, the youngest of the Shamrocks, but a "speed merchant on her feet, and a dangerous customer around the goal." Playing centre would be Connie Smith, who "follows her check around like a hawk and sees to it that her opponent does not do too much scoring." Opposite her would be Lottie Garratt, the "big noise of the London team," and an all-round player with an international reputation. Veteran Winnie Martin, "who knows the game from every angle and plays it with intelligence," would play forward and be guarded by Mary Clark, "a sturdily built young lady," new to the Shamrocks. Playing in the other forward slot was Dorothy "Dot" Johnson, a "natural lady athlete, a flash on her feet, who handles herself with grace and ease." Dot would be guarded by Mary Lindsay, whose speed, alertness, and aggressiveness caught everyone's attention last year. Substitutes were Elizabeth Elrick, who had already played for the Grads for five seasons although under women's rules; Nellie Perry and Daisy Johnson, members of last year's winning team; and newcomer Abbie Scott. Coaching the Shamrocks was Dr. George Smith, physical director at the University of Western Ontario, who had steered his team to victory against the best women's teams in the United States.[4]

Everything was ready for the most important basketball series ever held in Edmonton. Over 3,000 fans came to the Arena the first night and watched the Commercial Graduates defeat the London Shamrocks by a score of 17–6 in one of the fastest and most bitterly contested games seen in Edmonton. The *Edmonton Bulletin* called it a "wonderful exhibition of basketball—probably the best played anywhere in the world."[5] The Grads were faster and better shots, but more importantly, they displayed a style of play that would forever characterize their game. On attack, they used a system of sharp and accurate criss-cross passes, drawing their opponents away from their checks and eventually leaving one of their players free to secure a reasonably good shot at the basket. On the second night of the series, 4,000 spectators watched the Shamrocks again go down to defeat, 22–34, in an even better game than the first one. The Grads were simply superior. They were faster, heavier, and in better condition; they checked harder and closer, passed faster and more accurately, shot better and more often; they evaded the Shamrocks' checks at will and had a better system of play. In a word, they dazzled the fans. Coach Page also did something he would rarely do in the future. He sent in his substitute players—except for Eleanor Mountifield who stayed on the floor—for the last two minutes of the game. The Commercial Graduates had secured the Dominion title for the second year in a row and were now ready for a bigger challenge.

The series was not entirely a financial success, but Deacon White did not lose any money. Given the 50–50 agreed split on any profits, White and the Commercial Graduates Club each earned a little over $400 after all expenses had been paid. More importantly, the series had been hugely successful in introducing the game of basketball to Edmonton fans and in spreading publicity across the country, indeed throughout North America. The McDermid Engraving Company sent cuts of the individual snapshots of the Grads to eighteen of the leading newspapers in Canada and a syndicated story ran in major papers in the United States and Canada. As the Club pointed out in a letter thanking patrons for their support, "Edmonton is bound to derive more publicity from a sporting standpoint than it has ever received from any previous event."[6]

The Grads were now ready for stronger competition, which meant challenging a team south of the border. They chose the Cleveland Favorite Knits. Women's basketball, especially the industrial teams and leagues, was growing in the United States, just as in Canada. Businesses employing large numbers of young single women recognized the need to provide for their recreational and athletic needs. They constructed recreational facilities and sponsored teams that competed in intramural company events, in local industrial and municipal leagues, and occasionally in national competition.[7] Cleveland had been particularly successful at developing women's amateur and industrial basketball leagues, and with a huge 12,000 seat public auditorium suitable for basketball events, their teams could challenge and attract other teams.

By 1923, the Cleveland Favorite Knits, sponsored by the Favorite Knitting Mills and Sporting Goods Company, had been in existence for seven years. They consistently beat most of the teams they played. Individual players with names like Schier, Dachtler, and Haas reflected the team's German heritage. They also called themselves "world champions," with the temerity to print it on their uniforms. Most importantly, they played men's rules and had beaten the London Shamrocks, which made them worthy opponents for the Grads to challenge next. The Favorite Knits immediately accepted the invitation to come to Edmonton, an offer sweetened by $1,800 in expense money.

The Commercial Graduates Club again decided to engage the services of sports promoter Deacon White to look after everything connected with the series except the management of the team. They offered him two alternatives: one was a salary of $250 to assume all business arrangements, in which case the Club would protect him against any loss; the other was a commission of 33.3 per cent of the net profits, in which case he was to protect the Club against any loss.[8] White certainly recognized a good deal when he saw one, and despite the risk, he chose the second alternative. The Club was relieved because, given past deficits, they were in no position to suffer a financial loss. Priced from 50 cents to

1923 world champions. Back row: Dorothy Johnson, Connie Smith, Daisy Johnson, Winnie Martin, Abbie Scott; front row: Elizabeth Elrick, Eleanor Mountifield, Nellie Perry, and Mary Dunn. [CEA EB-27-11]

$1.25 depending on their location in the Arena, tickets were sold by mail order. Over 1,200 of the available 4,800 seats were ordered on the first day alone, and a few days later, tickets were mostly gone. The Grads were bringing big-time basketball to Edmonton.

The Cleveland team arrived in town to much fanfare and great anticipation on a sunny day in June. The local papers made certain that fans knew something about the Favorite Knits and each of its players, since Edmontonians were becoming increasingly familiar with the Grads and the players themselves. Observers predicted the Grads would have the hardest battle of their career because the two teams, as far as anyone could tell, were evenly matched. Aware that those attending the games were not entirely familiar with the rules of basketball, the Commercial Graduates Club took the unusual step of reminding fans that no "razzing" of an opponent should take place during a penalty shot (called a free throw today) otherwise a technical foul against the home team would result. They were especially concerned because so many of the Favorite Knit players were of "foreign birth," such that well meaning but misguided fans "might make use of this fact in giving colour to their 'rooting.'"[9] No spectator, they pleaded, should make any remark during the games that would be offensive, even to the slightest degree, to the visiting team.

The night of the first game arrived and the Arena was filled beyond capacity. The crowd was bigger than during the winter at the popular Western Canada Hockey League games featuring the Edmonton Eskimos. Scores of other supporters tuned their crystal sets to radio station CJCA, which posted an announcer with a telephone on the arena floor. The Grads shone, especially in their defensive work, and they beat the Favorite Knits 34–20 with better shooting, snappier passing, and surer ball handling. Anticipating an even more exciting second game, over 6,000 fans jammed into the Arena and watched the Grads win again, 19–13. The Grads never once lost the lead during this game. They were now "world champions," certainly a first for Edmonton, and the series was a financial success for both the Commercial Graduates Club and for Deacon White. The Grads' share of the net profits amounted to almost $3,000. For every dollar Deacon White made for himself, he had made two for the Club. Although this had been an astute business deal, Percy Page knew he could do the job just as well as Deacon White, and from then on the Grads never used a promoter to help organize a series. As for White, he became one of the Grads' strongest supporters primarily through his "Sport is My Subject" column in the *Edmonton Bulletin*.

Underwood International Basketball Trophy, 1923. [GA ND-3-2046]

By the end of the summer, three teams—two in the United States and one in Canada—had challenged the Grads for the right to compete for the new Underwood trophy (more properly known as the Underwood International Trophy), donated by J.J. Seitz, president of the Underwood Typewriter Company of Canada. Any team in Canada and the United States was eligible to challenge the holders of the cup—given first to the Grads to defend—providing they could prove to a board of trustees that they had a competitive record justifying the challenge. The Grads waived their privilege to question the credentials of the challenging teams because not only was this regulation vague, there was no time for the trophy organizers to establish a board of trustees. Besides, the Grads were ready to take on all comers. Edmonton City Council approved the use of the Arena, as long as the games were over before the hockey season began, at a charge of $250 for each two-game series. The guarantees for the three teams challenging the Grads came to a total of $5,200—not an insignificant sum even by today's standards. Any surplus would go into a trust fund to help the Grads compete in Europe the following summer, or alternatively, to undertake a playing tour of the United States. Percy Page was clearly now both coach and business manager of the Edmonton Commercial Graduates.

Aware of the unprecedented publicity the Grads brought to the city, Edmonton businessmen were becoming increasingly involved in the basketball club's affairs. Officers for 1923–1924 included honorary president John M. Imrie, publisher of the *Edmonton Journal*, along with the presidents of the Rotary, Kiwanis, and Gyro service clubs and the Edmonton Board of Trade acting as patrons. At the political and governmental levels, patrons also included the Lieutenant Governor of Alberta, the mayor of the City of Edmonton, the superintendent of schools, and the president of the Dominion Basketball Association. Aside from individuals who had an official relationship with the Commercial Graduates Basketball Club,

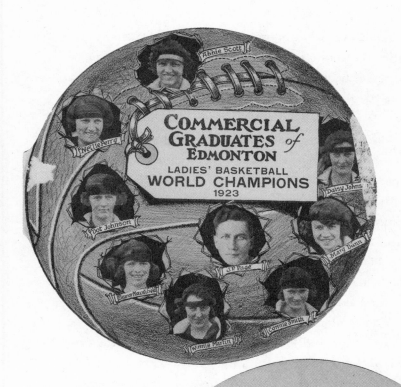

COMMERCIAL GRADUATES *of* EDMONTON
LADIES' BASKETBALL
WORLD CHAMPIONS
1923

Abbie Scott
Lavette Perry
Daisy Johns
Dot Johnson
J.P. Page
Mary Dunn
Eleanor Mountifield
Connie Smith
Winnie Martin

CHALLENGE SERIES

FOR THE

World's Basket Ball Championship, 1923

Toronto "Maple Leafs" - September 25, 27
Chicago "Uptown Brownies" - October 11, 13
Warren "National Lamps" - - October 23, 25

ALL SIX GAMES WILL BE PLAYED IN

The Arena

and the proceeds will be used to assist in sending the Commercial Grads. to the Olympic Games at Paris, 1924

Designed and Engraved by McDermid Studios, Ltd.
Printed by McKenzie-Stowe Press, Ltd.

Game program from Underwood International Trophy Series, fall 1923. [UAL] there was also a growing informal organization of businessmen who supported the Grads and acted more as "cheerleaders" by providing encouragement rather than financial support. John Michaels, owner of Mike's News Stand on Jasper Avenue between 100 and 101 Street, which was the ticket outlet for men's hockey, baseball, and football, agreed to sell tickets for the upcoming Underwood trophy series. This was the beginning of a long relationship between the Grads and Mike's, which lasted until the team disbanded. Charlie Hepburn ran an ice cream parlour and candy store, a favourite spot for service club luncheons and small banquets. Following an international series, the Grads and their opponents would often be entertained at a dance at Charlie's upstairs parlour. Other supporters included Jim McGavin and his son Bill of McGavin Bakeries; Maurice Brown, a businessman and active Rotarian, and Edmonton merchants Joe Moir and Bill Freeman.

The first challengers for the Underwood trophy were the Toronto Maple Leafs, the same all-star team the Grads had defeated in 1922 during their trip east. The Toronto Ladies Athletic Club, an exclusively women's organization with teams in several sports, sponsored the team, which included well-known athletes like sprinter Rosa Grosse and hockey star Grace Conacher. Also on the team was Alexandrine (Alex) Gibb, a founding member of the club, who would soon become Canada's pre-eminent woman sports journalist. The Grads prepared by practising against a team of boys from McDougall High School, which helped sharpen their knowledge of the men's game. When they appeared on the Arena floor to a wildly cheering crowd, they had ditched their restrictive bloomers and were outfitted in short-sleeved tops and knee-length shorts, with socks and kneepads covering their legs. "Distinctly athletic looking," according to one observer, they were doubtless more free to move about the court.[10] After a slow start, the Grads demolished the Toronto team by a score of 41–11, scoring 28 points to their opponent's 1 point in the last twenty minutes of the game. Although the crowd was smaller the first night, some 5,500 fans watched them crush the Maple Leafs 26–13 on the second night.

Next up were the Chicago Uptown Brownies, billed as the "Champions of the Middle States."[11] The team originated in 1916 through the Illinois Athletic Club and was one of several amateur women's teams in Chicago at the time. Early on they switched from wearing baggy bloomers to the more immodest boys-style uniforms, causing a public outcry. Because they had always worn brown uniforms, they were popularly known as the Brownies, and when they came under the sponsorship of a north side Chicago banker in 1921, they became the Uptown Brownies. In 1922 and 1923 they had won the central Amateur Athletic Union (AAU) tournament championship in the United States and were seen as worthy challengers to the Underwood trophy. The first game against the Grads was very close, but the Edmonton team squeaked out a victory with a score of 20–17. "These Chicago girls play basketball—real basketball," reported one sportswriter. "They are strong and heavy, fast in running and accurate in their passing, and they can shoot. Also they check close and hard."[12] They were very skilled at drawing the opposing guards out of position, which allowed one of their forwards, often the great Elsie Schreiber, to dribble the ball the length of the floor for a shot. The Grads had met their match for the first time, and it had taken time to adjust. In a bizarre twist, Percy Page— with permission from the Brownies—refereed the game. Demanding more remuneration than Page thought they deserved, basketball referees in the city had refused to handle the game. Most observers claimed he had been very fair under difficult circumstances.

Almost 9,000 spectators packed the Arena for the second game against the Brownies. Thousands more were disappointed that they could not get in. The short-lived referee dispute was resolved and Elwood Butchart and George Parney, both from the Varsity team,

Edmonton Grads versus Warren National Lamps, Edmonton Arena, 1923.

[GA ND-3-2145]

handled the game. The contest was neck and neck until the last
seven minutes when the Grads found the basket and scored three in a
row to win the game by 25–20. The arena crowd immediately jumped
to its feet and pandemonium reigned. Winnie Martin, Connie
Smith, Dot and Daisy Johnson, Mary Dunn, Nellie Perry, Eleanor
Mountifield, Abbie Scott, and young newcomer Helen McIntosh, still
a schoolgirl at Commercial, were Edmonton's favourite champions.

The last challengers for the Underwood trophy in 1923 were a
team from Warren, Ohio called the National Lamps, so named
because they were sponsored by a company that manufactured electric lamps. Despite bringing a large contingent of players, coaches,
and even a dietician to Edmonton, the Lamps were no match for the

Commercial Graduates. They played a rough and tumble version of basketball, yet the Grads kept their heads and beat them by a total score of 62–15 over the two-game series. Dot Johnson was the best sharpshooter for the Grads, and Mary Dunn did a magnificent job on defence.

This first international series had been a spectacular success for the Grads and for the city of Edmonton. The games had attracted thousands of spectators, who filled the arena to capacity each night, resulting in a considerable profit for the club. Percy Page had made the right decision to manage the business side of the series himself because, aside from paying out expenses, none of the proceeds had to be shared with an outside promoter. More important to the city, and especially the business community, the series generated unprecedented publicity. The Edmonton Commercial Graduates basketball story, with an accompanying group photo, was carried by most major newspapers in Canada and no less than 300 dailies in the United States; it also appeared in papers as far away as Hong Kong, Cuba, and the Philippines.[13] A group of Edmonton businessmen were so pleased with this publicity that they presented Page with a shiny new Chevrolet Coupe—fully equipped and insured—as a token of their appreciation for his work. Page, who had previously travelled by bicycle or streetcar, set about learning to drive.

Many of these businessmen were also Rotarians, as was Percy Page, and the Rotary Club began to play an increasing role in the success of the Grads. When the team returned from their first European tour in 1924 (see Chapter 3), Page addressed the Edmonton Rotary branch, acknowledging that they had "fathered" the Grads' organization from 1922 onwards, since it "had begun doing things in a big way."[14] The Rotarians did not provide direct financial support, but individual members did small favours for the Grads. As a group, they were highly enthusiastic team boosters. A select group of trusted advisors also provided Page with advice concerning the financial and

"The Gang" of supportive Edmonton Rotarians: Bill Freeman, Bill McGavin, Charlie Hepburn, Maurice Brown, Joe Moir, and John Michaels. [CEA EB-27-14]

business aspects of the team, something he rarely discussed with the players. Many years later, he explained his rationale: "It is very seldom that I ask them to bother about financial matters. I feel they have enough to worry about in keeping themselves in condition, and in playing their games. I usually accept the responsibility of deciding these other matters myself."[15] As their business manager, Page was firmly in control of the affairs of the club. He arranged all games and schedules; he negotiated with opponents regarding gate receipts and expenses; he dealt with the city and the Arena managers when the team played at home; he organized their travel plans and took care of everything when they were away. He was incredibly organized and fastidious, and no small detail ever escaped his attention.[16]

As time went on, more local businesses supported the Grads, whether it was through providing services for free or at a discount, giving them little gifts in appreciation of their efforts, or employing them full-time. When a local business hired a Grad, they were also prepared to arrange her vacation schedule or give her time off so she could travel with the team. In later years, when attendance at the games was flagging, businesses often provided one or two pages of advertising in Edmonton newspapers. Before the 1930 Canadian championship series against Toronto Lakesides, for example, readers of the *Edmonton Journal* were challenged to name the former and present Grads whose pictures appeared in the advertisements, which included stores, restaurants, hotels, a bank, and a variety of services. Six double free passes went to the "neatest and most correct answers."[17]

The affairs of the Commercial Graduates Basketball Club were always above board and carried out in the open, which contributed greatly to the admiration and public support enjoyed by the team. Their financial books were open for anyone to examine, with full statements sometimes published in the newspaper. As the Depression took its toll, the Grads faced greater difficulties in paying their way, and from a public relations perspective, it was important that their fans understood the implications of not supporting the team. A series at home generally cost about $2,000. The bulk of expenses were train fares and berths and hotel accommodation in Edmonton for the visiting team. Other expenses included floor painting, advertising, photos, telegrams, cartage, ticket seller, arena rental, taxis, officials, and a percentage (usually 10 per cent) to the Canadian Basketball Association.[18] The Grads were entirely dependent on gate receipts to acquire the necessary funds. Some series cost them money, but if the games were well attended, they usually made a profit. The money earned was also needed to pay for the club's ongoing expenses, which included

Advertising Edmonton's own Commercial Grads, 1926: Percy Page, Patricia Page, Elsie Bennie, Kate Macrae, Millie McCormack, Hattie Hopkins, and an unidentified gentleman. [CEA EA-10-2060]

equipping the Grads, Gradettes, and two school teams, the costs associated with their practices, and meals and incidental expenses when the Grads travelled. (The host team was usually responsible for transportation and accommodation.) In sum, all money earned through gate receipts was poured back into the club to keep it solvent. No one connected with the Grad organization ever received any money, although certainly many players benefitted indirectly from the opportunity to travel, all expenses paid.

Over the course of the team's existence, especially from 1922 to 1940, the Grads were unquestionably the best civic boosters in Edmonton's history. They brought attention to the city through their phenomenal success, and especially during their many travels throughout North America and Europe. They were superb ambassadors and the city became known as the "Edmonton of the Grads." After James Naismith, the founder of basketball, saw the team play in Edmonton in 1925 against a team from Guthrie, Oklahoma, he sent a letter to Page, which was subsequently syndicated and sent to newspapers throughout the United States. Although this brought invaluable publicity to Edmonton, there was also something instructive in Naismith's letter, part of which reads:

> I was particularly anxious...to see how the boys' style of games affected the social attributes and the general health of your players, and I can assure you that it was with no little pleasure that I found these young ladies exhibiting as much grace and poise at an afternoon tea as vigorous ability on the basketball court. I can only conclude that this is due very largely to the fine womanly influence of Mrs. Page, supporting your own high standards of sportsmanship and coaching ability.
>
> I feel sure that under proper management, and dominated with right ideals, basketball may be an efficient aid in developing in young women health, skill and refinement, and I would like to congratulate you and your team on the fact that while retaining their fine womanly instincts they have been able to achieve such marked success.[19]

Success on the basketball court, while at the same time retaining womanly attributes and instincts, was essential to earning respect and admiration for women athletes of the day. Almost from the beginning, writers and commentators noticed this quality among the Grads. Writing in *MacLean's Magazine* in 1923, Dorothy Bell observed, "There are two things besides the brilliant play of the Grads that have endeared them to the hearts of Canadian sport-lovers. One is the smile that shines on the face of each player through every battle, no matter how rough it may be; the other, their undeniable feminine charm that is their chief attraction."[20] She went on to say that even

Marching along Jasper Avenue during the Edmonton Exhibition parade, 1923.

[GA NC-6-10751]

though the Grads have battled teams from coast to coast, tussled with heavy boys' teams, stood up under stiff training and long hours of practice, they have lost none of their femininity. James Naismith would return to this theme several times. In his tribute to the Grads on the occasion of their twenty-first birthday in 1936, he wrote, "My admiration and respect go to you also because you have remained unspoiled by your success, and have retained the womanly graces notwithstanding your participation in a strenuous game. You are not only an inspiration to basketball players throughout the world, but a model for all girls' teams. Your attitude and success have been a source of gratification to me in illustrating the possibilities of the game in the development of the highest type of womanhood."[21]

The Grads were cherished ambassadors for the City of Edmonton and their winning ways brought acclaim and attention to the city, but at the same time, as individuals, they were expected to represent the highest ideals of womanhood. Percy Page insisted that his players be ladies first and basketball players second, and he kept a tight rein on their behaviour both on and off the court. Whether they were travelling across Alberta or the Atlantic, the rules were the same—no going out without permission, no smoking, drinking, swearing, or chewing gum, and always be smartly dressed. A lady is also polite, respectful, considerate, and discreet. On the basketball court, he demanded discipline and sportsmanship. Anyone whose behaviour did not measure up to that of a young lady well-versed in the social graces would simply not have become a Grad. In pre-World War II society, the term "lady" did not carry negative connotations, and individual Grads accepted the concept as the ultimate pinnacle of womankind.[22] They were also young working women earning their keep, although given the conventions of the day, still living at home. As expected, they would soon marry and withdraw from both the athletic and work world to become homemakers and mothers, and they accepted their future usually without question. As a team, and as individuals, they were probably the most successful and respected civic boosters Edmonton had ever seen. This became increasingly evident as they took on more and more opponents, and especially as they ventured beyond North America to Europe.

3   Taking On the World

THE COMMERCIAL GRADS had now defeated three teams from the United States, including one claiming to be "world champions." Although these were international matches, teams could not possibly claim a world title without first beating a championship team from Europe. By the early 1920s, the French were leading the way in international sport for women. Refused entry into the male sports world, especially in athletics, swimming, basketball, soccer, and cycling, women formed their own sports clubs such as *Fémina-Sport* (1911) and *Academia* (1915) in Paris. They sponsored matches, organized national championships, and formed a national federation. While much of this activity had originally been led by sympathetic men, it was a woman who emerged as the

49

leader of international sport for women. A member of the *Fémina-Sport* club, Alice Milliat was first treasurer and then president of the *Fédération des sociétés féminines sportives de France,* founded in 1917. This organization had successfully staged national championships in several sports, including basketball. It was time to petition the International Olympic Committee (IOC) to consider more women's events in the Summer Olympics, especially track and field.

Although the IOC had reluctantly allowed women's events in tennis, golf, archery, and swimming in the Summer Games between 1900 and 1920, it was adamantly opposed to opening the Games to female track and field athletes. Milliat and her colleagues were rebuffed, but not defeated. They persuaded the tiny principality of Monaco to host the first *Féminines Internationales de Monte-Carlo* in March 1921, where some 300 women athletes from France, England, Italy, Norway, and Switzerland participated in a variety of demonstrations and sports, including track and field and basketball. In the final of the basketball tournament, a team from England beat the *Fémina-Sport* team. Milliat also formed the *Fédération sportive féminine internationale* (FSFI), which, in August 1922, organized a spectacular international track and field meet—the *Jeux olympiques féminins*—in the Pershing Stadium in Paris. The event attracted 600 athletes from nine nations, including a team from the United States, and they competed before 15,000 enthusiastic spectators. The IOC was still unmoved and refused yet another plea to include women's track and field in the next Summer Olympics to be held in Paris in 1924; nor was the IOC interested in having basketball, let alone women's basketball, on their program. Women would have to be content with competitions in tennis, swimming, and fencing.

Canadian women did not compete in these first international women's track and field meets because the Amateur Athletic Union of Canada (AAU of C) had little interest in promoting the sport for women, nor did Canada send any women to compete in these early Summer Olympics. Basketball, on the other hand, was another matter. Certainly, Percy Page was following these developments and realized there was an opportunity for his team to compete in Europe—and soon. At the third *Féminines Internationales de Monte-Carlo* in April 1923, there were five nations represented in the basketball tournament—England, Italy, Switzerland, Czechoslovakia, and France. Italy and England won the first round, France having drawn a bye; France then defeated Italy in the semi-finals and England in the finals, thus giving the French team the European championship.

Page contacted the captain of the English women's basketball team and corresponded with Alice Milliat at the FSFI. Miss Birchenough, the English captain, replied enthusiastically that games could be arranged in England, and more importantly, Milliat invited the Grads to take part in a special tournament to be organized in Paris while the "men's Olympic contests" were taking place.[1] The only stipulation was that the team be officially recognized as Canadian champions by the AAU of C, which happened at its annual meeting in October 1923. They sanctioned the European trip providing that the Grads paid their own way. With their first international tour now a realization, all Page needed to ensure were the necessary funds for the trip—an estimated $7,500.

Although gate receipts from the Underwood trophy challenge matches in 1923 had boosted the Grads' trust fund considerably, they still needed to raise more money. After the ice went out of the Edmonton Arena in the spring and a new wooden floor was installed, the Grads took on several teams in succession, confident their fans would support them. First up was a return series with the Toronto Maple Leafs, who showed speed and aggressiveness but could not find the basket. They were beaten 26–6 in the first game and did not score a single basket—all their points were awarded on free throws. The Grads demolished them 23–14 in the

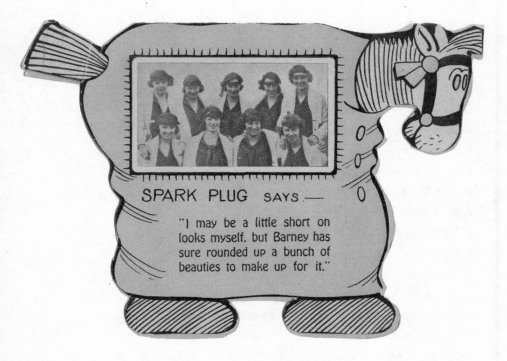

Game program in the shape of Spark Plug, official mascot of the Grads. [UAL]

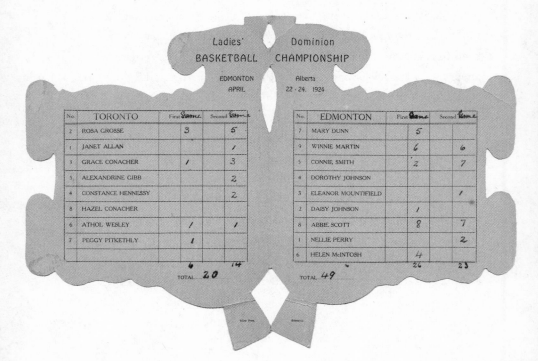

second game, which, according to Deacon White writing in the *Edmonton Bulletin*, "electrified, amazed, and thrilled" the capacity crowd.[2] Next was a series with the Chicago Lakeview Community team, who had an enviable thirty-four wins in thirty-five starts and had beaten the Chicago Uptown Brownies twice during the season. Again, the Grads were far superior, defeating the Chicago visitors 86–21 over two games, and prompting White to write, "It was simply a case of a bigger, faster, better drilled and more skilful collection of sharpshooters up against a team that was lighter, slower, inferior in combination, and lacking in expertness and accuracy in flipping the leather ball through the iron circle."[3] The Chicago coach, Harry Wilson, marvelled at how the Grads were supported in a city with a population of just 60,000, when at least 5,000 fans show up for their games every time. In the third and final series, the Grads handily beat the Cleveland Favorite Knits 22–7 and 40–19.

1924 European Tour and Paris Olympics

With enough money to finance the trip, and the expectation they would do well, the Grads set off on their first trip abroad proudly representing Edmonton and Alberta, and of course Canada. Their new uniforms, made especially for the tour, were a gold middy with black trim with "Commercial Grads" written across the front and "Edmonton" prominently displayed on the back along with the player's number. Down one side of their black knickers was the word "Alberta" with "Canada" displayed on the other side. Their little felt mascot, Spark Plug, a racehorse from the popular *Barney Google* comic strip, was comfortably ensconced in its own carrying case shaped like a boxcar. Mayor Duggan had presented it to them on behalf of the Rotary, Kiwanis, and Gyro service clubs. They also treasured a special silk banner given to them by the Great War Veterans Association of

Leaving for Europe, June 1924, with mascot Spark Plug in his own little box car.
[GA NC-6-11226]

Edmonton, who likened the Grads—true women and true sports—
to the Canadian nurses who served overseas during the war.

Serenaded by the Edmonton Newsboys Band and cheered by thousands of fans, the Grads embarked on their long journey to Europe on
June 19, 1924. The team consisted of Winnie Martin (captain), Mary
Dunn, Connie Smith, Abbie Scott, Dot and Daisy Johnson, Eleanor
Mountifield, and Nellie Perry. Accompanying them on the trip as far
as Montreal was "baby Grad" Helen McIntosh and her mother Ellen,
who performed chaperone duties since Maude Page was already
in the east and would join the team in Hamilton. They travelled

across Canada by train to Port Arthur, Ontario, and from there by steamer to Sarnia, eventually working their way by train and car to Quebec City. The Canadian Pacific Line ship *Montroyal* carried them across the Atlantic to Liverpool where they disembarked and began their travels through England and then on to Europe. They did not return to Edmonton until the end of August, some six weeks later.

Twenty-one-year-old Abbie Scott kept a detailed diary of their trip, which has luckily been preserved. Her observations are those of a young woman travelling afar for the first time and seeing the world. As they passed through small towns in Alberta, like Viking and Wainwright, crowds waved and cheered when the train slowed down. Rotarians met them at scheduled stops across the country, where they were entertained and shown the sights. On board the ship, they had a short workout each morning and then were free to do as they pleased, often dining at night at the Captain's table. Abbie notes that "Tottie" (Eleanor Mountifield) accidentally knocked the ball overboard on the last day during their workout. Docking in Liverpool, they were met by Edmontonian Ralph Forester, a former student of Percy Page, who had fought and been wounded in the war. He had agreed to take charge of their travel and accommodation arrangements throughout the entire trip. Travelling to London by train, they caught a glimpse of magnificent Wembley Stadium, where they hoped to play following their games in France. After sightseeing and shopping in London, they crossed the English Channel, landed at Bologne, and then boarded a train for Paris.

The Grads were scheduled to practise against a couple of pick-up teams in Paris, but they still had plenty of time to take in the sights, watch the track and field events at the Olympic stadium in Colombes, attend social teas and dances, and, of course, go shopping. Abbie bought herself a handmade Paris gown and wore it proudly to a special ball. At their first game, she described how they handily beat the opposition, even if they were hindered a little by unfamiliar rules:

Eleanor Mountifield and Dot Johnson with Commander Latta aboard the SS Montroyal en route to Europe, 1924. [CEA EB-27-21]

And what a game it was!! Of course, it was just a practice game so that we might become familiar with French rules. The man who refereed the game couldn't speak English, and it was too funny for words when he tried to explain things. It was easy to understand "marche," which of course meant walking with the ball, but one time one of the French girls pushed one of our girls, and in order to demonstrate, he got one of them to bend over and then kicked her. Well, it was one way of explaining a foul. Another time a French girl slapped Daisy, and he allotted her a free throw, but she didn't know what it was for so he marched up to her and slapped her on the wrist. So we learned some of the French rules, possibly the hard way. The score was 63 to 14, our favour, so it was an easy team to play against. In the two periods I played I got 23 points, which shows there was not much competition.[4]

In fact, there was little competition from any of the French teams. The Grads beat another Paris pick-up team 65–13 outside on a hot day, and when Abbie scored only 16 points, she attributed it to the heat. At the Pershing stadium, the *Fédération féminine sportive de France* had organized a one-day championship meet mainly for track and field athletes. Basketball was last on the program with the Grads playing an elite Parisian team, supposedly the French champions. They defeated them easily by a score of 69–7. Next up were the European champions, a team from Strasbourg, who proved to be stronger competition. Playing outside on a cinder court and before a large crowd, the Grads were proclaimed European champions by defeating the Strasbourg team 37–8. Abbie admitted in her diary that they "didn't have to put themselves out any, which is a good thing, as it was terrifically hot."

The remainder of their trip was spent mostly sightseeing as the team made its way along the Rhine to Mainz and Coblenz, and then to Luxembourg and Brussels. They spent several days visiting the most war-torn parts of Europe, including Ypres and Vimy, and stopped long enough to pick poppies in Flanders Field. The Grads played two more games against local French teams, one in Lille and another in Roubaix, each time demolishing the opposition. Percy Page, along with Winnie Martin and Daisy Johnson, went back to Paris to attend the third congress of the *Fédération sportive féminine internationale*, where Canada was admitted as a member. At the congress, the Grads were awarded the undisputed right to the world's basketball title until 1926 when the next *Jeux olympiques féminins* were scheduled to take place. As stated in the official FSFI congress report:

> *Canada's application to have the Commercial Graduates' Basketball Club of Edmonton, Canada, awarded the title of "World's Champions" was unanimously granted, after proof had been submitted showing that the Canadian team held the Championship of the United States as well as Canada. The Canadian team is entitled to hold this title until the next Olympic Games. The Congress went on record as being highly pleased with the showing made by the Edmonton ladies, the members expressing themselves as being especially grateful to the visiting team for their kindness in playing exhibition games.[5]*

Page and the others caught up with the team in Calais, where they crossed the channel to Dover, then took the train to Canterbury and on to London. They spent time in Wembley at the British Empire Exhibition, visited museums, including Madame Tussauds, and, of course, they shopped. On the final leg, they headed north to Scotland stopping in Edinburgh and Glasgow, but their promised game in Wembley Stadium against a British team never took place. Returning to Liverpool, they boarded the steamship *Montcalm* for the long journey home. Their ocean voyage was made all the more exciting in anticipation of Winnie Martin's impending marriage in Montreal to Dr. Robert Tait. On board, they had a small party and presented her with table linen in a chrysanthemum pattern, their club flower. The team celebrated with the newly married couple in Montreal, enjoying a huge wedding cake decorated with small dolls dressed as Grads.

Before arriving home, the Grads spent a weekend in New York City, long enough to sightsee and take in a Broadway show. Their train journey continued via Chicago and Winnipeg, but they were delayed a day due to a train wreck blocking the tracks in Unity,

(Top) Warming up for European championship game in Strasbourg, France, 1924. [CEA EB-27-31] (Bottom) 1924 European champions and their Great War Veterans of Edmonton banner. [CEA EB-27-30]

Troisième Année. — N° 94.   SAMEDI 19 JUILLET 1924   Prix : 30 Centimes

LES SPORTIVES
journal illustré féminin

✧ Rédaction, Administration et Publicité : 26, Rue Godot-de-Mauroy, Paris (9e) — Téléphone : Central 41-96 ✧

LE MATCH DE BASKET-BALL
du Stade Pershing

De gauche à droite : ELITE PARISIENNE : Walter, Paulette Puisais, Simone Puisais, Jousselin, Spiess.
EDMONTON CLUB : Eleanor Mountifield, Connie Smith, Nellie Perry, Winnie Martin, Mary Dunn, Dorothy Johnson, Abbie Scott, Daisy Johnson.

The Elite Parisienne team and the Grads are featured in the French journal Les Sportives. [GA M-329]

Maude Page (far left) and Grads holidaying in Malo-les-Bains, France.

[CEA EB-27-36]

Saskatchewan. Waiting for them at home was probably the biggest celebration ever accorded a victorious sports team. Special souvenir buttons displaying photos of individual Grads and their coach were sold to raise money for charity. Thousands of cheering fans met them at the train station when they finally arrived in Edmonton. Preceded by a police escort and two marching bands, they were driven downtown in specially decorated cars to Market Square (now Churchill Square). Twenty thousand excited spectators gathered at the Square shouting "we want the Grads!" The team and their proud coach slowly made their way to a specially built platform where the mayor and premier welcomed them home. The festivities ended with a large bonfire and impressive display of fireworks. The new world champions had been truly feted.

Throughout the next season the Grads held onto the prospect that they would travel to Europe in the summer of 1926 to defend their world championship and compete in the second *Jeux olympiques féminins* in Göteborg, Sweden. Under pressure from the IOC, Alice Milliat had been persuaded to drop the word *olympiques* and the event was now referred to as the *Jeux féminins mondiaux* or the Women's World Games. Much to everyone's disappointment, basketball was not among the sports included in the second Women's World Games, and there was no point in the Grads making the journey across the Atlantic. Instead, the team went on a gruelling two-week road trip to eastern Canada and the United States in April 1926 (discussed in Chapter 7).

Basketball was also not on the Olympic program for men or women, but in those days, each competing nation could ask for demonstration team games in two sports. For the 1928 Olympiad, the Canadian Olympic Committee had requested ice hockey and lacrosse, but they did so without consulting the Canadian Basketball Association, who in turn wrote to the IOC only to be informed there was no possibility of basketball being added to the program. After a highly successful international men's basketball tournament in Sweden, where several nations realized the potential of Olympic competition, the French representative asked again that basketball be a recognized fixture at the 1928 Olympic Games in Amsterdam. As 1927 drew to a close, the Grads were convinced they would be authorized to represent Canada at the next Olympic Games.[6] They had the backing of the Canadian Olympic Committee, but it was up to the IOC to decide whether to include basketball as an Olympic sport.

1928 European Tour and Amsterdam Olympics

Despite considerable lobbying, the IOC was unrelenting, and basketball was not to be part of the Amsterdam Olympics. However, all was not lost. As she had done before in 1924, Alice Milliat invited the Grads to take part in a European tour in conjunction with the Summer Olympics and to defend their world title providing, of course, that they were the official Canadian champions.

The Canadian women's championship in 1928 was determined by a series of playdowns between teams in the east and west. Claiming to be the winners of eastern Canada, the Toronto Lakesides journeyed to Edmonton in late April, where they were handily defeated by the Grads in a two-game series with a 62–49 score. Two weeks later, the Grads also defeated the western champions, the University of British Columbia, by a score of 65–45 over two games. Having defeated one team from the east and one from the west, the Grads considered themselves the Canadian champions and were preparing for their trip to Europe. Indeed, Alice Milliat had already announced their touring schedule and the teams they would play.

But all was not well in eastern Canada. A team from Dalhousie University in Halifax, winners of the Maritime championship, claimed they had the right to play Toronto Lakesides to determine who should have played the Grads. A lawyer was brought in by the Dominion association to sort out the mess. Lakesides were ordered to bring the Halifax team to Toronto or to play a sudden death game in Montreal. Regardless of their choice, Lakesides would be responsible for the expense. They promptly turned down both proposals and, as a result, the Eastern Canadian Basketball Association awarded the title by default to the Halifax team, who now had the right to play the Grads for the "real" Canadian championship.

The Grads had no choice but to accept the ruling because to refuse would jeopardize their European trip. The problem was that they were responsible for the Halifax team's travelling expenses as well as the cost of the two-game series—a total of $2,500. This was a blow to the Grads' organization because, instead of having sufficient funds for their long-planned travels in Europe, they would now have to call upon the public to help finance their trip. The two-game series against the Dalhousie team was an incredibly lop-sided contest with the Grads crushing the opposition by a score of 147–18. There was understandably little public interest, especially in the second game, which resulted in much reduced gate receipts. Realizing there was a shortfall, a group of Edmonton businessmen immediately went to work installing a battery of phones in a downtown office and calling other prominent citizens: "This is the headquarters of the Commercial Graduates Fund—how much can you give us?"[7] In less than a day they raised $1,600, and by the time they finished, they had more than $2,000. As Ken McConnell, sports editor of the *Edmonton Bulletin* and one of the team's most enthusiastic cheerleaders, pointed out, their trip would be welcome publicity and help dispel myths about the city of Edmonton:

> *Every newspaper in every country will carry results of the games and it will no doubt surprise many thousands of people to know that Edmonton, Alberta, Canada, exists and that the natives of the city have time enough, when not fighting off hordes of wild animals, battling the Indians and "mushing" over snow-covered trails, to place representatives, and good ones too, at the Olympic Games.*[8]

Consisting of Gladys Fry, Millie McCormack, Margaret MacBurney, Elsie Bennie, Kate Macrae, and Mae Brown, the team set off east by train on June 21, 1928, making two Ontario stops—Port Arthur and Hamilton—to play exhibition games. They were accompanied by Mr. Page and Elsie's mother, Mrs. Bennie, the latter acting as chaperone until Maude Page, who was already in the east, joined them. The party sailed from Montreal on June 30 and arrived in Liverpool a week later. Over the next two months they visited seven countries and played nine games, mainly against teams in France. While Percy Page sent home brief reports of their games, his wife Maude contributed an almost daily "Log of a Travelling 'Grad'" to the women's section of the *Edmonton Journal*. With characteristic wit and humour, her accounts provide an interesting and informative travelogue as well as insights into the rigors of travelling with a group of energetic and spirited young women. A cultured and educated woman, fluent in French, Maude and her husband encouraged the Grads to explore the cities they visited and introduced them to European culture through museums, plays, operas, vaudeville, and the like.

After arriving in Liverpool, the group motored north through the English Lake District to Glasgow and then to Edinburgh, Scotland. Elsie and her mother left the party to visit relatives in Sterling and Kate Macrae travelled further north to see her Scottish kin. From Edinburgh the team took the train south to London where they spent several days exploring the city and taking in a theatre production of Agatha Christie's *Alibi* starring Charles Laughton as Hercule Poirot. They were then on to Paris. Even with two games scheduled, the girls managed to fit in considerable sightseeing and shopping. They travelled to Lyons to play a game and from there to Geneva. In Geneva they were looked after by Lieut. Col. Georges Vanier, who would eventually become Canada's nineteenth Governor General (1959–1967). According to Maude, he was "courtesy itself and did everything possible to make our stop over a pleasant one."[9] Venice was next. They explored its canals by gondola, cooled off in the Lido, and attended an open-air performance of two Italian operas— *Cavalleria Rusticana* and *Pagliacci*. Milan was the next stop for a scheduled game, and from there they travelled through the Alps by train and steamer, arriving in Basel, Switzerland on August 1.

Their excitement mounted as they headed to Amsterdam in anticipation of cheering on the Canadian contingent, which, as it turned out, was doing rather well, especially the women. This was the first time women were allowed a full program of track and field events in the Summer Olympics. Canada's "Matchless Six," comprised of track athletes Ethel Smith, Myrtle Cook, Fanny "Bobbie"

At the 1928 Toronto Exhibition on their way home from Europe: Mildred McCormack, Gladys Fry, Kate Macrae, Mae Brown, Pat Page, Elsie Bennie, Percy Page, Margaret MacBurney, and Maude Page (standing). [GA NA-3578-7]

Rosenfeld, Jane Bell, and Jean Thompson, along with high jumper Ethel Catherwood, brought home four medals—two gold, one silver, one bronze—and won more points than any other nation. The Grads celebrated with the Toronto competitors in Amsterdam, several of whom they had met on the basketball court. The team then headed to Luxembourg, where another game was scheduled, and from there to Strasbourg and Rheims in France for two more matches, and finally back to Paris.

As for the games themselves, the Grads demolished every team they played, usually beating their opponents by 60 to 70 points, and no team scored more than 20 points against them. Often these games were played in less than ideal conditions on outside courts in unbearable heat. The forward line of Gladys, Millie, and Margaret was superb; Elsie and Kate formed an impenetrable defence; and Mae was always ready to substitute when necessary. Maude Page provided an excellent analysis of what ailed the European teams. Although they never let up and gave everything they had, they lacked the finesse required of a championship team, and perhaps thinking of her husband, she made clear that good coaching was the key:

> They are splendid athletes, but lack coaching in the finer points of the game. They also lack experience in playing against anything except their own type of game. Against the shifting styles which the Grads throw at them, they are helpless and it is almost pathetic to see such capable athletes unable to make use of their unquestionably latent ability. Give these French girls good coaching and they would hold their own with the best teams in the world.[10]

The Grads retained their world championship by defeating an all-star French team from Paris, Rheims, and Lyons. At 46–14, it was their lowest score, mainly because the game was played outside on a sandy court, which slowed up their play considerably. Leaving Europe, they sailed from Cherbourg to Montreal and returned to a triumphal homecoming in Edmonton on Labour Day. Thousands greeted them at the train station and lined the parade route cheering loudly and waving flags as the Grads, each carrying a beautiful bouquet of flowers, travelled through the city on a specially decorated fire truck with sirens blaring. Businesses along the route displayed flags, bunting, and welcome signs. Overhead, two planes swooped and circled, one of which was piloted by war hero Capt. W.R. "Wop" May. It was a fitting tribute to the world champions.

The next opportunity for the Grads to defend their world title would occur in 1930 at the third Women's World Games to be held in Prague, Czechoslovakia, and this time basketball was to be on the program. The Grads, however, declined an invitation to compete because they were saving money to travel to Los Angeles for the 1932 Olympic Games, where they had been invited to give a basketball demonstration. A team from the University of British Columbia (UBC) was chosen to go to Prague in their place. Through bake sales, teas, and bridge parties, augmented by donations from the university and the good citizens of Vancouver, the UBC team raised the necessary funds. When they arrived in Prague, they were shocked to discover that, instead of a tournament, they would play only one game before 10,000 spectators on an over-sized, outdoor cinder court, refereed by an Italian who spoke little English and barely knew the rules. As one member of the team remembered, "They crossed out all the rules in the basketball rule book they didn't like, and put in things they did like."[11] With no substitutions—unless someone was too hurt to continue—and no time taken between the quarters or half, several players did not play, but they were useful on the sidelines, quickly attending cinder-scraped knees. The UBC women beat France, the European champions, by a score of 18–14.

1932 Los Angeles Olympics

The 1932 Canadian women's Summer Olympic team was the largest yet in international competition with nine track athletes, nine swimmers and divers, and one lone fencer. Having a team of this size participate in international competition was a major accomplishment in the midst of the Depression. Basketball was still absent from the Olympic program, which Canadian sportswriters and commentators blamed on the country's sports officials, who, in their opinion, had made little effort to lobby for the inclusion of the sport, especially

1932 team destined for the Los Angeles Olympics: Doris Neale, Helen Stone, Edith Stone, Gladys Fry, Percy Page, Elsie Bennie, Millie McCormack (unable to travel due to illness), Margaret MacBurney, and Babe Belanger. [GA NA-3578-10]

given that Canada had a world-class team in the Grads. Entirely on their own, the Grads went to Los Angeles in August to take in the Olympics. Out of deference to the IOC, who urged that all unnecessary sporting events cease during the period of the Games, they did not play any exhibition games. Travelling with the team were Elsie Bennie, Mildred McCormack, Margaret MacBurney, Gladys Fry, Noella "Babe" Belanger, Doris Neale, and the Stone twins Edith and Helen, accompanied by Coach Page, his wife Maude, and their daughter Patricia.

On their way home, the Grads played several exhibition games. In San Francisco, they defeated an all-star team by 40–7; they vastly outshot the Victoria All-Stars 72–24; and in Prince Rupert they took on a young men's team and beat them by a slim margin of 32–26. They returned home victorious, but little had been accomplished toward their dream of one day competing in the Olympics. Perhaps in Berlin in 1936, it would be their time.

1934 Women's World Games

The fourth Women's World Games were scheduled for London, England in 1934 and basketball was again on the program. The organizing committee had decided that only one team could represent North America, and it would meet the European champions in a single world-title game. The Grads were confident they would be the team representing North America, and, to make their trip worthwhile, an extended European tour could be arranged. The Canadian Basketball Association and the Amateur Athletic Union of the United States agreed to a playoff series between the Canadian and American champions in order to select the team that would go London. This would be the first official North American championship in women's basketball.

Choosing the Canadian champion was fairly straightforward; the Grads won the western Canadian championship and easily beat the Toronto Ladies to win the title. In the United States, there were no national playdowns to choose a winner. Instead, the American champion was declared after winning a specially designated "national" tournament. In 1933, the winner was a team representing the Presbyterian College for Girls in Durant, Oklahoma. Given that the Grads played only men's rules, the fact that women's basketball rules were used at this tournament complicated the situation. Therefore it was decided that the Canada–USA series would consist of five possible games; the first team to win three games would be declared the winner. Furthermore, the games would be played using both sets of rules—the first game under men's rules, the second under women's, and then alternating. There was considerable difference between the two codes: five players for the men versus six for the women; where the men had full run of the court, the women were restricted to their own half; anyone could shoot in the men's game but only the forwards were allowed in the women's game; men could dribble down the entire floor whereas the women were restricted to a single bounce; and finally, the men could snatch the ball from an opponent, but this was not allowed in the women's game. Clearly, the rules would always disadvantage one team.

Located in southeastern Oklahoma, the Presbyterian College for Girls was a small junior college with less than 300 students, but it boasted a very strong basketball program. It was overseen by Sam Babb, whose administrative position in the state's school system allowed him to recruit widely and offer a college education to good players, some of American Indian heritage from rural schools. The students who came to the college were strongly motivated and grateful for the opportunity of an education in the midst of an economic depression. Coach Babb, whose rule was firm, stressed conditioning while creating a supportive, disciplined, instructive atmosphere, and he was particularly adept at the psychology of game preparation.[12] The Durant Cardinals, distinguished by their vivid red uniforms, were soon national champions.

In the spring of 1933, the Durant Cardinals made the long journey from Oklahoma to Alberta to play the Edmonton Grads for the inaugural North American championship. Aware they would need to be better skilled at the full-court men's game, the Cardinals partially financed their trip by playing against several men's teams along the way. They arrived in Edmonton on June 1, as prepared as they could be to take on the opposition. Playing for the Grads were Gladys Fry, Jessie Innes, Doris Neale, Margaret MacBurney, Babe Belanger, Evelyn Coulson, and twins Helen and Edith Stone. Interestingly, each team had twins in their lineup, with Vera and Lera Dunford playing for Durant. The Cardinals carried twelve players, as opposed to eight on the Grads, and they were taller and heavier than any team the Grads had played before. To balance things out, Page brought up Noel MacDonald and Mabel Munton from the Gradettes to play in the series.

The Grads had lost only three games in the last six years, and they were currently enjoying a thirty-four-game winning streak. On June 4, 1933, in the first game of the series, they were beaten 59–52 by the Cardinals, even though the Grads supposedly had the advantage of men's rules. They had met their match in the girls from Oklahoma, who featured a short passing game not unlike the one made famous by the Grads. The Cardinals also made the best use of their height by frequently intercepting Grad passes and upsetting their combination plays. In the final quarter, the Grads were forced to finish the game without Babe, Margaret, and Doris, each of whom had been sent off with the maximum number of personal fouls. Coach Page commented that the Grads had played one of their poorest games in years, but he was also surprised by the brilliance of the Durant team.

In the second game, the bewildered Grads frequently fouled under the restrictive women's rules and they lost again, this time by a substantial margin of 83–48. The crowd booed frequently at the referees' decisions because they simply did not understand the unfamiliar women's rules. Coach Page sent in Noel MacDonald, his tallest player, to play at the centre position so that Gladys Fry, who usually played centre, could assist on defence where her height was also an advantage. Page even called a time-out late in the game, something he never had to do before. Still, the Cardinals were too good and the Grads never had a chance.

So great was the interest in the third game that the rush seat section was completely filled fifteen minutes prior to the start of the game. With over 4,500 excited fans crammed into the Arena, a great roar went up when the Grads raced onto the floor and gathered in the centre to give their famous yell. They went through their pre-game drills watched by Spark Plug, their well-travelled mascot who was placed on the floor facing the Grads' basket. The game began and the crowd settled down, feeling confident the Grads would bounce back as they always did, especially with the more familiar men's rules in play. Both teams played a hard and fast game, checking their opponents closely, and the score remained close. At halftime it was 19–18 for the Grads, and at the end of the third period it was 29–31 for the Cardinals. A special phone number had been set up through the main telephone exchange where operators constantly updated the score. Over 50,000 people called the number, jamming the lines and causing the entire system to blow, resulting in a complete telephone blackout in the city for over twenty minutes. The score in the fourth and final period seesawed back and forth, but in the final seconds the Cardinals scored, winning the game by 45–43.

Pandemonium reigned in the arena as fans realized not only that the Grads had lost but that their opportunity to go to the Women's World Games in London had also disappeared. A small group showed their anger and apparently took it out on Herman Smith, the official from Oklahoma, who had been appointed by the AAU to referee the game along with George Parney of Edmonton. Coach Babb was also upset, claiming that a crowd surrounded his players at the end of the game and called them abusive names. There were counter charges by George Mackintosh, sports editor of the *Edmonton Journal*, to the effect that some of Herman Smith's calls against the Grads were questionable, and more seriously, Smith had assisted Coach Babb in coaching the Cardinals behind closed doors at their daily practices in the Edmonton Arena prior to the first game of the series. Never before had the Grad organization encountered such criticism and controversy. A committee of five prominent citizens (all men) was immediately appointed to investigate Babb's charges; they called in witnesses, none of whom could provide evidence of abusive behaviour on the part of anyone, and the Grads were exonerated. The general view was that Babb was an excitable coach prone to exaggeration. Nonetheless, the unfavourable publicity placed both the Grads and the City of Edmonton in a questionable light. Several months later, a top official from the AAU visited Edmonton for the next international series, which was against a team from Chicago, to see for himself how American teams were treated by their Canadian hosts. Everything went well.

At the Women's World Games in London in August 1934, the Durant Cardinals were unexpectedly on the losing end of a 34–23 score in the finals against a team from France. They returned home to persistent money problems, and, sadly, Coach Babb had to disband the team, but many of his players went on to play for other teams. As for Babb, he coached teams in Shreveport and in Galveston, but he died suddenly in 1937 at age forty-five.[13]

As for the Grads, Page took them on a three-week exhibition tour of eastern Canada in the summer of 1934 as a consolation prize for missing out on the trip to London. They played only four games—in Fort William, Montreal, Toronto, and on their return in Winnipeg—mostly for charitable purposes. They won all four games by a substantial margin. Eleven players, regulars and substitutes, made the journey, which was more vacation than playing basketball, with time spent in New York and Chicago. The only sad note was that they had to leave Doris Neale behind in Toronto because she had an emergency appendectomy.

1936 European Tour and Berlin Olympics

Despite uneasiness over increasing Nazi militarism and anti-Semitism, there was little support in Canada for a boycott of the 1936 Olympics in Berlin. Those who took an anti-Olympic stance came from a narrow group outside the established sports community,

En route to the Olympics in Berlin, June 1936. [PAA A11434]

namely members of Workers' Sports Association clubs, trade unionists, progressive churchmen and educators, left-wing political groups opposed to fascism, and various Jewish organizations.[14] Canadian sportswriters were mostly opposed to a boycott, and, in some cases, belittled attempts to organize one. Alexandrine Gibb of the *Toronto Star*, for example, was indifferent to the "rabid communists" who decried living conditions among the Canadian poor, when in her view they lived much better than a good many people in the Soviet Union. She had just returned from an extensive journey through Russia, sent by her paper to cover the "woman's angle." As usual, she made her position on the proposed boycott crystal clear:

> It's a certainty that no matter what country drops out of the Olympics the games will be held in Germany next summer—unless a war cancels the whole show. They will not be moved to any other country.

I can't help be amazed at the lack of knowledge of some of these athletes who think that if they decide not to go to that the games will be moved immediately somewhere else. It is your privilege not to try out for the games if you wish, but you can't move the Olympic games to any other country, and don't let anyone try to tell you it is possible.

On the face of it, it is ridiculous. Naturally it will be the Olympic committee which will deal with any Olympic matters, not some outside organization which suddenly has decided they want to handle the show.[15]

Although we will never know for certain, it is unlikely there was any discussion among the Grads about cancelling their third European journey, this time in conjunction with the Summer Olympics in Berlin. Although men's basketball had been added to the 1936 program as an official medal event, women's basketball was still forty years away from being granted Olympic status. As she had done in 1924 and 1928, Alice Milliat invited the Grads to Europe and arranged games for them throughout their tour. The Canadian Olympic Committee, through the efforts of Alexandrine Gibb, recognized the Grads as part of the Canadian contingent competing in Berlin; as a result, they were allowed to wear the official Olympic blazer and sit in the competitors' section at the stadium. The Grads took with them a fragment of the aircraft in which Germany's foremost air fighter in World War I, Baron Manfred von Richthofen, met his death. Given to them by Capt. W.R. "Wop" May, the Canadian wartime pilot responsible for the German ace's demise, the piece was to be presented during the Olympics to Richthofen's mother as an "act of friendship" between Canada and Germany.[16]

Making her first trip overseas with the team was Patricia Page, daughter of Percy and Maude, now twenty years old and working at the *Edmonton Journal* as a secretary. She was also writing a sports column for the paper called "Feminine Flashes," published twice weekly, which she worked on in the evenings. Although much of her subject matter was about the Grads and the Gradettes, she also covered girls' sport at the high school level, and women's sport throughout the city and sometimes in other parts of the country. Through her father she had an insider's perspective on the Grads organization with a view to promoting the team in her column, although she would occasionally complain about how difficult it was to get information out of him.[17] Armed with a brand-new portable typewriter given to her by the president of the Underwood Typewriter Company, as well as official press credentials for the Olympics, Patricia sent back detailed reports, published in the *Edmonton Journal* under her by-line. Similar to those of her mother in 1928, her accounts provide a detailed travelogue of the journey, although from the perspective of a young woman experiencing Europe for the first time.

The team left Edmonton on June 19, 1936 making their way east by train via Winnipeg and Chicago to Montreal, where they would sail across the Atlantic aboard the *Duchess of Athol*. Along the way they played exhibition games against all-star teams in Regina, Peterborough, Ottawa, and Montreal, with scores all over 90 for the Grads and never higher than 20 for the opposition, indicating the team was certainly ready to defend their world championship. Making the trip were Gladys Fry (now Mrs. Jack Douglas), Noel MacDonald, Babe Belanger, Etta Dann, Mabel Munton, Doris Neale, Sophie Brown, and Helen Northup. Gladys had only recently been married; Noel, Sophie, Doris, Helen, and Babe were all working as clerks, typists, or secretaries in Edmonton businesses; Mabel and Etta did not have jobs at the time. Along with Coach Page and his wife Maude—their long suffering chaperone—and Patricia Page, the group also included Mrs. Bennie and her daughter Elsie, who were again visiting relatives in Scotland.

After docking in Greenock, Scotland, the team travelled via Glasgow and Edinburgh to London, where they played their first

Strasbourg, France in 1936: Noel MacDonald, Gladys Fry Douglas, Mabel Munton, Sophie Brown, Doris Neale, Babe Belanger, Helen Northup, and Percy Page. Etta Dann is missing from the photo. [PAA A11433]

game. They routed the hapless London Pioneers by a score of 100 to 2. They then travelled to Paris, Marseille, Nice, and Monte Carlo. In Nice, the court was a concrete floor in the centre of town; in Monte Carlo they played on an outdoor asphalt court. The games attracted large crowds, even though in both instances the opposition was defeated by a very wide margin. The team then travelled to Italy, specifically Rome, Florence, and Milan, where again the European teams were summarily demolished. They spent a wonderful week in Switzerland sightseeing, swimming, eating, and sleeping before heading to Strasbourg and another game, this time against the French champions, whom they easily beat with a score of 83–25. Finally, on August 2, they arrived excitedly in Berlin to spend a week taking in the Olympics.

Patricia Page had a spectacular view of many Olympic events. Along with more than a thousand other journalists from all over the world, she occupied the press box situated in the centre of the stadium. Just a few seats away—"close enough so that I could toss him a basketball"—sat Hitler himself.[18] With considerable pride, she watched the Grads take their seats in the competitors' section smartly decked out in their white silk dresses and red Olympic blazers with white trim. Cheering loudly, they urged on the Canadian women sprinters, who were no match for the German athletes or world-class runners like the American Helen Stephens and the Polish-American Stella Walsh, who ran for Poland. The best Canadian performances were by Betty Taylor, who won bronze in the 80-metre hurdles, and the 4x100-metre relay team of Dorothy Brookshaw, Hilda Cameron, Jeanette Dolson, and Aileen Meagher, which also came third. High jumper Margaret Bell was a disappointing ninth in her event. As for the men, Patricia watched Canadian Phil Edwards win a bronze in the 800-metres at his third Olympics.

The men's basketball tournament, which included a team from Canada, was the most interesting sport for the Grads to watch. Patricia met with James Naismith, who was brought to the games as a tribute for his role in inventing and developing the game. Naismith told her that he never dreamed basketball would one day become an official Olympic sport, for men anyway. As for the Canadian team, she expressed shock and disappointment that they were nearly beaten by Brazil in the first round. Patricia observed, probably correctly, that the Grads could well have beaten some of the men's teams. On the second day of the tournament there were many requests from spectators for the Grads to put on an exhibition. Again Patricia commented, "Had they brought their uniforms

1936 team in their Canadian Olympic uniforms. [CEA A92-85 R925]

with them, I think an exhibition could have been arranged and it certainly would have made a hit with the crowd, for after watching the rather pathetic shooting on the part of some of the men's teams, I feel sure the Grads would have proved a revelation."[19] The Canadians persisted and ended up second among the twenty-three competing countries. The final game against the United States was played outdoors in a driving rain on a dirt court; in the resulting quagmire, the teams could not dribble and the score was ridiculously low at 19–8. Clearly the men would have benefitted from the Grads' short passing game and deadly accurate shooting even in the worst of conditions.

After Berlin, the Grads spent the remainder of their time in Europe travelling to Köln, Brussels, Ostend, and then to Douai in France, where they played another game, this time against a team representing a large oil refining plant. They ended their journey in Paris defeating two teams by substantial scores. In all, they had played nine games during this tour—all successful and with no team scoring more than 25 points against them. In fact, one of the teams they played in Paris, which they defeated by a score of 86-14, was basically the same team that unexpectedly beat the Durant Cardinals at the 1934 Women's World Games in London. In other words, the Grads might also have beaten the French team at the 1934 game in London had they not been shockingly defeated by the Cardinals in the run up to decide who would go to the Games.

When Patricia Page returned to Edmonton, she wrote a column about Alice Milliat and her persistent efforts to obtain more competitive opportunities for women athletes at the international level. She had met Mme Milliat on several occasions during their most recent travels, talked with her, and felt she had come to know her. "She struck me," wrote Patricia, "as a lady who had plenty of ideas, and one who was not afraid to express them, with the result that she ran foul of the men's organization on more than one occasion."[20] This was quite the understatement.

Under Milliat's leadership, the *Fédération sportive féminine internationale* had grown from five affiliated countries in 1921 to no less than thirty by 1936. She was the driving force behind no fewer than nine international congresses on women's sport, held in Paris, Göteborg, Amsterdam, Prague, Vienna, London, and Berlin. She helped organize four Women's World Games: Paris, 1922; Göteborg,1926; Prague, 1930; and London, 1934; and the fifth scheduled for Vienna in 1938. As Patricia reminded her readers, it was through Milliat's energetic efforts that the Grads had made three tours to Europe—the first in 1924, the second in 1928, and the last one in 1936. For more than fifteen years, Milliat had devoted her life to the betterment of women's sport, especially in Europe.

Enthusiastic crowd welcoming the Grads back from Europe, 1936. [PAA A11424]

Underlying these accomplishments was a constant struggle for women to gain access to international sporting competition, especially in track and field, while maintaining control of women's competition. As the FSFI became more successful, it was a serious rival to the International Amateur Athletic Federation (IAAF). Therefore, the IAAF decided to recognize Milliat's organization and persuade the IOC to include a few women's track and field events at the 1928 Olympics in Amsterdam. The FSFI continued to argue for the inclusion of more women's events at the Olympics, but the IAAF and IOC did little. Their inaction prompted Milliat in 1935 to ask the IOC to exclude all women's sport from the Olympics, which would leave the FSFI free to organize their own quadrennial games. The IOC ignored this request and also refused a proposal from the IAAF to include the discus and more running events for women in the 1936 Olympic program. In other words, the IOC was neither willing to allow women a full program of events in the Olympics, or let the FSFI run its own show. In 1936 the IAAF took complete control of all track and field by recognizing the FSFI world records, argued for a more complete program of women's events at the Olympics (which did not happen), and refused to allow the Women's World Games in 1938. These games did take place but were presented as the first women's European championships in track and field with no other sports on the program. The FSFI was finished and it never put on another event. Sadly, Alice Milliat left sport to live a life of relative obscurity until her death in 1957.[21]

There would be no more international travels for the Grads. The fifth Women's World Games did not take place in Vienna in 1938 as planned. The Grads disbanded in June 1940, well before the Summer Olympics, which were originally given to Tokyo and later moved to Helsinki, were cancelled due to World War II. Women's basketball was not included on the Olympic program until the Montreal Olympics in 1976.

4 The Grads 1915–1924

WHO WERE THE WOMEN who played on the Edmonton Commercial Graduates? Although the team began in 1915, those considered "official" Grads—thirty-eight in all—begin with members of the 1922 Dominion championship team and includes those who played until the team disbanded in 1940. So often the Grads are considered a homogenous group and no attention is paid to these women as individuals. Yet they span several generations, with the oldest born in 1899 and the youngest in 1922. And their lives, especially after they left the team, were very different. Almost all of them married, some more than once; most had children, but a few did not; many lived a long life and saw their grandchildren and great-grandchildren, and several died far too young.

This chapter discusses those who played between 1915 and 1924. Those who played in later years are remembered in Chapters 6 and 8. With one exception, the women here were born in the first few years of the twentieth century. Only two were born in Alberta. The rest were born either in Ontario, the United States, Scotland, or England. Most were young children when they came with their families to Edmonton prior to World War I; their fathers sought employment in the new and bustling city. All attended McDougall Commercial High School, coming under the influence of their teacher, J. Percy Page, who would become their coach when the team began in 1915. The women remembered in this chapter were members of the team that won the first Dominion championship in 1922, and, with one exception, they were also members of the first Grads team to travel abroad. Along with several others who played between 1915 and 1920, this particular group of women are among the Grad pioneers. They are Winnie Martin, Elizabeth Elrick, Eleanor Mountifield, Connie Smith, Daisy and Dot Johnson, Nellie Perry, Abbie Scott, Mary Dunn, and Helen McIntosh.

Winnie Martin Tait (1915–1924)[1]

Winnifred Amanda Martin's playing career with the Grads began when the team was first formed in 1915, and she was the only one of the original players to become a member of the 1922 Canadian championship team. Winnie was born in Petrolia, Ontario on September 28, 1899, but her family eventually settled in Edmonton. The second child of William and Margaret Martin, Winnie had two brothers—Kenneth, who was two years older than Winnie, and William, who was two years younger. Their father was a photographer and their mother was a teacher. When the commercial courses were introduced to Victoria High School in 1912, Winnie was among the first group of students. Along with her developing athletic

Winnie Martin Tait.

[CEA A92-85 R925]

skills, she was also becoming an excellent typist, regularly clocking over 100 words a minute and winning typewriting contests.

By the fall of 1915, Winnie had finished her schooling at McDougall Commercial and was back at Victoria High School to obtain her senior matriculation because she wished to become a teacher. With the formation of the Commercial Athletic Society, Winnie was eligible to play on the Commercial Graduates team, which she joined immediately. She was promptly elected the team's captain. A newspaper photo shows the "star performer" with long braids, crossed behind her head and tied with big butterfly ribbon bows.[2] After graduating from high school, Winnie attended Camrose Normal School to obtain her teaching credentials. The Commercial Graduates, just beginning their illustrious career, were very successful on the basketball court due in no small measure to Winnie's efforts on defence. She also won the 1918 Canadian Typewriting Championship in the open category, demonstrating speed and accuracy at 105 words per minute.

Winnie entered the University of Alberta in the fall of 1918 to begin her university studies. She continued to play basketball for Commercial, but also won the all-round championship in athletics at the University of Alberta. In 1921 she continued her university education at Queen's University in Kingston, Ontario, graduating first with a bachelor of arts degree, followed by a bachelor of commerce in 1923. She was one of only two women in Canada at the time to be so accomplished. At Queen's she was active in basketball and tennis, excelling at both. She also managed to compete at the world's typing contest in New York, scoring the highest of all the Canadian entrants. After Queen's, Winnie joined the staff at McDougall Commercial High School to teach and mentor the young women and men training for the business world. However, she did not stay at McDougall long.

Just prior to the Grads leaving Canada by ship on their 1924 European tour, it slipped out that Winnie was engaged to Robert (Bob) Tait, a Great War veteran and top athlete at the University of Alberta, who was completing his medical degree at McGill University. After the Grads docked at Quebec City on their return in August, Winnie left the group presumably to prepare for her wedding in Montreal. When the rest of the team arrived, they found Winnie and Bob already married, but forgave them at a celebratory dinner. The couple moved about in the United States first to Maine, then to New Jersey, and eventually to Spokane, Washington. Their family at this point had expanded to three children—Margaret, Winnie, and Bob. By 1930, they had settled in Vancouver, where Dr. Tait established his practice as a roentgenologist (radiologist) and three more children—Bill, Malcolm, and Logan—completed the family. A photo taken in 1940, captioned "Tait Family Orchestra," shows the six children with their mother, all dressed in similar outfits and each with a musical instrument. Winnie herself played the piano and composed music, but she was determined to have a family string orchestra to perform locally and at Kiwanis music festivals. Her son Malcolm became a well-known cellist and professor of music, performing and teaching throughout the world.

A woman of enormous energy and talent, Winnie engaged in a variety of projects and interests throughout her life. She assisted her husband in his medical practice, helping to run the business side. Along with her two brothers, and eventually two of her sons, she became highly involved in the mining business—gold in particular—especially at Manson Creek in northern British Columbia looking for potential mines. She spent a good deal of time in the area, and even took geology courses to learn more about mining, but in the end, she did not make her fortune. During the first years of World War II, with Dr. Tait concerned that the Japanese might attack the British Columbia coast, Winnie packed up her six children and moved to Edmonton, where she taught business essentials to recruits in the Royal Canadian Air Force Women's Division. The family returned to Vancouver after the war, and later Winnie worked as a court reporter.

Winnie also passed on her love of sports to her children. The oldest, Margaret, was a superb track athlete named to the Canadian Olympic team in 1948. Unfortunately, she had to withdraw because of an injury. Logan inherited his mother's love of basketball and was skilled enough to play for Canada in the 1960s. A chartered accountant, he settled in Lethbridge, Alberta and pursued a distinguished career in business.

Her heart failing, Winnie died in Vancouver on April 27, 1974 at seventy-four years of age, leaving her husband, who died in 1984, five of her children, and eighteen grandchildren.

Elizabeth Elrick Murray (1918–1923)

Elizabeth was born in Glasgow, Scotland on January 15, 1901. At
the age of eleven, she immigrated with her family to Canada. Her
father, William Elrick, whose occupation was listed as tinsmith,
arrived in Halifax in the spring of 1911. He immediately headed to
Alberta. The rest of his family, including his wife Margaret and five
children, made the journey a year later, arriving by ship in Quebec
City. Their destination was Strathcona, Alberta. Elizabeth was
the middle child. She had an older sister, Margaret, and an older
brother, Alexander and two younger sisters, Barbara and Nora.
After attending McCauley and Norwood public schools and then
Victoria High School, Elizabeth completed her secretarial training
at McDougall Commercial. She graduated in 1918 and immediately
went to work as a stenographer with the Canadian National Railway.

While at Commercial, she played on the school team for two seasons, and because she was good enough and certainly keen, she
continued to play with the Commercial Graduates team after graduation. Although Coach Page wanted her on the team that went east
to play the London Shamrocks for the Canadian championship in
1922, Elizabeth was unable to persuade her employer to give her the
necessary time off. When the Grads changed to men's rules in 1923,
she was disadvantaged because she had only played the women's
game and, as a guard, had not developed an accurate shot. During
the 1923 season, she was a substitute guard, but when she did get
to play, the *Edmonton Bulletin* commented, "She is a steady, reliable
player who can be depended upon to watch her check closely."[3]

Elizabeth moved to Vancouver in the summer of 1923 for the
"benefit of her health," followed soon after by her fiancé, Richard
(Rex) Murray, who also worked for the Canadian National Railway.[4]
They were married in September and returned to Edmonton soon
after. Elizabeth continued to play basketball, but this time for

Elizabeth Elrick Murray.

the Morris School of Physical Culture, which entered a team in the 1924–1925 season of the city's mercantile league. Two daughters, Maureen and Rhoda, soon followed, and by 1942 the family was living in Winnipeg. In 1957, they moved to North Vancouver. Wherever she lived, Elizabeth was an active member of the United Church of Canada, especially the United Church Women.

Elizabeth Murray died in Winnipeg on June 29, 1984 at the age of eighty-three. Her husband predeceased her in 1981. At the time of her death, she had five grandchildren and one great-grandson. It would seem that Elizabeth had put aside her days with the Grads because she did not attend any of their reunions or functions held over the years. But there was another reason. Her daughter, Rhoda Collins, in a letter to former Grad Betty Bawden Bowen, written on the day of her mother's death, stated, "Mom was always very humble about basking in the successes of the Edmonton Grads. She really feels she had been one of the lesser players and didn't deserve the fame. I know she cherished her years with the Grads and had great respect for you all." Betty responded that many Grads felt the same way, but it was a team sport and their continuing friendship over the years after the team disbanded was special. It seems a shame that Elizabeth Elrick Murray, throughout her long life, did not benefit from getting to know this amazing group of women.

Eleanor Mountifield Vogelsong (1919–1924)

"Tottie" to her teammates, Eleanor was born in Fort Yukon, Alaska on May 20, 1902 to Henry R. Mountifield and the former Margaret Houghton. Her parents settled in Seattle for a short while, but then came to Edmonton in 1904 because her father, originally from England, wished to live in a country that recognized the British flag. When they arrived in Edmonton, Eleanor was the third of four children, but eventually the family expanded to three boys and six girls. Their father, a real estate broker, was a fine athlete and encouraged all his children, including the girls, to be athletically active. Tall and willowy, with a halo of golden hair, Eleanor was equally at home on the basketball court, the golf course, and the skating rink.

A graduate of McDougall Commercial High School, she joined the Grads in 1919, and played in the centre position under women's rules. When the Grads switched to men's rules in 1923, Eleanor changed to defence, playing at right guard, which prompted a sportswriter for the *Edmonton Bulletin* to comment, "Her passing to teammates is uniformly good, and at times it reaches the high level of genius, for she seems to sense where to pass that ball....This is a mark of the finished athlete in any team game. At guarding Captain Eleanor ranks with the best in the game and she is likely to break away any time and electrify an audience with a sparkling basket."[5] Very popular among her teammates, she became captain of the team for a short period while Winnie Martin was away studying at Queen's University.

Eleanor Mountifield Vogelsong.

Eleanor resigned from the Grads in the fall of 1924: "I no longer wish to play basketball (too old)."[6] After graduating from Commercial, she worked as a bookkeeper at a local business, but in 1925, she decided to leave Edmonton. She moved to Seattle, where she did secretarial work at the General Insurance Company. It was here that she met her husband, Charles D. Vogelsong, and they were married in the summer of 1927. Eleanor played basketball in Seattle for a team called the Rhodes. A son, also named Charles, was born while the couple lived in Seattle. By 1937, they had moved to Lewistown, Idaho. They lived in Edmonton briefly during the 1940s, possibly due to the war. During their time in Edmonton, Eleanor also coached a basketball team. At some point, she and her husband divorced. By 1946, Eleanor was back in Lewistown, and a couple of years later she went to work for the Potlatch Corporation, retiring in 1967 as supervisor of their steno pool. She died on February 5, 1985 in Lewistown, where the epitaph on her tombstone reads "Gold medal athlete."[7]

Connie Smith McIntyre (1920–1926)

In 1923, when the Grads switched from women's to men's rules, Coach Page needed a centre player, someone tall who could jump high and consistently tip the ball to a teammate. He found her in Connie Smith. At 5'9" Smith was certainly tall enough, and according to the *Edmonton Bulletin*, she was "a bear at tipping the ball and is fast enough to stick like a leech to her opponent."[8] When Winnie Martin left the team after their European trip in 1924, Connie took over as captain and remained so until she retired from the game in the fall of 1926.

Like many of her teammates, Constance M. Smith, was born in the "old country," which in her case was Walsall, Staffordshire, England. She was born on October 5, 1903. Less than a year old, she travelled across the Atlantic by ship with her parents, Daniel and Emily, and three older brothers—Daniel, Samuel, and Alfred. They arrived in Montreal in the summer of 1904, and the family soon made its way to Edmonton by train. Her father had been a farmer in England, but like so many men seeking a better life on the prairies for their families, he became a building contractor and eventually a government building inspector. Connie and her brothers attended McKay Avenue School.

By 1920, Connie had graduated from McDougall Commercial High School and was employed with Alberta Government Telephones as a stenographer. Alongside Winnie Martin, she was playing on defence for the Commercial Graduates. She was one of the younger players on the 1922 Canadian championship team, but she continued to mature and improve, especially when she became their captain. Frederick (Ted) Watt, a journalist and long-time Grad supporter, caught the essence of her playing skills in the following ditty:

Captain Connie is as fleet
As the god with winged feet.

Connie Smith McIntyre.

Quick to start, she leaves her check
Far behind, a nervous wreck.
Certainly, we're all too glad
To admit she isn't bad.
If you want a proper tip
On the art of marksmanship,
Come and watch the long shots soar
Through the hoop from centre-floor.
We'd be modest if we could,
But we must admit she's good.

Captain Connie, we must state,
Does not lack for solid weight.
There have been a few who've tried
Roughly pushing her aside—
They aver they'd sooner fall
Up against a nice stone wall.

Captain Connie, when she's pressed,
Just continues with her best—
Going may be mighty tough
But her "best" is quite enough—
Not in word alone, by hang!
Is she captain of "the gang."[9]

In 1927, Connie married Lloyd McIntyre, a "brilliant athletic luminary and prominent vendor of automobiles."[10] Baseball and hockey were Lloyd's sports. In 1925–1926, he played professional hockey with the Edmonton Eskimos of the Western Canada Hockey League. His hockey career continued for another decade with teams in various minor professional leagues. The couple had one child, Alan, and a long marriage, celebrating fifty years in 1977. Lloyd died in 1984. They had moved to Viking, Alberta in 1945 where Connie was a charter and life member of both the Eastern Star and Royal Purple, charitable organizations dedicated to the promotion and support of community needs.

Connie died in Viking on January 9, 1990 at eighty-six years of age and was survived by her son, two granddaughters, and three great-grandchildren.

Daisy Johnson (1920–1927) and Dot Johnson Sherlock (1921–1927)

Daisy, named Margaret Jane at birth and the older of the two Johnson sisters, was born on November 26, 1902 to Angade (Andy) and Elizabeth Johnson. Her sister Dorothea Lily, who preferred Dorothy or, better still, just Dot, was born four years later on January 22, 1906. Along with two brothers, Victor and Harold, they lived on a farm in Jumping Pound, Alberta, a small community west of Calgary and just south of Cochrane. By 1911, the Johnson family had moved to Edmonton, where their father, a

Daisy Johnson.

[CEA EB-27-45]

real estate broker, took advantage of the city's pre-war housing boom. Daisy and Dot went to public school at McKay Avenue.

Both sisters attended McDougall High School for a year. Dot then took the two-year business course at Commercial and Daisy transferred to Victoria High School in her quest to become a teacher. They both played basketball on the various school teams. By 1920, Daisy had graduated and was completing her teacher training at Edmonton Normal School, where she played on the basketball team. She also played for the Commercial Graduates, and was on the team in December 1920 when they first travelled outside Alberta to Saskatoon to take on the local YWCA and the University of Saskatchewan. Meanwhile, Dot was a member of the McDougall senior high school championship team, but both were on track to become Canadian champions.

When Percy Page decided to try for the Dominion basketball championships in 1922, he had five excellent players, but women's rules, which were to be used in two games against the London

Dot Johnson Sherlock.

[CEA A92-85 R925]

Shamrocks, required six players. Daisy was now teaching in a rural school at Jarrow, south and east of Edmonton, and she had little opportunity to practise. Page wrote to Daisy asking if she would join the team and travel to London. "I'd been a teacher for ten months but I set up a hoop on a granary wall and my eye was in. Mr. Page played the basics—passing and shooting—so I thought I could pull my weight," Daisy told journalist Ted Watt many years later. "You didn't think he was asking a lot of you?" suggested Watt, and Daisy regarded him as though she only half understood the question: "He was giving me my chance wasn't he?"[11] At sixteen, her sister Dot was the youngest member of the 1922 team. Dot had just graduated from Commercial and was enjoying her first job as a steno at the DeLaval Company in Edmonton.

Local sportswriters were entirely complimentary about Daisy and Dot, who were still in the early stages of their basketball careers. Dot was the faster and flashier of the two: "Miss Johnson is a whiz at getting around the floor, quick as a flash in darting away from her check, and she can shoot baskets from almost any position. Believe me she can shoot baskets, and she gets them away quickly. She is a wonderful natural athlete, playing with the grace and ease of a finished performer."[12] As for Daisy, playing at left forward, reporters wrote, "Although she is not as fast a player as her sister, she is remarkably steady and can always be depended upon to turn in a finished performance."[13]

The two sisters played standout basketball over the next five years while also pursuing their respective careers as teacher and stenographer. Dot "Flash" Johnson, so named because of her spectacular style and illusiveness, was frequently the leading scorer, whereas Daisy was considered the steadiest and most consistent player on the team. When Connie Smith resigned from the team in the fall of 1926, Dot took over as captain and Daisy was elected president of the Commercial Graduates Basketball Club. Both were leaders and looked up to by the other players. They left the team in the fall of 1927, although Coach Page was anxious to have them stay on, especially with an impending trip to Europe the following summer. "No," they replied, "if we stay on, it means that some other girl won't get the chance to go over. We had our chance in 1924, and it's someone else's turn now."[14]

Daisy continued her teaching career in Edmonton, primarily at Eastwood and Woodcroft Elementary Schools. She never married and retired in 1968 after forty-seven years in the classroom. She enjoyed retirement for a decade, but unfortunately died of cancer on March 16, 1979 at age seventy-six, survived by her brother Victor and her sister Dot.

Dot chose a different path. From 1924 until 1934, she worked as a stenographer at E.N. Moyer, a school supplies company. She also became a star in the local five-pin recreational bowling league. Along with her sister and widowed mother, she lived in the family home until she married accountant Ronald F. Sherlock on December 28,

1934. They had one child, Elizabeth Ann, better known as Betty. Dot's husband died in 1987, and she eventually moved to Kelowna to be closer to her daughter, two grandchildren, and eventually four great-grandchildren. She died at age ninety-seven on March 20, 2003.

Nellie Perry McIntosh (1921–1924)

Known as Nellie all her life, she was born Ellen Perry in London, England on February 4, 1903 to Joseph and Mary Ann Perry. She immigrated with her parents to Saskatchewan in 1906, where her sister Ethel and brother Herbert were born. Sometime between 1911 and 1916, the family moved to Edmonton. Jobs were hard to come by in those days but their father found work as a car mechanic. Nellie attended McKay Avenue and Oliver schools, and by 1917 she was a student at McDougall Commercial High School. In a photograph of the 1919–1920 basketball champions of Commercial High School, Nellie is identified as a "graduate," at which point she was working briefly in a local business before settling into a job as a clerk at Canadian Pacific Railway for the next several years.

Since the Grads played no official games in 1921, Nellie first shows up in a media report about the team in January 1922, clearly impressing the *Edmonton Journal* sportswriter, who observed, "Miss Perry, on the forward line, was easily the outstanding player....[She] does not shoot an overhead ball such as characterizes the average lady player but snares the ball on the run and shoots with deadly precision that might well be the envy of many of the male players around the city."[15] Soon after this observation, in a game against the University of Alberta where the Grads won 29–9, Nellie scored all but one of her team's total. The Grads went on to play the Lethbridge Barons for the provincial championship in 1922, where Nellie and teammate Daisy Johnson scored on more than 50 per cent of their tries, a noteworthy statistic

Nellie Perry McIntosh.

[CEA A92-85 R925]

among women players in those days. Both players were members
of the team that won the first Canadian championship in 1922.

Like many of the players before her, Nellie had to switch to
the men's five-player game in 1923, but she adjusted well and her
remarkable shooting ability carried her through. She was handicapped more by her office duties at Canadian Pacific, which
often prevented her from turning out to practice. Something
must have been worked out because she was a member of the
team that toured Europe for six weeks in the summer of 1924.

Like several others, she left the team at the end of the 1924 season. She married Gordon McIntosh in 1927 and by early 1930 had two
children. Eventually, she had seven children—Tim, Bud, Alan, Rod,
Barbara, Carol, and Wendy. The family lived for a time in Winnipeg,
where Nellie was active in her church, played five- and ten-pin bowling, and managed junior bowling teams for many years. She died
after a short illness in Victoria on April 16, 1991, at eighty-eight years,
survived by six of her children, fifteen grandchildren, and seven

great-grandchildren. In June 1991, her daughters planted a tree in her memory in the Edmonton Grads Park located in the Inglewood neighbourhood, recognizing her basketball accomplishments and treasured lifetime friendships. As her obituary noted, "She wanted to be and will be remembered for her sense of humour."[16]

Abbie Scott Kennedy (1922–1924)

Abbie Scott played only a short time for the Grads, but her efforts on the court were often recognized as superb. Her full name was Abigail Esther and she was born in Cheyenne, Wyoming on October 6, 1902, the youngest of four children born to Frank and Salome Scott. Abbie's father left Scotland in 1878 and came to what was then Fort Edmonton to work for the Hudson's Bay Company. After several years of travel, he decided to return to Edmonton in 1911, where he was a machinist with the Canadian National Railway. The following year he sent for his family, and they moved into a little house near Norwood Church on Edmonton's north side. Interested in local politics, Frank was elected to the Public School Board in 1919 and continued to serve until 1923. One of his two sons, also named Frank, joined the Canadian Over-Seas Expeditionary Force in 1916 and fought in the war.

Abbie attended several public schools, including Oliver, Parkdale, and Norwood before moving onto McDougall High. She completed her secretarial training at a business college, and soon after was employed as a stenographer at the Coca Cola Company in Edmonton. Having played basketball throughout her schooling, Abbie continued to polish her basketball skills with a team that played in the ladies' mercantile league. In the fall of 1922, when Coach Page wished to groom a player who could replace the great Daisy Johnson when necessary, he chose Abbie Scott. At the time, Daisy was teaching in a rural school outside of Edmonton, which

Abbie Scott Kennedy.

[CEA A92-85 R925]

made it difficult for her to attend practices and scheduled games.
Page saw something in the young understudy, and so did the sportswriters: "Abbie has inherited the stamina of the bucking broncos
of the plains, and goes down the floor regardless of three or four
checks who may try to block her path."[17] She continued to improve
over the 1923 season; by 1924, she was no longer a substitute player
and took her place on the regular lineup. Deacon White seemed
to have a particular soft spot for her. He praised her abilities in his
Edmonton Bulletin column several times. Here's a typical example:

> *Miss Abbie Scott again demonstrated that she was not only Mr. Page's*
> *scoring ace, but that she was the best lady athlete on the floor. Of*
> *the 42 points rung up by the Grads [against Lakeview Community*
> *League of Chicago], she was responsible for 15, which is more than*
> *one third, and she did not play in one period at all....Class is writ-*
> *ten all over this young lady. When she leaned back, checked in front,*
> *and shot a basket with both hands on the ball, tossing it directly*

over her head, she showed that she had everything in the reper-
toire of the expert male sharpshooter. Yes, Miss Scott is one sweet
basketball player. She has height, weight, strength, noteworthy abil-
ity above the shoulders, and wonderful coordination when it comes
to tossing the ball through the ring at any old distance at all.[18]

After returning from their first European tour in August of 1924, and following the series against American teams later that fall, Abbie decided to resign from the team. Her letter of resignation stated simply that she had "finally decided to give up active participation in the game."[19] She married Robert Kennedy in August 1928, and their daughter Lois Anne was born the following year. Abbie did not work outside the home but was involved in a variety of women's organizations throughout the years. She lost her husband in 1952, and later made this comment about her relationship with the Grads: "Whether I had played with them or not, the Grads became the best friends I've ever had. When I was widowed twenty-three years ago they saw me through the dark days—and still do. I've held office in many women's organizations, but, in the end it has been primarily to raise money for good causes. With the Grads there's a plus."[20]

Abbie died in Edmonton on February 24, 1991 at the age of eighty-eight. She was survived by her daughter, three grandchildren, and one of her brothers. Allan Stein and Mairi MacLean, who were responsible for *Shooting Stars*, the award-winning documentary film about the Grads, paid Abbie the ultimate compliment—they named their daughter after her.

Mary Dunn Dickson (1922–1926)

"Wee Mary," as she was affectionately nicknamed, joined the team in the fall of 1922, replacing Winnie Martin at guard. A small 5'4" sturdily built dynamo, she was fast on her feet, fit enough to run the

Mary Dunn Dickson.

[CEA A92-85 R925]

entire game, and revelled in rough and tumble play. "The main business of a guard is to stick close to her opposing forward," wrote an *Edmonton Bulletin* sports reporter, "and here is where Mary shines. She hangs around like a necklace. At the same time she was a constant threat to her opponent at shooting baskets for Mary can dart away occasionally into a good opening and hoist the ball into the goal."[21]

Born in Hamilton, Scotland on March 6, 1902 to William and Margaret Dunn, Mary was the middle child with three older and three younger brothers. To better their fortunes, the Dunn family immigrated to Canada in 1913 and chose to live in Edmonton, where an uncle and aunt had settled a decade before. Mary's only sister was born in Canada a year after the family moved. Like most men from the "old country" who emigrated during this period, Mary's father found that jobs were scarce and had to scrounge for work. Mary's father first tried coal mining; then he set up a general store, which failed; next, he unsuccessfully sold insurance; and finally, when war broke out, he joined up and went overseas along with his two older sons.[22] All returned safely, and Mary's father went back to coal mining.

The family lived on the north side on 95 Street just north of 118 Avenue. Mary went to public school at H.A. Gray and then moved onto McDougall High for grades nine and ten. She learned the rudiments of basketball in public school, but with no indoor court, the game was played outside. At McDougall, she was introduced to more sophisticated basketball by Mr. Page, who was just beginning to establish his basketball dynasty. In 1919, and just seventeen, Mary went to work at the Soldier Settlement Board as a stenographer where she was paid sixty-five dollars a month. The Soldier Settlement Board had been established in 1917 to help returning servicemen set up farms. Mary worked in the "salvage department," responsible for selling a farm and its contents if the unfortunate farmer could not make a go of it, which often occurred when the land was poor. Still living at home, she turned over her salary to her mother. After a couple of years, she became dissatisfied with her job at the Settlement Board because they were expanding and hiring new people who were paid more than Mary, but whom she had to train. She had a friend working for the Northwest Company, a subsidiary of Imperial Oil, so she applied and got a job at eighty-five dollars a month with the possibility of earning a whopping one hundred dollars in six months time. As the assistant to the manager, Mary worked from nine to five on weekdays and until one in the afternoon on Saturdays, leaving her evenings free for the twice-a-week basketball practice.

Although small, Mary was an exceptional basketball player, and what she lacked in height, she made up for in speed and sturdiness. She played the left guard position, but she could also shoot: "When once on the move, it would take a freight train to stop her, and woe betide the forward who takes any liberties with 'wee Mary.'"[23] In her more than three years with the team, Mary was a perennial star. Her biggest thrill was travelling with the team to Europe in 1924 in

conjunction with the Paris Olympics. Many years later, she still marvelled at how, as a young working woman with limited means, she
had been given the opportunity of a lifetime to travel abroad.[24]

Mary's basketball career came to a sudden halt in early 1926 when
she became engaged on January 16 and was married on February 3.
Once married, the players normally could not stay on the team, but
many years later Mary suggested she was ready to quit anyway. Her
new husband was Robert G. Dickson, otherwise known as "Speed"
due to his prowess on the basketball court. He worked at Imperial
Oil, but in his spare time played and coached basketball, including
the YWCA team on which Mary was an early member. Eventually the
couple had four children—Mary, Bruce, Joan, and Jean. The latter two
children were twin girls. World War II interrupted most everyone's
lives, including Mary's family as her husband spent five years overseas
with the Royal Canadian Engineers. The family moved to Calgary in
1950, where Mary continued to live after her husband died in 1955.

"Wee Mary" lived a long life. She was ninety-four when she died
on August 4, 1996, survived by her four children, eight grandchildren,
and four great-grandchildren.

Helen McIntosh Davidson (1923–1924)

Often given to hyperbole and occasional sexism, sportswriter Deacon
White compared Helen to the mythical Helen of Troy, who, he
suggested, "had nothing on this young damsel for looks and intelligence." About Helen the basketball player, White was effusive:

> Yes, she was easy to look at. But her looks did not bother her any. She
> was out there on the floor to play basketball, and, take it from us, she
> can play. This young miss has everything that goes to make a success-
> ful basketball player. To begin with, she has style and poise, the very
> two things that you find in all the big leaguers. Without these two

Helen McIntosh Davidson.

[ASHFM]

qualities you never find a player sticking very long in the fast com-
pany. The public likes to look on the player who handles himself or
herself gracefully, nonchalantly, and in good form. Miss McIntosh
has speed, weight, intelligence, and uncanny ability to shoot bas-
kets in good style. She can take a pass, and is so unselfish that she
seems to prefer to pass to another member of her team rather than
take a shot at the basket herself, when within scoring distance.[25]

Unfortunately, Helen's career with the Grads was short—just
over a year. She was given her first opportunity to play with the
team in October of 1923, when she was in the lineup as a substitute for an international series against the Chicago Brownies, after
two years as star player on the senior team at Commercial High
School. Helen, nicknamed the "Baby Grad," did not get to play in
the series, although she played against the Warren National Lamps
who were up next. By the following spring, Helen was touted as
the most improved player on the team with a great pair of hands

who gets the ball away fast. It was at this point that Deacon White made his observations about Helen, but she still remained a spare because Connie Smith, Winnie Martin, and Abbie Scott were Page's top scorers. On the 1924 European summer tour, Helen and her mother accompanied the team only as far as Montreal. Cost was no doubt a factor in this decision, and also Page had the players he needed. When the team resumed play again in the fall, Helen was yet again a spare and rarely played in any of the series. She resigned from the team at the end of the year along with veterans Eleanor Mountifield, Nellie Perry, and Abbie Scott.

Born on December 23, 1905, into a large Toronto family, Helen was the only girl among six brothers, five of whom were older than she. Her parents, James and Ellen McIntosh, moved the family to Edmonton sometime between 1911 and 1916, perhaps for more land and better opportunities. After graduating from Commercial, Helen took a job as a steno at Woodland Dairy, where she worked until she was married in November 1927 to Victor Floyd Lees of Edmonton, an electrician with the provincial government. Helen and Victor had three sons—Keith, Larry, and Fenton—but the marriage ended and they both eventually remarried. Aside from the twenty-fifth anniversary reunion of 1947, when she was still Helen Lees, there is no record of Helen attending any other Grad reunions. Her second husband was George Davidson. From 1954 onwards they lived in Chilliwack, British Columbia. He died in 1967 and Helen passed away on October 28, 1975 at sixty-nine years of age. She was survived by her three sons, eleven grandchildren, and her younger brother.

5 Keeping It Simple

"WE TRY TO DO THE SIMPLE THINGS a little more efficiently than our opponents," Coach Page once explained to a sports reporter. "I've always stressed the two fundamentals, passing and shooting, and ignored almost completely the complicated plays which are featured by other teams."[1] Harold F. Cruickshank, one of the Grads' more astute observers, wrote, "Thousands of fans have imagined that the Grads have a whole hatful of streamlined, magical razzle-dazzle plays, the key to which no opposing team or fan could ever find. The Grads certainly give that illusion. They specialize in baffling short passes, pivots, tricky cut-ins, aerial and bounce passes and a myriad of other eye-bulging shifts and shots, but they are merely perfected elemental plays."[2] Coach Page often attributed the team's success to teamwork and shooting accuracy, which were achieved through the continuous and repetitive practice of basketball fundamentals. But there was much more to the Grads' phenomenal record than the simplicity of their plays.

The Basketball Factory

Clare Hollingsworth, who eventually became Percy Page's son-in-law, began teaching at McDougall Commercial High School in 1934 and coached the junior girls' basketball team. He described the school as a "regular basketball factory."[3] There were four feeder teams providing as many as forty aspiring players each year: the junior high school team for the youngest and most inexperienced players; the Comets, the senior high school team; the Cubs, a junior ladies' team for those either still attending McDougall or who had recently graduated; and finally the Gradettes, an intermediate ladies' team also for graduated players with the potential to one day join the Grads. The 1928 Gradettes team, for example, was composed of eight players, six of whom eventually made it to the Grads: Edith Stone, Helen Stone, Jessie Innes, Doris Neale, Mae Brown, and Evelyn Coulson. The two who did not become Grads were Kay Mets and Marian Kinney. (Marian's younger sister Margaret, however, played as a Grad the next year.)

Some never played beyond the school teams because they were not interested, did not have the ability, or just as importantly, failed to measure up to Page's standards of acceptable behaviour. This included not just their skills and teamwork on the basketball court, but how they conducted themselves off the court. Any member of the Grads, Page insisted, must be a lady first and a basketball player second. Over a period of twenty-five years only two members of the Grads had not been students at Commercial High School. As

1934–1935 Gradettes: Babe Daniel, Mary Killick, Betty Ross, Isobel McNeil, Mary McConkey, Coach Bill Tait, Jean Williamson, Winnie Gallen, Hilda Hughes, Cal Holmgren, Edith Power, and Edna Reilly. [PAA BL2658/2]

Page explained, "By the time a girl has worked her way from the junior high school team to the Grads, she has learned all I can teach her, and if she has a certain amount of natural skill and the determination to succeed, she will probably stick. As students I have an excellent chance to watch these girls, and if anyone fails to measure up to Grad ideals she is weeded out before she has been with us very long."[4] Although a public invitation was extended each fall for girls in Edmonton who were interested in playing basketball to turn out for the first practices of the Gradettes, it was almost impossible for an outsider to break into the ranks. In 1935, a Commercial Girls' Basketball League was formed from a group of the best city high school players. The league consisted of three teams—the Macs, Dougs, and Coms. The teams were provided with shirts by the Grads organization, and eventually the twelve best players were given a chance to try out with the Gradettes.

Coach Page was amazingly adept at picking just the right girl to fill a spot on the upper-level teams. This was not a hit and miss affair. Rather, he made a calculated effort to know everything about the players and to win their confidence. In his words, "My plan, and it has worked successfully for over twenty-one years, is first to study each playing member as she steps up into the ranks of the Grads. I must know her capabilities, her limitations—her every whim; and at once I set out to win her full respect and confidence. What more is necessary?"[5] Year after year, Page was able to put together a successful team not only because he instructed them in how to play winning basketball, but also because he taught them the value of character and instilled a profound loyalty to each other and to him. Even though others became involved with the team over time, he was still their leader, and for some, a father figure. Long after players had retired, Mr. Page was still their respected mentor.

The "Grad Machine," as some sport reporters called this well-organized and effective feeder system, took several years to develop. In October 1924, the Grads decided to enter a team, under the name Gradettes, into the provincial league. At the time, the team was composed primarily of senior players who were still attending Commercial. Combined with the junior and senior high school teams, this was the beginning of a more formal farm system. The Gradettes competed at the intermediate level in provincial competition paralleling the Grads in the senior division. Page also decided another coach was needed, someone he could work with, and who would primarily be responsible for coaching the Gradettes. He chose William T. "Bill" Tait, a forty-eight-year-old physical education instructor with the Edmonton School Board, who also had substantial coaching experience. Born in Toronto into a large Scottish

Going up against the Boy Grads, November 1939. [PAA KS31/2]

family, Tait had coached his younger brother Jack, a highly successful middle-distance runner with the West End Toronto YMCA and
a member of the 1908 and 1912 Canadian Olympic teams. Bill was a
track coach with the Canadian team in London in 1908. After World
War I, in which both brothers fought overseas with the Canadian
Expeditionary Force, Bill came to Edmonton because he was hired
by the school board as an instructor and by the University of Alberta
as the track coach. A tall, distinguished-looking gentleman with
white hair and a moustache, he was highly respected and liked by
the young women basketball players under his charge, who found
him less severe than Coach Page. Nonetheless, the two men were in
complete agreement as to the emphasis on teamwork and shooting accuracy, and for any of his players lucky enough to make it
to the Grads, the transition was easy and smooth. The Gradettes
also provided scrimmage opponents for the Grads in practice, and

occasionally when a player was injured or ill, a Gradette might be moved up temporarily to take her place during an important series.

Another aspect of this remarkable basketball factory, and one important to the Grads, were the Boy Grads. After the Grads switched from girls' rules basketball to the five-player men's game in 1923, it was important that they practise this version of the game against skilled players who would constantly challenge them. Initially, they played against the Commercial High boys' team, who usually entered men's intermediate competition. Like the Grads, the young men who graduated from Commercial wanted to continue playing together, and in 1927 they became an official branch of the Commercial Graduates Basketball Club, continuing to compete in the intermediate provincial league. Players on the Boy Grads were usually between seventeen and twenty years old, obviously bigger and stronger than most of the Grads, thus providing a team of extra height and speed against which they could practise. There is no official record of these contests over the years, but reading about them in the newspapers, one gains the impression the Grads got the best of the Boy Grads as many times as they were beaten by them. There is also no listing of the young men who played on these teams, and their names rarely appeared in the newspaper accounts. Although mostly forgotten, the Boy Grads contributed to the Grads' success, certainly initially, because they helped sharpen their instincts on the court and made them realize they could easily outsmart the heavier and taller women's teams they encountered.

In September 1935, Percy Page made a completely unexpected announcement: he planned to retire as coach of the Grads in six months and turn the team over to Arnold Henderson, who was currently his assistant. Page would continue as the team's manager, leaving Henderson more time to coach. Increasing responsibilities at his school, Page explained, meant that he was unable to give the time and attention he felt the team deserved.[6] Considerably younger and originally from Vancouver, where he had played and coached basketball for the University of British Columbia, Henderson was a teacher at McDougall High School and responsible for coaching the boys' senior team. However, by the fall of 1936, and following the Grads' summer tour through Europe, including the Olympics in Berlin, Page was still firmly in control as coach, and it would appear he had changed his mind about retiring. Former Grads have said the players made such a fuss that Page reconsidered. Others have intimated something happened between the two men, but none were willing to divulge any details, and they probably did not know themselves. Whatever the issue was, the two worked it out, and following Bill Tait's retirement in November, Arnold Henderson took charge of the Cubs and Gradettes. He was ably assisted by Clare Hollingsworth, who also continued to coach the senior high school team. There was no further discussion of Page retiring as the Grads' coach, and he continued in that position until the team was permanently disbanded in June 1940.

Game Preparation

For much of the basketball season, which normally extended from September until June, the teams practised only twice a week. Practices were usually held on Monday and Thursday evenings from eight until nine-thirty in the Commercial High School gymnasium. Unless the Grads were working out against the Boy Grads, which usually happened when a series against a team from the United States was imminent, the Gradettes and the Grads practised together. Players were expected to be ready to start on time and lateness was not tolerated. Coach Page, assisted first by Tait and later by Henderson, ran a very tight practice, which varied little in format and execution. Observing an early fall practice, with over thirty girls—Grads, Gradettes, high school players, and some senior public school girls—one sportswriter commented, "Every second of the evening's performance was efficiency plus. Not a minute was wasted; the coach knew exactly what he wanted. Everything was carefully explained and illustrated. The movements began slowly—to accommodate the girls who have had little experience. Before each exercise was completed and a new one started, the girls were letter perfect in what they were trying to do."[7] This particular practice consisted of various shooting and rebounding drills, and a series of exercises designed to simulate a variety of game situations, which were more fun for the players.

The Grads were famous for their short-passing game, which was dictated by the fact they practised in what today would be considered a tiny gymnasium space. The space that the Grads used for practice currently holds the library at the refurbished McDougall Public School. Radiators stuck out from the wall right behind the basket. "You had to watch out," remembered Babe Daniel, one of the later Grads, "because when you went in for a lay-up shot, if you didn't turn quickly, you'd hit the radiator."[8] Their game was also improved through hours and hours of monotonous drill, and as Coach Page conceded, "The girls have confidence enough in my judgment to accept these drills as part of our necessary routine, and they go through them without complaint."[9] Drills may have been repetitive, even boring, but when asked about these practices years later, Grads remembered them as interesting and fun. Even injured or recovering after an illness and only to able to watch, the girls were expected to attend practices. Helen Northup Alexander recalled, "Mr. Page was there all the time, and he always expected us to be there. I broke my arm but I still went out to practices. He told me: 'You can learn something from watching.'"[10]

As the season progressed, the Grads would spend one of their practice nights playing in a game situation, sometimes with the Gradettes, but more often against the Boy Grads. These

Edmonton Stock Pavilion, later known as Edmonton Gardens or Arena, c. 1914.
[CEA EA-45-1124]

would usually take place in a larger gymnasium such as the one
at the University of Alberta. These practice games were played
as if they were the real thing, with referees, scorers, and tim-
ers to replicate the situations they would encounter when it
counted. A week or so before an international series with an
American team, the Grads and Boy Grads would hold workouts
in the Edmonton Arena, mainly so the players could get accus-
tomed to the larger playing area. Interest in these workouts
was high and several hundred fans often came out to watch.

Originally called the Edmonton Stock Pavilion, the Arena was
a barn-like structure built in 1913 on the exhibition grounds. It
was a popular indoor setting where 6,000 spectators could watch
"circuses, pageants, athletic contests, hockey matches, skating,
theatricals, to say nothing of horse shows, live stock exhibitions and

Lining up in the Edmonton Arena before the start of an international series in the mid-1930s. [GA PA-3128-191]

motor shows."[11] The Arena was the largest of its kind in Canada. Amateur and professional hockey teams played there during the winter, and the ice was made from scratch each year—it simply melted away when the temperature rose because there were no facilities to maintain it. The Grads first played in the Arena in 1923 when they brought the London Shamrocks to town for the Dominion championships, and from then on it was the site of their many victories and a few losses, primarily against teams from the United States.

Several wooden floors had been specially built over the years to accommodate a basketball court in the middle of the Arena. Around mid-April, after the hockey season finished and the spring horse show had taken place, the floor was placed over a layer of dirt and sawdust on the slowly melting ice. The last one was built in twenty-four sections, each weighing from 900 to 1000 pounds, with a total weight of over 11 tons; it had a maple top and measured 75' by 40', with a 5' margin around the outside. Setting it up required a dozen workers to prepare the underflooring, handle the sections, and make certain it was level. Built by the city at a cost of $1,400, it was paid for in instalments by the Grads each time they used it for an international series.[12] With everything ship-shape at the Arena, and the opposition in town, the now familiar refrain was heard across the city: The Grads are playing tonight!

Game Night

Individual Grads began arriving at the Arena an hour or so before game time, most coming directly from work. They would head first to the northeast corner, just past the horse stalls, where two rooms with no running water, mirrors, or even a coat hook—just bare board benches and a slab table—had been set aside as changing areas for the teams and coaches. Edith Stone Sutton, a player in the early 1930s, remembers it clearly: "In order to get to this hideaway, it was necessary to pass through a miasma of odours—a rich mix—beginning with a strong reminder of the housing of recent horses. Add to this the smells now beginning to drift in from the activities of the various concessionaires preparing their hot dogs, hamburgers, french fries, brewing coffee and frying onions."[13] As the crowd gathered and took their seats in the Arena, they were serenaded by the Edmonton Newsboys Band.

After warming up, and just before the opening whistle, the Grads would carry their droopy little mascot Sparky onto the centre of the floor. Sportswriter Harold Cruickshank describes what happened next: "With arms about each other's shoulders, heads respectfully bowed over Sparky, feet tapping a jungle-drum type of accompaniment, they invoke the aid of the gods of basketball—or so we have been lead to believe. Many have probably imagined that through some mystic power of Sparky, the Grads became attuned, possibly, with those ancient gods of the idol-worshipping, basket-ball-playing Mayas of Yucatan."[14] And what was this famous chant?

> *Pickles, ketchup, chow, chow, chow,*
> *Chew 'em up, eat 'em up, bow, wow, wow;*
> *Hannibal, cannibal, sis, boom, bah,*
> *Commercial Graduates, rah, rah, rah!*

Style of Play

The Grads' unique style of offensive play changed very little over the years. Basically, it was run, pass short, and shoot, which characterized their fast-breaking game. As far back as 1924, when the Grads demolished a Calgary all-star team 28–0, local sportswriters witnessed their spectacular combination play, and made several observations: "The Grads bunch together and go down the floor with machine-like regularity, utilizing a very short passing game and check hard."[15] "There was always someone in position and open to take a pass whenever the Grads were in possession....Throughout the performance the Grads showed a complete understanding of the system of play, the rules and the movements of their mates. They combined their efforts wonderfully, and their catching and passing was almost faultless."[16]

Coach Page was once asked by a reporter, "To what extent is the girls' play mechanical?" He laughingly recalled a remark he overheard when the Grads played an all-star team in San Francisco in 1932. The coach of a famous men's team was watching the game very closely. When asked his opinion of the Grads at halftime, he remarked, "A

Dot Johnson and Connie Smith practising their skills, 1926. [CEA EB-27-67]

wonderful team, but the signals they use have whiskers on them."
Page was not in the least offended by the remark for the simple reason that the coach was basically correct: "Many of our plays are old
ones—plays which I have picked up from many years' observation—
but the Grads have them down in such a manner that they 'click.' Far
too often teams are burdened with signals and plays which are far
too intricate, and are worse than useless. We use very few set plays,
and when the time comes to use them, I can always count upon the
girls to play them perfectly."[17] Gladys Fry Douglas, the Grads' centre
from 1927 to 1936, also confirmed there were only a few basic plays,
usually those initiated from throw-ins and jump balls. In those days,
a centre jump was taken after every basket. One player was responsible for giving a signal, such as a finger rubbing the seam of the

shorts or scratching a shoulder. Their signals were similar to those given by the third-base coach in baseball. They indicated where the centre was to tip or throw the ball and the sequence of passes to the basket was set from there.[18] Even as the years went by and the game changed, for example, with the increasing use of screen or post plays, the Grads stuck with the more basic run-pass-shoot type of offence.

Defensively, they began early on to utilize a "man-to-man" system, and this too did not change much over the years. It was during their first international series in 1923 against the Cleveland Knits in Edmonton that the Grads first used the set five-man defence system, where each defensive player guards a specific opponent and tries to prevent them from taking action. The puzzled Cleveland team was unable to penetrate it, and time after time, they stood back in their own end passing the ball trying to draw out the Grads, who would not be enticed out of position. Reminiscing about this several years later, Coach Page observed, "So far as I am concerned, I really originated what is known as the 'five-man defence' system. I had the thing all planned in my own mind and drilled the girls so that Cleveland had the hardest job in the world to break through. I was really taking a little credit to myself for having thought out something which worked. However, the joke was on me, for a short time later I ran across a book in which exactly the same system was explained, and had probably been used by several teams before I had thought of it myself."[19]

With the Grads beating their opponents almost all the time, and sometimes by a substantial margin, it was natural for commentators to suggest they should "ease off" when the score became ridiculously high against comparatively easy opposition. Coach Page made it abundantly clear this was never an option:

In fact, well-meaning friends who have watched the crowds dwindle away from thousands to a few hundreds have suggested time and

Taking a break in a game in the Edmonton Arena, 1938. [CEA EA-160-1167]

again that it might be good policy to drop a game or at least win by smaller margins. My answer to that suggestion—and the same thing goes for the girls—is that every game we have ever played, or will ever play, has been and will be absolutely "on the level." We play the game for the game's sake, and not for the gate receipts. We go on the floor to give the fans the finest demonstration of basketball we know how, and if in doing so it means that we run up a score of 100 points or more, it's just "too bad" for our opponents. If the time comes when the fans won't go out to watch us play, merely because they take the result for granted, we are perfectly ready to quit. In doing so, we shall at least be able to hold up our heads and know that we have given our best.[20]

Giving their best also meant playing cleanly. Harold Cruickshank once observed, "There is a tendency in the heat of battle to start retaliating with hips, wrists and elbows, but never in all their quarter of a century of brilliant accomplishments have the Grads had as many fouls called on them as have been called on their opponents."[21] Although there are no statistics to support this claim, reading the game reports year after year certainly leads one to the same conclusion. In fact, the question of why American teams committed more fouls in games against the Grads was addressed in an interesting article by Arnold Henderson, who at the time was the assistant coach of the Grads.[22] His first point was that visiting teams, especially those from the United States, were sometimes not familiar with the rules or their interpretation because they played under two and sometimes three different rule codes, whereas the Grads played only under the men's code. Second, the American teams favoured a slow-breaking game, and when they were required to check the quick-breaking Grads, they found it impossible to avoid fouling. Also, because of their fast-breaking style of game, which demanded more action and was physically harder on the players, the Grads were generally in better condition than their competitors. Tiring under the Grads' style, American players were more likely to commit fouls. Henderson's third point addressed the objection that Alberta officials called the "guarding from the rear" rule too closely. He argued that guarding from the rear should result in a foul if there is any contact, no matter how slight, because strict adherence to the rule would stop players from trying uselessly to check from behind. Fourthly, he addressed the controversial notion of "intentional fouls," whereby it makes sense to stop an opponent who has a clear break to the basket for a lay-up shot. Some coaches claim this to be a "smart play" because a basket will result in two points, whereas there is only a 60 per cent chance that the fouled player will make her foul shots. Henderson made clear that he and Coach Page considered these plays not smart at all; indeed they were unsportsmanlike and should be penalized as disqualifying fouls. Finally, Henderson pointed out that from the time players turn out for the feeder teams in the Grad organization, they are taught "the game is the thing" with a specific emphasis on clean checking. Every scrimmage was played under the watchful eye of competent officials; every foul was accurately recorded in a scorebook and discussed with the player so that errors in technique could be immediately corrected.

During their long career, the Grads were rarely accused of rough play. Mentioned earlier was an incident that occurred in 1920 in a game against the University of Alberta. The Grads were so shocked by accusations of roughness that they refuted the charges in a lengthy letter published in the local newspaper. In the previous seven years, they pointed out, no team had ever defaulted a game; no team had ever protested a game; and only one player on any of these teams had been expelled from a game for too many fouls.[23] Although it did occur on occasion, fouling out of game was something all players obviously tried to avoid. (In those days, four personal fouls was the limit.) Once, when an unnamed Grad fouled out in a game against a team from eastern Canada, she immediately broke into tears because it had never happened before.[24]

Percy Page as Coach

No matter what happened in a game, or how the play was going, his players never knew from his expression if Coach Page was "mad, glad, or worried."[25] He would only call a time out in dire circumstances. The very few times Page ever showed anger were remembered vividly by the players many years later. In a very close game in 1940 against the Vancouver Westerns for the Canadian championship, the Grads could not seem to get going, and at halftime, they were only two points ahead. They came to the bench for the break and Page, as was his usual habit, fanned them with a towel. On this occasion the Grads noticed that, instead of flapping gently, the towel was moving so vigorously it made snapping sounds. Although clearly perturbed,

Coach Percy Page instructing his team, 1939. [PAA KS31/1]

Page spoke in his usual manner. In another game, his concern over a foul committed by the Grads produced an "Oh, no" so loud that the referee gave him a technical foul, much to the shock of his team.[26]

Page's behaviour on the basketball court over twenty-five years was a model of restraint and he rarely let his emotions show. During the game he sat quietly on the sidelines with his substitute players, legs crossed and tapping his foot. When one of his team passed him and he felt some admonition was necessary, the most he would say was "Oh dear, Oh dear" with the player sometimes wondering what she had done wrong. If it was serious, he would take her aside after the game and explain the problem, but he never embarrassed a player in front of her teammates. She might also receive a brief note explaining the problem. A compliment or good word from the

Percy Page and Etta Dann, 1936. [PAA A11425]

coach was similarly hard to come by. In an interview decades after she had played on the team, Mary Dunn Dickson still remembered one of Page's compliments. In October 1923, the Grads were challenged by the Toronto Maple Leafs for the "world" championship played in Edmonton. It was Mary's task to guard Rosa Grosse, who at the time was also the Canadian sprinting champion. The Grads handily beat the Toronto team in two straight games, due in part to Mary's brilliant work checking Grosse. Page acknowledged this and complimented Mary directly: "You did a very nice job on her."[27]

Most of Page's teams were comprised of eight players—five regulars and three substitutes. Often his first-string players would stay in for the entire game. He would not necessarily play each substitute, even when his team had a substantial lead, which they often did. His philosophy was that fans wanted to see excellent basketball, something best accomplished through the regulars. Of course this meant that his players, especially the regulars, had to be very fit and able to play an entire game. There is no indication that Page had them do regular conditioning exercises either during practice or on their own; this was long before the days of weight lifting and systematic training. Several players have mentioned that they had to walk everywhere, especially with money tight during the Depression, which probably kept them reasonably fit. Aside from time off in the summer months, if they weren't touring they were either practising or competing, which meant that they had little opportunity to lose fitness. Many Grads played other team sports, especially baseball and softball. They were allowed to play these other sports only during the summer, however, because Page did not want his players to risk injury. Downhill skiing was also out, but he had no objections to skating, swimming, tennis, golf, curling, and the like.

A Team versus All-Stars

Back in 1924, Deacon White had the audacity to suggest that the Toronto Maple Leafs, a team handily defeated by the Grads for the senior ladies' Canadian championship, were nothing more than a "clique of girls that hang together."[28] Needless to say, the Toronto team took umbrage over this description, but White had a point, which was that, aside from players like Rosa Grosse and Grace

Toronto Maple Leafs, who the Grads beat in 1924 for the Canadian title.
[GA ND-3-2327]

Conacher, the Maple Leafs was not a team of "selected" athletes like
the Grads. It is also interesting to note that Grosse had made her
mark as an outstanding track athlete and Conacher, like her brothers, was known more for her ice hockey skills. Nonetheless, White
had touched upon a theme that goes a long way to explaining the
Grads' phenomenal success over twenty-five years and why they continually beat all-star teams, especially those south of the border.

Even though Page had his favourite players, those he could
depend upon all the time, there were no "stars" among the Grads.
Page insisted on teamwork. While a player might be tempted
to try for a basket, if someone else was in a better position, she
passed the ball—or else. "There was not one selfish girl on the
team," Helen Stone observed, "Nobody wanted to be a star. I wonder now, how can an All-Star team play together if they're all

stars?"²⁹ Many an American team thought it could beat the Grads if it bolstered its lineup with one or more star players, sometimes enticed from another team, or even a player picked up on the way to Edmonton. These strategies rarely worked. Even when their opponents were bigger and stronger, the Grads still beat them.

During the Grads' entire existence, Coach Page always sidestepped the issue of who were the best players, certainly when asked to name them by the sports media. Several years after the team disbanded, he finally broke down and named his all-time five best players. For forwards, he chose Margaret MacBurney (1926–1935), "a deadly sniper and one of the most remarkable foul shot artists in the history of the game," and Gladys Fry (1927–1936), a natural "southpaw" who could score baskets from the left side when least expected. At centre, it was Noel MacDonald (1933–1939), the highest scoring Grad of all time. In the guard positions were Connie Smith (1920–1926), who, besides being tall and fast, was one of the most powerful players ever to play on the team, and Etta Dann (1935–1940), who was so versatile she could handle a forward or guard role equally well. Page also picked his "choices" from among the Grads since 1915: fastest player, Babe Belanger; most colourful, Connie Smith; most graceful, Helen Northup; most accurate shot, Margaret MacBurney; most elusive, Dot Johnson; most cheerful, Gladys Fry; most inspiring captain, Elsie Bennie; most reliable guard, Mabel Munton; and the fans' favourite, Mary Dunn.³⁰

EDMONTON COMMERCIAL GRADUATES BASKETBALL CLUB

WORLD'S CHAMPIONS

Gladys Fry
CENTRE

CAPTAIN
Elsie Bennie
GUARD

ed
nack
RD

6 The Grads 1925–1930

THE PLAYERS DISCUSSED in this chapter all joined the team between 1925 and 1930. Since several Grads resigned at the end of 1924, there was a considerable changeover of players at the beginning of the 1925 season, with Kate Macrae, Elsie Bennie, and Hattie Hopkins joining the team. As players left in successive years, spots opened up for others: Marguerite Bailey, Mildred McCormack, and Margaret MacBurney in 1926; Joan Johnston, Mae Webb, and Gladys Fry in 1927. The last three players in this group—Babe Belanger, Doris Neale, and Margaret Kinney—were added in 1929. Some played for as little as one year, and others for almost ten. The period between 1925 and 1930 was a busy one for the Grads with the increasing number of Underwood trophy series, exhibition tours throughout Canada and the United States, and most important of all, the 1928 European summer tour, including exhibition games in connection with the Amsterdam Olympics. The women in this group were born prior to World War I, some in Edmonton or Alberta, but most elsewhere. In each case, they arrived in Edmonton as young children with their families. All but two—Gladys Fry and Mae Brown—attended McDougall Commercial High School.

Kate Macrae Shore (1925–1929)

Like many of her contemporaries, Catherine "Kate" Macrae was born in the "old country," which in her case was Glasgow, Scotland. She was born on July 16, 1905 as a sister to Edward. In 1910, their father Angus immigrated to Canada, followed a year later by his wife Margaret and the two children. Settling in Edmonton, Angus was a teamster who worked for the city until starting his own hauling business. Florence, a younger sister to Edward and Kate, was born in Edmonton. Kate went to public school at Westmount and Norwood and then to high school at Commercial, graduating in 1921. She went to work immediately as a steno in a doctor's office before being hired by the Hudson's Bay Company in 1924. The company magazine, *The Beaver*, reported, "Miss Kate Macrae is filling the position as stenographer in the advertising department left open by Miss Nellie Nicholson. It is said that Katie is a regular wizard at typing."[1]

Not only was she a whiz at the typewriter, Kate was also gaining a reputation on the basketball court while playing for several teams. She had first learned the fundamentals under Percy Page at Commercial High School, and by late 1924, she was back playing with the newly formed Gradettes. She also played on a team representing the Morris School of Physical Culture, and when she went to work at the Bay, she was immediately recruited to the Hudson's Bay Trappers, who played in the city's mercantile league. Tall, wiry, and

Kate Macrae Shore.

[PAA BL2637/7]

slim, Kate was a rising star, but the press had difficulty spelling her last name correctly:[2]

> *The stalwart Kate MacRae at centre was the indisputable star of the game. She was everywhere at once, stepping into many dangerous gaps left by some of the less experienced team-mates. It kept her hopping but she proved equal to the task. Though only scoring one point, she was the centre of the attack, the game being built around her.*
>
> *This girl, when hitting on all six, is all that the most ardent fan can desire for action and the opposition will know that they have been in battle when they stack up against her.*
>
> *Miss McCrea is one of the most promising players in the city. She was pilot of the Hudson's Bay Fur Trappers and was the high scorer in practically every game she played in.*

Kate's first game as an Edmonton Grad was on February 22, 1925 in a game against the Varsconas for the Northern Alberta Ladies' championship. She was a reserve player, substituting on defence for either Mary Dunn or Elsie Bennie. This time the press was not only effusive, they also got her name right: "Kate Macrae got her chance to play in the big company and this player certainly showed herself to be the goods. The latest addition is strong enough to spill most incoming rushes and with this intention she was sent into the game, and many of the Varsconas will vouch that Kate Macrae is good."[3] Over the next four years, partnered on defence with Elsie Bennie, she got better and better and was frequently singled out as a star. She was likely at her peak during the international series in Edmonton on June 10, 1929, which would also be her last game: "Kate Macrae...was a tower of strength to the Grads in their close game with the Detroit Centrals. Besides playing her defence position to perfection she figured in numerous attacks that got points for her team."[4] The Grads played no further games until October, and by then, Kate Macrae was married and no longer a Grad.

Her engagement to Saskatchewan-born Eddie Shore, hockey star and bruising defenceman for the Boston Bruins, was announced in August and the popular couple were married in Edmonton on October 8, 1929. Not quite nine months later, their son and only child Edward (Ted) W. Shore, Jr. was born. Eddie Shore had played hockey with the Edmonton Eskimos before being sold to the NHL Bruins, who were looking for exciting and colourful players to attract fans. Occasionally controversial and always popular, he remained with the team for fourteen seasons. After the Bruins, he played with the New York Americans for a year and then left to concentrate on his new roles as owner and coach of the American Hockey League's Springfield Indians, a team he had purchased in 1939. Although Kate and Eddie spent the winters in Boston and later Springfield, from April until September they could usually be found on their farm near Daugh, about sixteen miles northeast of Edmonton, until it was sold in 1942. Both also became American citizens.

Kate was a wonderfully talented athlete. She loved to skate and probably would have made a great hockey player had basketball not been her game of choice. Also an outstanding golfer from an early age, she began playing golf competitively when she was a Grad. She was still improving in 1943, when she made it through to the semi-finals of the City of Edmonton ladies' golf championship. Her son remembers her as a great cook, willingly feeding a dozen or more hungry threshers on their farm during harvest, all from a wood and coal stove. Tragically, she died all too young at the age of forty-one after being ill for a year with breast cancer. She passed away on September 17, 1945 in Springfield, and as Percy Page put it so well, "It seems to be an irony of fate that the first member of our club to be called was one of the most rugged girls we ever had."[5]

Eddie Shore remarried in 1952 and his second wife died in 1981; he passed away in 1985 at the age of eighty-five, survived by his son Ted and four grandchildren.

Elsie Bennie Robson (1925–1934)

Elsie had an exceptionally long career with the Grads—almost ten years—and she was captain of the team for at least half of those years. In the fall of 1924 she was a member of the newly formed Gradettes. When several Grads retired from the team after the European tour, a few places on the team opened up, and on February 2, 1925, Elsie gained her first chance to play as a Grad in an exhibition game against the Winnipeg All-Stars. Amazingly, the match was played on the stage of a packed Empire Theatre, in downtown Edmonton, with ropes stretched across the front apron to prevent players from tumbling into the first-row seating. A year later, when guard Mary Dunn left the team to be married, Elsie filled her spot and stayed there for most of her career.

Elsie Bennie Robson.

[PAA BL2637/1]

Elsie Norrie Bennie was born on May 10, 1908 in Stirling, one of Scotland's oldest towns. In April of 1913, the family, including Elsie, her parents Alexander and Margaret, and her younger brother Alex, arrived by ship in Portland, Maine and made their way to Edmonton. By 1916, the family, which had expanded to include a niece, Margaret's mother, and four male boarders, was living in a house in northeast Edmonton. Elsie's father had been a butcher in Scotland and he took up the same trade in Canada. As a student, first at McCauley Public School and then at McDougall Commercial High School, Elsie honed her typing and basketball skills. By 1924, she was employed with the City of Edmonton in her first job as a stenographer. Unfortunately, by then her mother had been widowed, and to make ends meet, Margaret went to work as a sales clerk at the Johnstone Walker department store. Years later, Elsie noted that her mother had been very supportive of her athletic pursuits and never missed a game.[6] In fact, on a few occasions Mrs. Bennie took on the responsibility of team chaperone during their trips away.

One of the reasons for Elsie's long career with the Grads, aside from the fact that she was a talented and steady player, is that she did not marry until she was thirty years old, which was unusual in those days, at least among the Grads. From early in 1925, until Kate Macrae left the team at the end of the 1929 season, Elsie and Kate were the Grads' very effective defensive duo: "At the other end of the court, the Bennie-Macrae stalwarts loom up like the rock of Gilbralter before the in-coming rush of the opposing forwards, and whoever gets by this pair deserves every point that is made."[7] Both players were also capable of tearing down the floor on a scoring rampage of their own. After Kate Macrae left the team, one of Mae Brown, Doris Neale, or Margaret Kinney was paired with Captain Elsie on defence. For some unexplained reason, Elsie left the team and relinquished her captaincy at the end of the 1932 season. Yet, strangely she returned to the Grads in the spring of 1934, played in several series, and was a member of the team that toured eastern Canada and the United States that summer. She does not, however, appear in the 1934 team photograph and there is no evidence she was still with the team during the 1935 season.

From 1924 until 1937, Elsie continued to work in the Treasury Department at City Hall. Toward the end of her basketball career, she also helped coach the YWCA women's team and was involved in the administration of the game as second vice-president of the Canadian Amateur Basketball Association. In 1940 she was named honorary president of the Commercial Graduates Club in recognition of her long service with the team.

Elsie married W. Donald Robson on November 20, 1937, and in the absence of Elsie's father, Percy Page proposed the toast to the bride. The couple lived first in Regina and then moved to Calgary, eventually having two daughters, Margaret and Beverly. She was a long-time member of several service organizations, including the Order of the Eastern Star and the International Order of Job's

Daughters. Elsie died in Calgary on June 15, 1999 at the age of ninety-one, predeceased by her daughter Beverly and her husband Don, and survived by her other daughter Margaret and two grandchildren. As her obituary noted, she would be most remembered for her "caring and giving nature, her affection and good humour, and, above all, her tolerance of others."[8] She was indeed a role model and leader.

Harriett (Hattie) Hopkins (1925–1927)

Harriett McCleave Hopkins was born in Bangor, County Down, Northern Ireland on March 12, 1908. Her parents were Emily and David Hopkins, and she had an older sister May and older brother Robert. When and why the family came to Canada is a mystery; they cannot be found in either the 1911 Canadian census or the 1916 Prairie census.[9] What we do know is that Hattie attended public school in Edmonton beginning in 1914, followed by Victoria High School, where she completed grade eleven. A good athlete, she enjoyed badminton, tennis, swimming, skating, and especially basketball. In 1924–1925, Hattie attended McDougall Commercial for the one-year business course, where she played on the Gradettes.

In April of 1925, having just turned seventeen, Hattie made her first appearance with the Grads as a substitute in the Dominion championship series against Toronto's Young Women's Hebrew Association (YWHA) team. The *Edmonton Bulletin* reported, "She is fast on her feet, has a nice shot, and only needs to learn how to control her passes in order to rank with the best of them."[10] She remained a substitute player for most of her playing career, although a valuable one because she could play equally well on both offence and defence. Occasionally, when Dot Johnson's trick knee gave out, Hattie was called into the game. But her career with the Grads was a short one because she resigned from the team in the fall of 1927, along with the Johnson sisters and Marguerite Bailey.

Harriett (Hattie) Hopkins.
[GA ND-3-3089]

As a stenographer and secretary, Hattie was employed by a variety of Edmonton organizations between 1925 and 1942, including the Alberta Government, Weber Brothers Agencies, Chapman-Slessor Agencies, International Harvester, and L.C. Smith and Corona Typewriters. For most of this time, she lived with her sister May, a long-time teacher at Highlands Public School, and her brother Robert, who worked for the *Edmonton Journal.* In January 1942, Hattie enlisted in the Royal Canadian Air Force Women's Division. As a clerk stenographer she was originally posted to Edmonton, but throughout the war she was moved to stations in Toronto, Dauphin, Ottawa, and finally Calgary, rising to the rank of sergeant. Hattie was honourably released due to medical reasons in October 1945.[11] In January 1946, she was awarded the British Empire Medal with the following commendation:

An energetic and efficient worker whose extreme devotion to duty has been an example and inspiration to all those serving with her. Sergeant Hopkins' experience has been applied to Air Force Administration in such a manner that, as non-commissioned officer in charge of postings, she has received the praise and respect of all ranks. She has initiated drawings and procedures in her work that have been used as a model in other units. She takes a very keen interest in the welfare of the airwomen and is active in promoting their welfare activities.[12]

Suffering from endometriosis, a debilitating gynecological medical condition, Hattie was advised that full-time stenographic work would place too much strain on her health. As a veteran, and eligible for further training, she took a one-year course in handicrafts at Macdonald College in Montreal, with the goal of becoming a handicraft teacher and opening her own shop in Edmonton. Hattie returned to Edmonton in the fall of 1947, and because there were no jobs available to teach handicrafts, she was employed as a steno at an insurance agency. One year later, she got a job at the Charles Camsell Indian Hospital, which had opened in 1946 as a tuberculosis sanatorium primarily for Aboriginal patients from the North. Hattie's responsibilities were to teach and later supervise the handicraft program, an important aspect of occupational therapy for patients.[13] She worked at the Camsell until the summer of 1953, when a curious note appeared in the hospital newsletter: "Miss Harriett Hopkins, accompanied by her sister, Miss May Hopkins, will leave at the end of June by car, for Vancouver, BC. There they will be the guests of their brother, Mr. Bob Hopkins."[14] Harriett died suddenly in Vancouver on August 13, 1954. She was forty-six years old, and although the cause of death is not known, we can assume her health problems were a contributing factor.

Harriett M. Hopkins, former Edmonton Grad and World War II veteran, was buried in Vancouver, survived by her sister May in Edmonton and her brother Bob in Vancouver.[15] Neither sibling appears to have married or had children, which made it impossible for me to trace any relatives.

Marguerite Bailey Jacobs (1926–1927)

In a wonderful photo in the *Edmonton Bulletin* in October 1926, Marguerite ("Ronnie") Bailey is shown suited up in a Grads uniform assuming a classic basketball stance ready to pass the ball. At the time she was making a bid for a place on the Grad regulars. The previous year she had been a member of both the Commercial High School senior team and the Gradettes, and in April 1925, she was chosen to be part of the Grads as they travelled to the west coast for a series of exhibition games against opponents in Vancouver, New Westminster, Victoria, and Kamloops. The caption below her photo went on: "Although short, she is of stocky build and will remind the fans of Connie Smith in her ability to 'bust through' wherever an opening presents itself."[16]

Rita, as she liked to be called, was born in Toronto on October 31, 1906, not long after her parents, Andrew and Mary Bailey, and older sister Hilda had emigrated from England. By 1911, the family, which now included Hilda, Rita, and their younger brother John, was living on a farm in the Battleford district of Saskatchewan. Their father, a farmer and house painter, decided to move further west, and by 1916 the family—including another son, George— was living in Edmonton. As a student, Rita attended Sacred Heart Public School and Victoria High School, followed by business training at McDougall Commercial. She was obviously a good athlete, and at 5'6", not so short. In August 1923, when she was sixteen, she ran in the 1924 Olympic trials at the South Side Olympic Grounds in Edmonton, coming third in the 100-yard dash.

Her basketball career with the Grads, although brief, was certainly a busy one. In April 1926, Rita and two other Gradettes

Marguerite Bailey Jacobs.
[CEA EB-27-87]

accompanied the team on a two-week intensive road trip throughout eastern Canada and the U.S., which also included the Dominion
championships against Toronto Lakesides. The Grads played ten
matches in seven cities in thirteen nights and won six of them,
but the three Gradettes saw little action. Rita became an official
Grad in October 1926 and was a reserve player in two international series—one with the Guthrie (Oklahoma) Red Birds and the
other against the Detroit Nationals. She played with the team,
mostly as a substitute, from January until May, but resigned in
the fall along with Dot and Daisy Johnson and Hattie Hopkins.

Rita's first job was as a clerk at Woolworth's in Edmonton, but
around 1926 she settled into a position as a stenographer at the
University of Alberta, where she worked until at least 1942. She married Horace Jacobs on March 2, 1943, and after this, she is difficult
to track. At the time of the Jubilee reunion of the Grads in 1955,
she was living in Los Angeles and was unable to attend the reunion. Ten years later, she flew in from her home in Hawaii for the 1965

Grads reunion. She lived in Hawaii until the mid-1980s and somewhere in that time was divorced. Rita died in Vancouver on October 28, 1992, just two days shy of her eighty-sixth birthday. Her obituary mentioned her sister Hilda, also living in Vancouver, and two sisters-in-law, but no children.

Mildred McCormack Wilkie (1926–1932)

"I have never seen more accurate or more graceful shooting," an American coach once said of Millie McCormack, "and this goes for men as well as for girls."[17] According to Percy Page, Millie was probably the finest ball handler ever developed by the Grads. Paired with Margaret MacBurney on the forward line for most of her career, Millie was one half of a formidable twosome.

Mildred Ruth McCormack was born in Buffalo, New York on June 21, 1909. Three years later she and her older sister Ellen came with their parents, Samuel and Cora, to Edmonton. Why the family chose Edmonton is unclear, but their carpenter father eventually took a job as the caretaker at Highlands School, where he worked for many years. Millie went to school at McCauley, Highlands, and Victoria High, and by 1926, was finishing up her last year at McDougall Commercial and playing for the Gradettes. Along with Marguerite Bailey and Margaret MacBurney she was chosen to accompany the Grads in April on their gruelling road trip through eastern Canada and the United States. That fall she went to work at the United Typewriter Company as a cashier. A couple of years later, she was a stenographer and bookkeeper at the same business. She also played baseball and was a member of the Edmonton Toddies, who won the senior ladies' championship in 1926 and 1927.

Quiet and unassuming, Millie was known for her consistency during her career with the Grads. She was a substitute player for most of the 1927 season, but by 1928, when the Grads went to Europe, she

Mildred McCormack Wilkie.

[PAA BL2637/24]

was on the starting lineup. Paired with the more dazzling Margaret MacBurney, she always held her own and often shared high scoring honours. Plagued by illness, Millie was unable to play early in the 1932 season and she tendered her resignation on May 9, 1932. As reported in the *Edmonton Journal*, "Few more capable or popular players ever graced a Grad uniform than the 'flaxen flash,' and her loss will be regretted alike by the Grads and their supporters."[18] She played in ninety-four games, scoring a total of 924 points for an average of 9.8 points per game, making her the fifth top scorer of all time.

Millie continued to work at the typewriter company until she was married in December 1936. Her husband, Walter Wilkie, was a lacrosse player with the New Westminster Salmonbellies, the team that represented Canada at the 1928 Olympics in Amsterdam where lacrosse was a demonstration sport. Perhaps they met there. Regardless, the couple took up residence in New Westminster, British Columbia, and two sons, Maurice and Jack, soon followed. Millie died on May 10, 1991 at eighty-one years of age, predeceased by her husband. Her brief obituary provides no clues about her life after the Grads.

Margaret MacBurney Vasheresse (1926–1935)

By the time she retired from the team in October 1935, Margaret MacBurney had played in 164 games, scoring a total of 2,079 points for an average of 12.6 points per game. Next to Noel MacDonald, she was the second highest scoring Grad, and along with Winnie Martin and Elsie Bennie, she was one of the longest playing Grads. A bad knee had forced her into retirement. Barely 5'4" tall and a dynamo on the basketball court, she was very fast and a remarkably accurate shot.

Margaret was born in Fernie, British Columbia on April 9, 1909. Not much is known about her family except that her older sister Olive joined the Barnum Bailey Circus at sixteen as a trapeze artist and that she had a younger sister named Alberta. Apparently their mother Sarah outlived three husbands. When Margaret was young, the family moved to Edmonton where she attended Garneau and Queen's Avenue public schools, followed by high school at McDougall Commercial. Like most Grads, she honed her basketball skills playing on the high school teams and then on the Gradettes. Still in high school, she got her first chance to play with the Grads when, along with Marguerite Bailey and Millie McCormack, she was brought along as a spare on the infamous road trip of April 1926. She earned a permanent spot on the team later that fall, ably slipping into the position left vacant by a retiring Connie Smith. When she brought home the gold and black uniform, she told her mother that it was the happiest day of her life.

Margaret was short, never built for speed, and handicapped by poor eyesight, but she made up for these deficiencies through an unbelievably accurate shot from just about anywhere on the court.

Margaret MacBurney Vasheresse.

When she was on, she was unbeatable, and often the high scorer
in the game. In 1931, she sunk a remarkable sixty-one free throws
in succession, beating the world record. She was a member of the
team that travelled to Europe in 1928 in conjunction with the
Amsterdam Olympics and to the Los Angeles Olympics in 1932 on
the exhibition tour. In recognition of her leadership capabilities and
playing abilities, she captained the team between 1932 and 1935.

Beginning in 1928, Margaret worked at the *Edmonton Journal*
for nearly ten years as a stenographer and billing clerk, but in
1937, for unknown reasons, she decided to move to Vancouver.
Missing basketball, she played for a short while with the Vancouver
Spencers. There she met her husband, Victor Vasheresse, and
they were married in July 1939. The couple had no children, and
Margaret continued to work as a stenographer. She retired in
1970 when she was seventy. She kept fit through swimming and
bowling. When Victor died in 1977, Margaret moved into a senior's residence in Burnaby. She was very active in volunteer work,

especially as it pertained to seniors. She struggled with arthritis and helped establish the Burnaby Arthritis Support Group.

In 1994, Margaret moved back to Edmonton to assist her sister, Alberta Attridge, who was suffering from Alzheimer's, and to be closer to her extended family. She followed sports avidly and took pleasure in watching the youngest family members play hockey. As she aged, and became one of the few Grads still alive in Edmonton, she undertook considerable volunteer work to keep their memory alive by speaking to children, students, and interested groups. Always readily available for an interview, she could be depended upon to tell a good story, but never at the expense of upsetting the long dead Mr. Page.[19] Margaret always said she wanted to live until she was ninety-nine, hockey player Wayne Gretzky's number, but she died peacefully on June 27, 2007, a few months short of her goal.

Joan Johnston McEwen (1927–1929)

Joan Johnston is another player about whom we know very little. She played on the team for a short time and it is not entirely clear whether she attended or graduated from McDougall Commercial High School. According to the 1911 Canadian census, she was born in Alberta, perhaps Edmonton, sometime in April of 1907, with a given name of Joanna. Her parents were Joseph and Anna Johnston, and she had two older brothers, Stanley and Rodger. In 1911, the family was living in Onion Lake Village in the Battleford district of Saskatchewan, but by 1916 they had relocated to Strathcona, which by then had amalgamated with Edmonton. Her father had been a farmer in Saskatchewan, and in Edmonton he was manager of a city dairy.

From the sketchy biographical information available, we know that Joan learned to play basketball in Castor, a small community about ninety miles east of Red Deer. A photograph found in the

Joan Johnston McEwen.

[PAA BL2637/21]

Glenbow Archives shows "Joanna" with her team in 1923 when they won the Central Alberta championship.[20] She subsequently played for Strathcona High School and for the Camrose Normal School, which indicates that she may have trained as a teacher following high school. Joan makes her first appearance with the Grads in mid-October of 1927, when her photograph appears in an Edmonton paper indicating that she is one of two new players, both of whom were substitutes. The only indication about where Joan came from is the note that she "hails from Caster, although she has been in the city during the last couple of years."[21] She had possibly been playing with the Gradettes. Since several Grads had left the team after the summer, Page needed to find new players quickly to fill his roster for the 1927–1928 season.

Joan's first chance to play was during an international series in Edmonton against the Chicago Taylor Trunks. In the final period of the first game, Page substituted her in, but she was so nervous that she forgot to report to the referee and the team received a technical foul. Fortunately, she redeemed herself in a later series with the Minnesota Bankers and got her picture in the paper because she played a "splendid" game. Nonetheless, she remained a substitute forward throughout her short career. The fabulous shooting duo of Margaret MacBurney and Millie McCormack rarely required much assistance.

In the summer of 1928, when the team was gearing up to leave on their European and Olympic tour, it was clear that they only had sufficient funds to carry six players, even though there were seven players on the team at the time. A meeting was called to discuss who would be left behind. The discussion had only begun when Joan spoke up and asked to be the one dropped because she felt her playing was not up to the standard of the others. The following spring, Joan was still on the team as a substitute player with reports that she "looked good whenever she was on the floor."[22] However, by the middle of April she is no longer listed on the roster. Another young player, Babe Belanger, had been brought up from the Gradettes, and perhaps Joan saw the writing on the wall. She would never become a regular Grad.

What happened to her after that is a complete mystery. At some point, she married and became Joan McEwen and had a son. She did not participate in any of the team reunions over the years. According to a list in the City of Edmonton Archives, she died in December 1989, but an obituary has not been found.

Mae Brown Webb (1927–1930)

With the exception of two players, all of the Grads either attended or graduated from McDougall Commercial High School. There was no firm rule that you had to have been a student at Commercial to become a Grad, but in the normal course of events, a player would work her way through the junior and senior high school teams, possibly be chosen to play with the Gradettes, and eventually make it to the Grads. Mae Brown did not attend Commercial, and even came from a different city. In April 1925, she was a member of the Vancouver All-Stars, one of several teams to play the Grads, who at the time were making their way through British Columbia. Two years later in March 1927, Mae was playing for the Vancouver Canucks, a team sponsored by the Young Liberal Club, when they came to Edmonton to challenge the Grads for the Western Canadian championship. By the end of November the same year, it was announced that Mae would play with the Grads.

Born to Scottish pioneers Archie and Isabella Brown, Mary "Mae" Margaret arrived on August 15, 1903, not long after the family, including brother Archie, immigrated to Canada. They first settled in Minnedosa, Manitoba, where Mae was born, although the family soon homesteaded in the Lougheed area of central Alberta. Three more siblings, Irene, Gordon, and Norman (Buster) were born in Alberta. Her childhood spent on the family farm, Mae learned to play basketball using a bushel barrel for a basket. She completed her schooling in Lougheed. After attending Alberta College in Edmonton, Mae decided to move to Vancouver where she found work, and at the same time, sharpened her basketball skills by playing for the local YWCA team.

Mae's first opportunity to play with the Grads was early in December 1927 in an international series against the Minnesota Bankers. By then she had returned to Edmonton and was working as a stenographer at the Canadian Credit Men's Trust Association. Perhaps the promise of a tryout with the Grads brought her back to Edmonton. Coach Page was having some difficulty getting a team together that fall because several players had not returned after the summer break. Although he chose two players from the Gradettes, namely Margaret Nairn and Joan Johnston, fate intervened. Margaret

Mae Brown Webb.

[PAA BL2637/15]

was forced to give up all strenuous exercise on doctor's orders after playing with the Grads for only a few weeks, and Joan was seriously injured in a skating accident just days before the Minnesota series. Although Joan recovered sufficiently to play in the series, Mae also got on the floor and proved she was ready for senior competition.

During the early part of her career with the organization, Mae appears to have played for both the Gradettes and the Grads. In March 1928, for example, there is a photo of Mae with the Gradettes in the *Edmonton Bulletin*, and on the same day, the *Edmonton Journal* carried a picture of the Grads that also included Mae.[23] When playing with the Grads, she was mostly a substitute, and a valuable one at that, because she could play either the forward or guard positions with equal ability. She was known in those days as a "utility" player. Nonetheless, she was a regular member of the Grads when they toured Europe in the summer of 1928 and when they went on an extensive trip to the west coast of Canada and the United States in the summer of 1930. In October 1930, Mae announced that she was leaving the team because "she had played long enough and will hereafter follow the games from a seat on the sidelines."[24]

After retiring, Mae continued to work as a stenographer until she was married in September 1937 to Bruce Webb, a manufacturer's agent. Together they raised their family in Edmonton, which included son Gary and daughter Jane. With her husband constantly travelling, Mae ran the household and undertook volunteer work. In the 1950s and 1960s, for example, she was very involved with the Edmonton YWCA as a board member and executive officer; she was awarded a life membership in 1971 in recognition of her service to the organization.[25]

After fifty-nine years of marriage, Mae was widowed in 1996. Unfortunately, she suffered a stroke about a year after her husband died and was thereafter confined to bed. She passed away on April 7, 2000 at the age of ninety-six, survived by her children and their spouses, two grandchildren, and four great-grandchildren. Her daughter Jane recalled that her mother loved to talk about her days with the Grads: "What she brought to the Grads was always seen in the family in terms of dedication, determination and energy."[26]

Gladys Fry Douglas (1927–1936)

Gladys Alberta Fry was different from most other Grads. She was the first "south side girl" to join the team, which meant that she was a product of Edmonton's south side schools and the University of Alberta. In other words, she was not a graduate of McDougall Commercial. She was also the first Grad to play on the team after she was married. Or rather, she was the only player that Coach Page *knew* to be married. At just over 5'9", she was certainly one of the tallest Grads, and she was the only left-handed player in the team's history.

Gladys Fry Douglas.

[PAA BL2637/18]

Gladys was born on February 26, 1907, on a homestead in Alberta. Her father, John W. Fry, trained as a teacher, but when he married her mother, Maria, he established a homestead near Kitscoty, a small rural community east of Edmonton near the Saskatchewan border. In 1911, he moved his family, which by then consisted of Gladys and her sisters Dora and Ruth, to Edmonton, where he took up the contracting and real estate business. Another daughter Clara and a son Jack, both born in Edmonton, completed the family. Later on, John W. Fry entered municipal politics and served as a city alderman from 1932 until 1937 and as Edmonton's mayor between 1937 and 1945.

Gladys attended Queen Alexandra Public School followed by Strathcona High School. In the spring of 1927, she was playing for the Varsconas, a combined team from Strathcona High and the University of Alberta, which the Grads had soundly beaten to win the city championship. Come fall, Coach Page remembered the tall Varsconas centre and asked her to try out for the Grads. At first

Gladys refused because she was university student, studying home economics, and felt she would not have the time. Page tried again and this time Gladys agreed.[27] She played her first game as a Grad in an international series against the Chicago Taylor Trunks at the end of October 1927 when she replaced retiring centre Daisy Johnson. For the next three years, until she graduated with her bachelor's degree in 1930, Gladys played for both the Grads and the University of Alberta. Normally this would not have been a problem because by then the Gradettes, not the Grads, competed in the city's senior league and the two teams rarely played each other. However, both Varsity and the Grads reached the finals of the 1930 provincial championship, and of course each wanted Gladys on their team. To solve the problem, the two teams played a special game without Gladys in order to decide who would have her services. Gladys would play on the winning team. The Grads, especially forwards Babe Belanger, Millie McCormack, and Margaret MacBurney, smothered the University of Alberta team by a score of 50–7, and it was settled beyond any doubt that Gladys would play for the Grads.

Gladys had a long and illustrious career with the team. Harold Cruickshank called her the "genial centre, who packs a permanent smile together with a wicked sizzling shot."[28] Her specialty was to follow up on her own rebounds, and, being a "southpaw," she slammed in baskets from the left side when least expected. When centre Noel MacDonald came up from the Gradettes in 1933, she began to relieve Gladys, who eventually was moved to defence. After the team's Canadian exhibition tour during the summer of 1934, it was announced that Gladys was among the several players leaving the team. However, by late fall she was back playing, and when Margaret MacBurney retired in the fall of 1935, Gladys took her place as captain. In the spring of 1936, when Gladys was married, it was assumed she would immediately leave the team, but Coach Page persuaded her to come overseas on their European tour in connection with the Berlin Olympics. It was her second time abroad and she finally retired when they returned. In all, Gladys played in 161 games for the Grads scoring a total of 1,679 points for an average of 10.4 points per game, which made her the fourth highest scorer of all time. In fan ballots at the end of the final series in 1940, she was voted number four on the all-star team.

Prior to her marriage, Gladys worked as a lab technician at the University of Alberta. On May 2, 1936 she married Jack Douglas, who followed a career in banking. The couple had two sons, John and Jim, and eventually moved to Calgary. Gladys was active in sports all her life. She also willingly volunteered her services to various charitable organizations. Along with the honours she received as a member of the Grads, she was inducted into the University of Alberta Sports Wall of Fame in 1986 for outstanding achievements in basketball and track. At age eighty-four, suffering the aftermath of a stroke, Gladys died in Calgary on March 17, 1991. She was survived by her husband Jack, her sons and their spouses, two grandchildren, and several of her siblings.

Noella "Babe" Belanger MacLean (1929–1937)

Why Noella Belanger was called "Babe" is not clear, possibly because she was small. Nevertheless, it is the name she preferred all her life. Born in Edmonton on May 8, 1911 to Fred and Georgiana Belanger, who were originally from Quebec, Babe had an older brother Louis, and a younger brother and sister, Morris and Blanche. Their father was a cableman who worked for the city telephone company. Like so many of the Grads, Babe attended Parkdale Public School and then went to McDougall Commercial for high school. An all-round athlete, she was an exceptionally fine sprinter and, despite her short stature, a good high jumper. She once competed against Olympic gold medallist Ethel Catherwood in a high jumping demonstration before a

Noella "Babe" Belanger MacLean.

[PAA A11430]

capacity crowd crammed into the grandstand at the Edmonton exhibition grounds. Ethel easily cleared the bar at 5', while Babe, who was just less than 5'3" tall, came second with a jump of 4'5".[29]

Babe got her first chance to play with the Grads in March 1929 when Coach Page brought her up from the Gradettes as a substitute in an international series with a Seattle team. She did not leave the team until she retired eight years later. Initially, she was used as a relief forward for either Margaret MacBurney or Millie McCormack, but when Millie became ill in the spring of 1932 and had to resign from the team, Babe filled her spot. She was a perpetual star from then on, and "one of the classiest little forwards ever seen in the game."[30] A vivacious brunette, she could run like a rabbit, often galloping the entire length of the floor and winding up below the basket for a set-up shot. She was also deadly accurate at shooting baskets. Between 1929 and 1937, she was a member of teams that travelled throughout Canada and the

United States and also to Europe in 1936. Throughout her career, she played in 136 games, scoring a total of 1,441 points for an average of 10.5 points per game, the third highest scorer of all time.

Babe announced her retirement from the game in June 1937 after an international series against the Tulsa Stenos. In her *Edmonton Journal* "Feminine Flashes" column, Patricia Page wrote the following tribute:

> *The passing of Babe Belanger from the ranks of the Grads will be regretted by the thousands of fans throughout the country who have seen her play. One of the smallest girls ever to wear a Grad uniform, she was probably the fastest and certainly one of the most colourful. Down in Montreal last summer, her fellow Frenchmen took her to their hearts, and every time she got hold of the ball and sailed toward the basket she got a great round of applause—much the same as greeted her out at the arena on Monday night when she got back into the game after a brief illness. She will certainly be missed, and we are sure every fan who has watched or listened to the games will join us in wishing her all the luck in the world in her future career.* [31]

Although working as a steno at the *Edmonton Journal* when she retired from basketball, Babe's future career soon turned out to be marriage and a family. A year after leaving the Grads on September 6, 1930, she married Ian MacLean, an undercover RCMP officer, and moved to Verdun in Quebec. They eventually had two children, Neil and Heather, and in the early 1950s they moved back to Edmonton, where Ian was an athletic trainer for several professional hockey and football teams. Babe was apparently quiet and modest about her days with the Grads, especially to her children, who had no idea about their mother's basketball stardom until much later. [32] She was widowed in 1975, and toward the end of her life, diabetes took its toll, robbing her of her sight and much of her hearing. Babe Belanger died at eighty-three years of age in an Edmonton nursing home on January 7, 1999.

Doris Neale Chapman (1929–1936)

Imagine playing your first basketball game in a Grads uniform only to discover that the person who invented the sport was in the stands. This happened to Doris Neale. In late October 1929, the Grads were to play a two-game international series in Edmonton against a strong team from Cleveland, the Blepp-Knits. While travelling to Edmonton, the Blepp-Knits had added several players from the Chicago Taylor Trunks to bolster their roster. This would be the Grads' first series without the services of guard Kate Macrae, who had just been married. Mae Brown was filling her spot, but in a practice game against a men's team just before the series, Mae tore the ligaments in her ankle and was out for the season. Coach Page immediately looked to the Gradettes and chose Doris to team up with Elsie Bennie on defence. The Grads beat the Blepp-Knits by a wide margin in the first game with a score of 50–31, and it was noted that Doris "gave a remarkably fine display."[33] Watching the second game was none other than James Naismith, who came all the way from the University of Kansas just to see the Grads in action. They defeated the Cleveland team again and received nothing but praise from Naismith. Doris Neale continued to play as a Grad for another seven years.

Born in Ottawa, Canada's capital, on June 26, 1911, Doris was the youngest of Arthur and Mabel Neale's four children. When she was two years old the family moved to Edmonton, where two more children were born, giving Doris five siblings—Gordon, Margery, Lorne, Norval, and Olive. Tragically, Doris's mother died in childbirth with her seventh child, Alice. The baby was sent to be raised by relatives in Saskatchewan and a housekeeper was employed to help Arthur,

Doris Neale Chapman.

[PAA BL2637/27]

a pressman working in a printing business, with his large family. No doubt Doris learned a great deal about survival and independence as she was growing up, traits she would need herself later in life.

After attending H.A. Gray and Parkdale public schools, followed by three years at McDougall Commercial, Doris was ready for the work world. Her first job was as a steno at Northern Hardware, but she soon found more interesting work with the Radio Department of the *Edmonton Journal*, where she worked for several years. As for basketball, she had learned the fundamentals at Parkdale and the finer points at Commercial, and in 1927, she was chosen to play for the Gradettes. Only 5'3" tall, Doris was speedy, tenacious, and a fine ball handler. Although she could shoot, Coach Page decided she was best suited to the guard position.

By 1936, Doris was working as secretary to Dick Rice, the co-founder of Sunwapta Broadcasting and radio station CFRN. It would also be her last year as a Grad; she retired after the team returned in September from their European tour. She continued to work at CFRN until she was married in the fall of 1938 to Edwin (Ed) Chapman of Toronto, where the couple lived. In January 1939, she was invited to play basketball with the Toronto Ladies, who were about to take on the Grads. She declined this offer. A son, Peter, was born later in 1939 and her daughter, Judith, was born in 1942. Another son, Randall, arrived in 1949. At this point, the family was living in Kitchener, Ontario. Sadly, the marriage fell apart, and in 1953, Doris moved with her three children to High River, Alberta, where she worked as a secretary. A few years later, she had the opportunity to return to Edmonton and again work for Dick Rice as his executive secretary at Sunwapta. Although she retired in 1976 when she was sixty-five, Doris soon became bored and she went back to work for another five years, retiring for good at age seventy.

In an interview, her daughter Judy remarked that family and work sustained Doris. She was a private person who simply got on with life and made the best of her circumstances, something she had learned as a child when her own mother died. Judy summed up her mother by saying "she was a tough lady."[34] Doris died of cancer at age eighty on February 27, 1992, survived by her three children, seven grandchildren, and one great-grandchild as well as two brothers and a sister.

Margaret Kinney Howes (1929–1930)

At just under a year, Margaret had one of the shortest careers with the Grads. In November 1929, she was added to the team as a substitute, and in March of the following year, it was announced that she was officially a member of the team. By the fall of 1930, she was back playing with the University of Alberta because new regulations prevented her from playing on two teams that played in the same league. Born in Edmonton on February 1, 1912, Margaret was the youngest child of James and Olive Kinney. Hers was a large and athletic family. Her two brothers, Wilf and Jim, were well-known for their

Margaret Kinney Howes.

[PAA BL2637/14]

prowess in hockey; her sister Marian was a member of the Gradettes
for two years, while another sister, Dorothy, played basketball for the
Victoria High School team. In 1925, Dorothy and Marian founded
the Kinney School of Dancing and Physical Culture in Edmonton,
where they both taught. Margaret attended a number of schools
and colleges, including Victoria and McDougall Commercial high
schools, Edmonton Normal School, and the University of Alberta.

In 1928–1929, she was playing basketball alongside Gladys Fry on
the University of Alberta's Varsity team and, at the same time, was a
regular on the Gradettes. Her first game with the Grads was as a substitute, along with Babe Belanger, in an exhibition game in Regina
before 3,500 enthusiastic spectators against a team called the Torrid
Zones. Although Margaret continued primarily as a substitute, she
was kept busy by the Grads in the 1930 season, which included the
usual provincial, western Canadian, and national championships;
two Underwood trophy challenge series, one against the Seattle
Ferry Lines and the other with the Chicago Taylor Trunks; and a

summer tour through British Columbia and down the west coast of the United States in lieu of a trip to Prague for the Women's World Games. The Grads played no more games in the fall, and Margaret returned to Varsity competition as a member of both the women's basketball and track teams.

While on campus, she was also a part-time worker for the Student Christian Movement. Founded in 1921 and rooted in the social gospel movement, the group was inspired by the Christian tradition of fighting oppression and struggling for a better world. Upon graduation in 1932, Margaret became national secretary to the organization, and based in Toronto, she travelled across the country organizing conferences at various universities. In 1941, Margaret was appointed national industrial secretary to the YWCA, working with women employed in Canadian war industries. She was married in 1943 to Dr. Frederick S. Howes, an electrical engineer on the staff of McGill University, who initiated training and research in electronics and radio communications. In Montreal, Margaret worked on a volunteer basis for the Canadian Association of Adult Education until 1946 when she was hired as a producer for the CBC to fill in for a male employee who was serving in the armed forces. She stayed at the CBC for twenty years and eventually became a regional supervisor, responsible for English language public affairs radio and television programming originating in Montreal and Quebec City.[35]

Fred Howes retired from McGill as professor emeritus in 1964 and Margaret retired from the CBC in 1966. Realizing they would never be promoted, many key women at the CBC either left or retired in this era. Fred and Margaret had no children and were married for fifty-two years. They also had a long and hopefully enjoyable retirement, since Fred was in his ninety-eighth year when he passed away in January 1995. Several months later on September 9, 1995, Margaret died at eighty-three years. Her obituary read, "Margaret lit up the

lives of all who knew her. She was a woman of great heart and quest-
ing mind whose lifelong concern was for people and their needs."[36]

7 Rhythm of the Years

THE EARLY HISTORY of women's basketball in Canada is marked
by uneven development across the country and significant east–
west divisions. The most controversial issue causing these divisions
was gender-based rule codes. In many ways, these factors explain
why Percy Page looked primarily to the United States, rather than
Canada, for competition to challenge his team. There was also
a steady rhythm to the Grads' basketball season, which usually
extended from November until June. Each year was more or less
the same. The team organized in the fall—decisions about new
players were made and they might also schedule an Underwood
International Trophy challenge series with an American team if
the Arena was available. The provincial, western Canadian, and

Dominion championships were completed by March, and one or more international challenge series usually took place later in the spring. Usually in the summer months, although sometimes in April or May, there was a one- to three-week exhibition tour somewhere in Canada or the United States. The team also went on lengthy European trips during the summers of 1924, 1928, and 1936. The regularity of the basketball season was determined not only by the limited number of American teams willing to make the journey to Edmonton, but also by the availability of a suitable venue to attract a crowd large enough to bring in substantial gate receipts. The only appropriate space in Edmonton was the Arena, which was unavailable during the men's professional hockey season from December until mid-April. The lack of large venues to attract spectators also posed a problem for the American teams, most of whom played basketball in the winter, and, therefore, they were forced to travel to Edmonton outside of their competitive season.

Gender-based Rules

The controversy over rules, especially those used by women's teams, is deeply embedded in the history of basketball. When James Naismith created this vigorous indoor game, it was designed to help keep his young male students at the YMCA Training College in Springfield, Massachusetts in shape between the football and baseball seasons. Naismith had five fundamental principles in mind when he devised the game: (1) There must be a ball; it should be large, light, and handled with the hands; (2) There shall be no running with the ball; (3) No man on either team shall be restricted from getting the ball at any time it is in play; (4) Both teams are to occupy the same area, yet there is to be no personal contact; and (5) the goal shall be horizontal and vertical.[1] Women teachers from a nearby school came to watch these first games, and within weeks they asked

Naismith if he would show them how to play. They were soon proficient enough to teach their young female students the fundamentals; the game for girls began to spread as rapidly as the boys' game.

Women physical educators soon recognized basketball's potential, but if played by girls and women, they were convinced that the rules needed modification to control unnecessary roughness and encourage more teamwork. Senda Berenson, physical director at Smith College in Massachusetts, was the first to develop a set of rules especially for girls and women, which were approved by the American Association for the Advancement of Physical Education in 1899 as a way to standardize the game nationwide.[2] These modified rules discouraged personal contact and tussling through stringent penalties. Most importantly, the rules limited each player to either half or one-third of the court, depending on its size or the age of the girls. Women physical educators argued that women's basketball was not a weak or emasculated form of men's basketball, but a different game that required different rules because girls were physiologically weaker than boys:

> The game subjected the player to a test of physical endurance which was beyond the capacity of any but the most vigorous. The panting, gasping and calling for "time" by the player of ordinary strength, as well as the disproportionate fatigue that often accompanies a game, showed that the heart was being forced to carry an unusually heavy load. It was seen that the game which made such heavy demands on organic vitality was ill-adapted to the rank and file of girls and that its range of usefulness was much limited thereby. It was also recognized that the dangers from collision, violent contact and falling were more serious for the girl than for the boy.[3]

Many women physical educators, especially in the United States, were opposed to high level sport for girls and women, and they promoted "play for play's sake," stressing the enjoyment of sport and the development of good sportsmanship and character rather than the breaking of records and the winning of championships. Their philosophy was encapsulated in the creed "a team for every girl and every girl on the team," which was best accomplished through a broad-based intramural sports program that exposed students to a variety of athletic experiences. Also popular were "play days," where girls from different institutions, whether elementary or high schools, colleges or universities, industrial, civic or church groups, met for a day of games and athletics. Play days, women physical educators argued, would effectively eliminate spectators, publicity, gate receipts, and individual stars—indeed all forms of commercialization and exploitation. To remove all traces of the "evils" of men's sport, they advocated a separatist philosophy whereby only women administered, coached, officiated, and controlled girls' and women's sports.[4]

Beginning in 1901, the American Sports Publishing Company issued the annual *Spalding's Official Basket Ball Guide for Women*, which contained the Spalding rules, although they were more commonly referred to as girls' rules. Six players were restricted to a particular section of the court—front, centre, or back—depending on their position; the ball could only be dribbled once (later changed to three times); and snatching or batting the ball from a player's hands was prohibited. This was in contrast to the five-player boys' or men's rules in which players could use the full court with fewer restrictions on dribbling and guarding the offence. Influenced by their American counterparts, women physical educators in central Canada and the Maritimes enforced the Spalding rules in schools and universities, although the more vigorous boys' rules were often used—not without condemnation—in YWCA, community, or church leagues outside of the control of physical educators. Basketball as played by the Toronto Ladies and Young Women's Hebrew Association (YWHA), commented a Toronto sports reporter in 1924, is "entirely

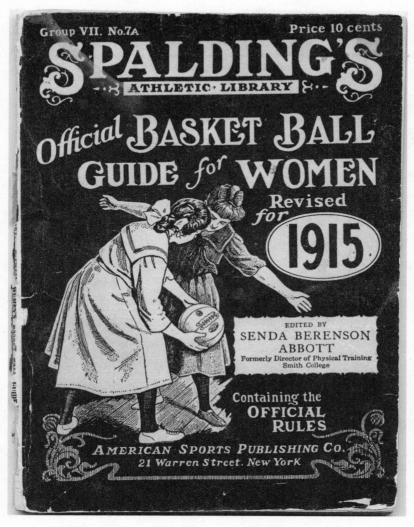

Cover of Spalding's Official Basket Ball Guide for Women, *1915.* [SCA 5782]

too rough a game for girls."[5] This particular YWHA team, including star player Bobbie Rosenfeld, went on to win the Toronto Ladies' Basketball League, and after defeating the Ottawa Alerts, travelled to Edmonton in 1925 only to be beaten by the Edmonton Grads. In 1921, with the formation of the Canadian Women's Intercollegiate

Basketball League (CWIBL), the Spalding rules were modified to permit each player to cover two-thirds of the floor. The CWIBL decided to publish its own rulebook. With some success, they canvassed all high schools and universities in eastern Canada to use these rules.

The situation was considerably different in western Canada. The relative scarcity of women physical education teachers meant that most teams were coached by men and played by men's rules in both educational and community settings. In 1923, the Alberta Basketball Association declared there would be two leagues for women players—a junior and a senior—whereby the Spalding women's rules would be used in the junior league and the men's rules in the senior. Although the Grads had started out playing the Spalding rules, they switched in 1923 to comply with the Alberta Basketball Association ruling and never looked back. The CWIBL, very much eastern-based, lobbied for use of their modified Spalding rules across the country and were not impressed when the Grads went to Europe in 1924 and played under men's rules. Members of the CWIBL were upset enough to send a letter of protest to the secretary of the Canadian Olympic Committee (COC) and the president of the Amateur Athletic Union of Canada (AAU of C).[6] The CWIBL was also unwilling to recognize championships that did not use women's rules, and it put pressure on both the COC and AAU of C to prevent the Grads from defending their world title at the Women's World Games in 1926.[7] As it turned out, basketball was not on the program and the Grads did not go to Europe that year.

During the twenty-five years of the Grads' existence, the Canadian rule problem was never resolved. Dorothy Jackson, a physical educator at the University of Toronto, conducted a national survey in 1941 to ascertain what rules were being used across the country. She discovered there was still an even east–west split with British Columbia, Alberta, Saskatchewan, and Manitoba governed almost entirely by men's rules, whereas Ontario, Quebec, New Brunswick, and Nova

Scotia accounted for most of the 53 per cent of teams who were using girls' rules. She also noted that a handful of women physical education teachers in private schools, a few high schools, and YWCAS had introduced the girls' game in the west with limited success. Similarly, there were organized leagues using men's rules in eastern Canada, but they were almost entirely outside the schools, universities, and teacher training colleges.[8]

The contentious issue of gender-based basketball rules, in both Canada and the United States, had deep roots in the philosophical divide between middle-class, university-educated, professional women physical educators and the promoters of popular sports, many of whom were men. Where physical educators condemned commercial and industrial sport for women as exploitative, sponsors and promoters saw it as the only opportunity for the thousands of young women who worked in the factories, shops, and downtown businesses to play sport. Local businesses were also not indifferent to the added benefits of publicity when their name was splashed across player uniforms. Alexandrine Gibb, the leading Canadian women's sports administrator of the 1920s and 1930s, and a firm believer in commercially-sponsored sport for women, argued, "The girls lure the commercial firms into supporting them, so they can play ball under proper circumstances, be properly clad with clothing and have bats and balls and fun." She was also quick to condemn the situation in the United States, where young women athletes were sometimes enticed by industrial concerns solely for the publicity and benefits these firms derived from sponsoring high-profile teams. She also argued for the necessity of gate receipts: "Who would buy the uniforms and pay the expenses of securing an amateur card and the resultant doctor's fee for physical examinations? Who would pay the coach?"[9]

Although Percy Page was never paid as a coach, and his players were strictly amateur, he believed in the value of providing quality competitive opportunities for working women. Unfortunately, we do not have the benefit of anything he might have said or written on the philosophical debates concerning basketball rules or industrial sport, but his actions demonstrate that he was clearly in favour of allowing women to play the full-court men's game and using gate receipts to finance his teams and their travels. As for the belief that the men's game was too strenuous for females, Page insisted that the required procedure before a girl became a Grad would eliminate any who were unfit; each player had to have a doctor's certificate indicating she was in good health before being issued an amateur card. When pressed, Page relied on his observation that former Grads were now in the business of producing babies; clearly, vigorous basketball had not in any way damaged their reproductive capacity.[10] Where he stood with regard to commercial sport, whereby teams were sponsored by industrial concerns or small business, is not known. Page was certainly proud, however, that, with the exception of a small sum donated to the team when they made their second tour of Europe in 1928, "every dollar which has been necessary to finance the girls' trips from year to year has come from careful financing on the part of the club."[11] He was also totally committed to maintaining the amateur status of his players:

> No collection of athletes in any part of the world has a better claim to the word "amateur" than the Edmonton Grads. These girls, without exception, are working girls who play the game for the game's sake—practising faithfully twice a week throughout the year, except for June, July and August, and in their own spare time, rather than that of their employers. Not a suspicion of professionalism has ever been raised against any member of any Grad team.[12]

Best Team in Alberta, the West, and Canada

"Girls' basketball in the Cow Town has in the past been of a negligible quantity and quality, and it is hoped that real opposition comes from the south in the years to come, adding both competition and encouragement to the Edmonton enthusiasts who have been at it so long without much gained for themselves in the way of outside contests," observed an Edmonton sportswriter after the University of Alberta decisively defeated the Calgary Buccaneers in the lead-up to the 1924 provincial championship.[13] The Grads went on to beat Varsity to win their tenth consecutive provincial championship. When it became obvious that no team in the province could match the Grads, the Alberta Basketball Association suggested that they accept a bye and not compete during the regular season, but meet the winner of the senior league in home-and-home games for the provincial championship. From 1927 onwards, the senior league winner was either a team from Calgary or the Gradettes, who had become too good for intermediate competition and were entered into the senior tournament. With the exception of the Calgary Central Grads, a team comprised of graduates of Central High School, the other Calgary opponents were industrial teams. The Beavers were sponsored by the Hudson's Bay Company, the Wittichens by a financial brokerage firm, and the Buffaloes by the Calgary Brewing and Malting Company. The only times the Grads did not compete for the championship, letting the Gradettes do the job instead, were in 1936 because of their European tour, and in 1939 and 1940 when they were granted a bye into the Canadian final. Between 1915 and 1940, the Grad organization never lost a senior provincial championship.

Just when the western Canadian basketball championships began for women is not entirely clear. Regardless, the major opposition for the Grads in the west always came from a team in Vancouver. The Grads first ventured across the Rockies in the spring of 1925 to play a four-game exhibition series against all-star teams from Vancouver, Victoria, and Kamloops. They beat all comers, and it is possible that the two-game series against the Vancouver team was considered a western final. With no team from British Columbia entering the Canadian playdowns in 1926, the Grads met the Vancouver Canucks the following year in what was officially described as the western Canadian championship. The Canucks were sponsored by the Young Liberal Club, whose politics at the time promoted amateur sport for women. With a similar style of play to the Grads, the team had dominated competition in the lower mainland and Vancouver Island. However, they were no match for the Grads, who beat them in two games straight with scores of 34–19 and 30–18. The University of British Columbia also had a strong team, but the Grads easily defeated them in the western final the following year, as they would again in 1930. No final was held in 1929 or 1931. Throughout the 1930s, the Grads consistently defeated a Vancouver team for the western Canadian championship: first the Witches, then Province, and finally the Spencers. They won their last championship in 1938 by defeating the Victoria Superiors, who unexpectedly beat the Vancouver Spencers. Including their byes into the Canadian finals in 1939 and 1940, the Grads never lost a western Canadian championship.

The same was true for the Canadian championship, which they won perennially beginning in 1922. Women's basketball did not develop across the country to the extent that every province was able to enter regional playdowns. The most successful teams came from Vancouver, Edmonton, Toronto, and Windsor. There was also the problem of gender-based rules. Although basketball was well-established in many universities in eastern Canada and the Maritimes, most of these teams played only women's rules and competed in their own leagues. After defeating the London Shamrocks in 1922 and 1923, the Grads often faced a team from Toronto for

1923 Canadian champions: Eleanor Mountifield, Connie Smith, Abbie Scott, Dot Johnson, Nellie Perry, Winnie Martin, Elizabeth Elrick, and Mary Dunn.

[PAA A11413]

the Canadian title—Lakesides, YWHA, Ladies Athletic Club, and British Consols. None were ever able to come close to beating the Grads. The Windsor Alumnae thought perhaps they could do it in 1934 and 1935, but they too were soundly beaten. The Grads never lost a Canadian championship series. They played thirty-one Canadian championship games, losing only two—once to the London Shamrocks (see Chapter 1) and once to the Toronto Lakesides.

United States Challengers

In his continual search for worthy teams to challenge the Grads, and to make the games sufficiently interesting to draw large crowds, Page looked to the United States, where there were more

Chicago Tri-Chi basketball team in Edmonton, December 1925. [GA ND-3-3037]

commercially sponsored teams and certainly more who played
men's rules than in Canada. From 1923 onwards, over thirty different American teams came to Edmonton to challenge the Grads,
some more than once. Most travelled from states located far from
Alberta—Arkansas, Idaho, Illinois, Iowa, Kansas, Ohio, Oklahoma,
Michigan, Minnesota, and Missouri. During the depression-laden
thirties and before the days of commercial air travel, it was a remarkable testament to Page's ability to raise enough funds to allow
the club to help pay the travelling expenses of visiting teams.

During the 1920s and 1930s, the city of Chicago was a hotbed
of women's basketball. In fact, by 1926 there were more than 100
teams organized into nine leagues. Between 1923 and 1940, no city
sent more women's basketball teams to Edmonton than Chicago.
The first of these was the Chicago Uptown Brownies, who challenged the Grads for the Underwood International Trophy in the fall

of 1923 because they had won the Central AAU Women's Basketball Championship in both 1922 and 1923. Held annually in Chicago since 1919 in conjunction with the men's championship, the Central AAU tournament used men's rules and attracted teams mostly from the Chicago area, although it billed the winners as "champions of the Midwest." Since the national AAU championship for women was a few years away yet, and the Uptown Brownies had at least distinguished themselves in a major tournament, Page took a chance when he first invited them to Edmonton. He was not disappointed, nor were the thousands of fans packed into the Arena, who witnessed two closely fought games that were remembered for years as among the most exciting ever played: "For spills, thrills and chills, that series has probably never been equalled anywhere, and when the two teams left the floor at the end of the second game, it will always be a moot question as to who was the most nearly exhausted—the spectators or the players themselves."[14] The Grads won that first series 20–17 in the first game and 25–20 in the second. They would play the Uptown Brownies three more times—in 1924, 1928, and 1929—and retained the Underwood trophy each time.

The Brownies' main competition in Chicago came from the Chicago Lakeviews, founded in 1920 as the Lake View Community Girls. They beat the Brownies in the Central AAU championship in 1924 and 1925. In 1926, under the name Tri-Chi Girls, they took their third championship. Sponsored by the T.J. Taylor Company, a trunk manufacturer, they became the Taylor Trunks Tri-Chis. By the fall of 1927, the Taylor Trunks were no longer considered an amateur team by the AAU because two of their members were playground instructors. Since they were making money through sport, they were considered professionals. Consequently, their team was barred from playing other AAU teams. Managed by the genial Harry Wilson, who would become a great friend to the Grads, the team first came to Edmonton in 1924. They returned in 1925–1926—the series was played over New Year's—and in 1927 and 1930. The Taylor Trunks had accumulated an admirable record by 1930—winning 220 games and losing only nine. During that last series with the Grads, they nearly beat them. Up to this point, the Grads had seventy-eight consecutive wins, and had not been defeated in seven years, but on May 4, 1930, in the first game of the series, the Taylor Trunks won by 10 points with a score of 34–24. A crowd of nearly 7,000 packed the Arena for the second game. Cheering and clapping wildly, they helped their team handily beat the Taylor Trunks by 40–13, and the Grads won the series. The *Edmonton Journal* had set up a special telephone number for fans who were stuck at home to find out the score. An estimated 100,000 to 150,000 calls flooded the system, blew the main exchanges, and disrupted telephone service throughout the city. When the final whistle sounded, thousands of spectators swept down onto the arena floor and the Grads were hoisted shoulder high to receive their accolades.

Several other teams came to Edmonton from Chicago over the years: the Forest Park Cardinals in 1931, the Red Devils in 1932 and 1933, the Spencer Coals in 1934, the Usherettes in 1935, the All-Stars in 1938, and finally the Queen Anne Aces in 1939 and 1940. All were typical industrial teams of the era. The Spencer Coals were sponsored by Spencer Brothers Company, a coal supply business; the players on the Usherettes were employed by Harry Frain, who operated the concessions for ushering at many stadia and convention halls; and the Queen Anne Aces were sponsored by a candy company of the same name. None ever beat the Grads except the Queen Anne Aces (coached by Harry Wilson), who won the final game of a three-game series in 1939 by matching the Grads in speed, ball handling, combination, and shooting. But the Grads took the series by an aggregate score of 120–98.

The first AAU (United States) women's national tournament was held in 1926 in Pasadena, California, although most of the

St. Louis Curlees and the Grads lined up at the start of a game in the Edmonton Arena, June 1926. [GA ND-3-3215]

better teams from across the country did not show up and the event became just a small, west coast meet. A team from the Pasadena Athletic and Country Club won the tournament; the Grads had soundly beaten them the summer before on their exhibition tour through Texas, California, and British Columbia. The AAU boldly decided to use men's rules for the tournament, but they permitted a longer rest between halves. As in Canada, there was a geographical divide between the two sets of rule codes: men's rules predominated in the northern and eastern states, whereas women's rules were the norm in the western and southern states.[15] The official national tournament was not held again until 1929, this time in Wichita, Kansas, with teams playing under women's rules. Because of these rules, the Grads did not play any of the national tournament winners until they were forced to play the 1933 winners—the

Oklahoma Presbyterian College Cardinals from Durant—for the first North American title to decide who would represent the continent at the Women's World Games in London the following year. This series was discussed in Chapter 3; it was a disaster for the Grads even though the first and third games were played using men's rules. They never had a chance in the second game under women's rules. Page always insisted that it was easier for a team to change from women's rules to men's rules than for a team to change from men's rules to women's rules because of the many restrictions in the latter. When American teams challenged the Grads for the Underwood International Trophy, they had to agree to play by the men's code because this was stipulated in the trophy regulations.

Even the AAU began to realize the standard six-player women's game needed changes to make it faster and more exciting, yet they were hesitant to convert entirely to the full-court game. At first they tried two parallel national tournaments, the "softie" for those who played women's rules, and the "tomboy" for the few teams playing men's rules. The Chicago Spencer Coals won the latter tournament. Not long after, however, in an Underwood trophy series with the Grads in Edmonton, they were demolished in the first game with a score of 100–39 and somewhat exonerated in the second, 46–37. The biggest rule change came in 1936 when the AAU instituted the "running" or "shooting" guard, later called the "rover." This new rule permitted one guard to cross the centre-line and participate in her team's offence, although it had to be the guard who passed the ball into the offensive end. An opposition forward would follow the guard in order to defend her, putting eight players at one end.[16] Combined with the limited dribble and three-second rule, the rover rule made for a game with more passing and outside shooting, not unlike that already played by the Grads.

Certainly, from 1934 onwards the Grads tried to play the winners or runners-up from the AAU national tournament, or at least teams

Tulsa Business College Stenos, National AAU champions, 1934–1936. [CEA EB-27-98]

among the top four, but only under men's rules. The Tulsa Business College Stenos from Oklahoma, or simply the Tulsa Stenos, became the first team to win three consecutive AAU championships—in 1934, 1935, and 1936. Coached by Steve Beck, they first came to Edmonton in 1934 after their AAU win. With star players like Hazel Walker and Alberta Williams, the Stenos outweighed and outreached the Grads; even still, they could not mount a strong enough attack and were beaten in three straight but close games. Of all the American teams who challenged the Grads, the Tulsa Stenos probably came the closest to beating them, and each year the series was the most thrilling to witness. The Grads won again in 1935, but only after the Stenos took a game and forced the series to four games. Writer Harold F. Cruickshank contributed a special ditty to the occasion, part of which went:

GRADS!...GRADS! *Just too tough a proposition*
For the Beck-coached gals to take.
GRADS! GRADS! *Who defy all opposition*
When they need the points they make.
Here's a hand to Page's champions—
With a cheer from every fan—
Neale, MacBurney, Fry, Belanger,
Munton, Noel, and Etta Dann.[17]

The Stenos again pushed the team to four games in 1936, and with close-scoring games, the Grads' high percentage of successful free throws helped them. For the third time in three years, they extended the Grads to four games in 1937, when a total of 13,000 excited fans paid to see the series. As George Mackintosh, writing in the *Edmonton Journal*, commented, "When you consider that many of these fans bought tickets knowing well in advance that they would only be able to see one of the baskets, no further proof is necessary that this city is the 'Edmonton of the Grads.'"[18]

Barnstorming Throughout North America

Percy Page believed wholeheartedly in the sport of basketball for girls and women. He also realized, as the Grads' reputation grew, that they could play an important role in promoting their version of the game across Canada and the United States. He was supported in this view by other basketball coaches and managers, who recognized that appearances by the Grads would give a much-needed boost to women's basketball in their locales. Wherever they went, certainly in the United States, the team brought favourable publicity to the city of Edmonton, especially through articles in local newspapers, and people were curious to learn more about Alberta's capital. After their triumphal trip to London, Ontario in 1922, where they

Returning from a trip through eastern Canada and the United States, April 1927.

[CEA EB-27-70]

won the first Dominion championship, the Grads embarked on an exhibition tour somewhere in North America almost every year of their existence—except on the three occasions they travelled abroad to Europe. Even then, they often stopped several times along their way across Canada to play exhibition games. In 1936, for example, they played teams in Regina, Winnipeg, St. Paul, Peterborough, Ottawa, and Montreal before heading across the Atlantic.

These trips also provided an opportunity for the young working women who comprised the team each year to travel and see much of the continent—something they could not have done on their own. When the Grads travelled to British Columbia in April 1925 to play a four-game exhibition series in Vancouver, New Westminster, Victoria, and Kamloops, only one member of the team had been west of the Rockies. Certainly none had been as far south as Fort

Worth when the team went on a four-week barnstorming tour in the summer of 1925 through Oklahoma, Texas, California, and British Columbia. Against the Guthrie Red Birds in Oklahoma, with James Naismith among the spectators, the Grads received a fine tribute from the sport's inventor: "It is doubtful if any girls' game previously played has ever equalled that of tonight in all round strategy, brilliance of play and doggedness, both in attack and defence."[19] The Grads won the two-game series by a total score of 45–19 and amazed the Guthrie fans with their ability. They followed this up with a 47–6 victory over a team in Fort Worth, and then headed to California, although they did not get there in time to play a team in San Diego. In Pasadena, they romped over a team from the Pasadena Athletic and Country Club, who went on to win the first AAU women's championship the following year. They overwhelmed a hapless all-star team in San Francisco 62–2, which was "simply a case of a well-drilled machine against a willing but hopelessly outclassed opposition."[20] It took a team of boys to finally beat them in a game that had been hastily arranged to satisfy hundreds of local fans. The San Francisco YMCA boys' team, the Pacific Coast 135-lb conference champions, with the advantage in height and weight, won by a score of 42–15, although the Grads refused to wilt and fought back tenaciously for every point. On their way home, they trimmed the Victoria All-Stars, and got their revenge in Kamloops against an intermediate young men's team by beating them in a close game.

Page took his team on the road again the following April for an ambitious two-week tour through eastern Canada and the United States, where they played ten games in seven cities in thirteen nights, but came away with a disappointing win-loss record.[21] They did well against a team in Winnipeg, and also against the Chicago Tri-Chis, where some of Chicago's most prominent sportswriters came to observe. One wrote, "Ten bob haired girls checked their powder puffs and maidenly manners in the dressing rooms of the Broadway armory last night, galloped out on the basketball floor, and for forty minutes fought the rip roarinest battle 6,000 fans ever saw."[22] He was also amazed at how tough the Grads were: "Pretty little Dot Johnson once fell with a knee out of joint. She lay on the floor and waited to have the leg jerked back into place. And jerked it was. Sister players held her shoulders and the good leg flat on the floor while another sister pulled and pushed at the leg that was awry. A husky football player might have called for an anesthetic. Dorothy called for a time out. The leg finally cracked into joint and Dorothy hobbled back into play."[23] Next up were the Warren Elks, who the Grads had beaten twice before in Edmonton, and they did so again in Ohio, which, according to the local paper, was the biggest basketball event in the history of Warren.

The Grads then travelled to Cleveland, where they would play a four-game Underwood trophy series against the Newman-Sterns, with two games in Cleveland and two in New York. The Newman-Sterns beat them in the first game possibly because the glass backboards, which the Grads had never encountered before, played havoc with their shots. Admittedly, the Grads simply did not play well. When word of their loss came to the Alberta Legislature, the leader of the opposition made an informal proposal to recognize the sterling effort of the Grads and the fine advertising they brought the province. Nellie McClung stood right up and put the seal of approval on it: "We should be proud of those girls. Proud of their bright-eyed girlishness, their athletic prowess, their sweet womanliness, and we should strive to emulate them, and all grow up to be girls like them."[24] The Grads redeemed themselves by defeating Cleveland in the second game, but they were beaten in the third, which was played in New York. Again the Grads were bothered by the glass backboards, which prompted Page to ask that a white oil cloth be pasted over the back of the glass during the final game. It didn't help and the Grads lost again, losing the series by a score of 72–60.

Back in Canada, the Grads played Toronto Lakesides for the Canadian championship, and lost the first game of a two-game series. It was too much for Coach Page, and in a rare moment of frustration, he let loose:

> Frankly, I have analyzed the girls' play from one end to the other, studied the score sheets, talked over with the players the work of the opposing team, and done everything possible to detect the source of the thing which is responsible for the really pitiable exhibitions the girls are turning in. It simply can't be done. The girls assure me that they are not exhausted, as one might expect, but whatever it is it's a certainty that they lack the aggressiveness that they have always shown at home. They have forgotten completely the old fighting spirit which has won for them many a game in the past. Their work is crude and quite on par with the rankest novice.[25]

With a startling reversal of form, the Grads won the second game against Lakesides by a wide margin, and therefore won the Canadian championship. Page was forgiving and laudatory, calling his team "the gamest bunch of girls in athletic history."[26] A wildly cheering crowd of 10,000 welcomed the Grads when their train pulled into Edmonton and four bands led a motorcade carrying the team down Jasper Avenue. A letter from the club executive appeared in the *Edmonton Journal* a few days after their return explaining why they had crowded so many games into two weeks rather than over a month as originally planned. It had been impossible for some team members, and for Page himself, to obtain a leave of absence for longer. Even though several games were lost, they never failed to garner the attention of sportswriters, and thus "we believe that we have done a good deed for Edmonton everyday."[27]

Although the Grads were interested in promoting basketball throughout Canada and North America through their barnstorming

Edmonton Grads versus Gradettes in Wainwright, Alberta, August 1931.

tours, they were also committed to seeing the sport grow in their
home province, especially in the rural areas. In 1930, just before
the start of their summer tour to the Pacific coast, they honoured a
request by the citizens of Wetaskiwin to stage an exhibition game.
Playing on a hastily constructed outdoor court, with the Gradettes
as their opponents, the Grads delighted several hundred spectators, many of whom had travelled a long distance to see the famous
team in action. After the game, the teams were entertained at a
banquet at a local hotel. Again in 1931, the Grads and Gradettes
played a series of exhibition games in Wetaskiwin, Wainwright,
Lloydminster, and Vegreville with record turnouts. Later in the
fall, the teams travelled to Camrose to play an exhibition game
at a school tournament before 900 enthusiastic fans, something
they repeated in 1932. According to Page, the Grads received invita-
tions from dozens of towns throughout the province, but because

it was difficult for his team members to get time off work, they were able to accept just a few. For the lucky towns, it was one way of thanking its citizens for supporting the Grads over the years.

The Grads' Amazing Record

The Grads accumulated a remarkable win-loss record over a period of twenty-five years. It was not until 1922, when the team first won the Canadian championship, that sufficient interest was taken in the team to justify the keeping of accurate records. The Commercial Graduates Basketball Club presented these records several times in official booklets.[28] The last one was issued in 1975. The club has also acknowledged the efforts of Gerald Whitley and Jake Buisman, who painstakingly recorded the details of every Grads game since 1922, and who provided statistical summaries of games, scores, and player achievements.[29] According to the official records, the Grads played 375 official games between 1922 and 1940. But the team also claimed to have played 147 games between 1915 and 1922, before official records were kept. The total of these two figures is 522, which has been accepted over the years as the total number of games played during their twenty-five-year career. In fact, this statistic is quoted over and over in articles about the Grads. Since they purportedly lost only twenty of these games, their overall win-loss record would stand at 96.2 per cent, an amazing achievement in the annals of sport.

It would seem that the 522 figure for total games played is too high. For example, a thorough analysis of newspaper reports from 1915 to 1922 puts the number of official games at forty-nine, almost all against local opponents.[30] Of these, the Commercial Graduates lost only six. The discrepancy can be explained by the fact that the games played by McDougall Commercial's junior and senior high school teams, and not just the Grads, were included in the original figure of 147. Among the 375 games supposedly played between 1922 and 1940, some were played prior to 1922 and have therefore been counted twice. Also, the numbers in the categories that make up the 375 games (e.g., North American, Underwood International Trophy, Canadian Finals, Western Finals, Alberta Finals, Canadian Exhibition Games, American Exhibition Games, European Games, and Men's teams) do not always tally with the published accounts of these games. Added to sixty-one games in the Canadian Exhibition category, for example, are "35 others against Edmonton teams" with no indication of the teams or scores. Finally, and especially in the 1975 booklet, *Edmonton Grads: 25 Years of Basketball Champions 1915–1940*, where every effort is made to be accurate, the statistical summary for a specific game category often does not match the information provided in the summary chart of games played supposedly from 1922 to 1940.

Given these problems, the total number of games played by the Grads between 1915 and 1940 is more likely to be in the neighbourhood of 412, rather than the often quoted 522. They lost very few of these, and the number twenty is often cited, which appears to be accurate given the newspaper accounts. They lost so infrequently, it was big news. Therefore, this would give them an overall win-loss record of 95 per cent, which is still amazing.

8 The Grads 1931–1940

THIS ERA OF THE GRADS was marked by almost yearly additions to the team as well as the unusual practice of bringing players up from the Gradettes for a tryout, sometimes more than once, only for them to be sent back down to the farm team. Coach Page was continually tinkering with his lineup. The players discussed in this chapter became Grads after 1930. Several of them were still playing when the team disbanded in 1940. Like a few players before them, some in this group first learned the fundamentals of basketball at Parkdale School, one of Edmonton's oldest public schools. At Parkdale, they were taught by Miss Olive Thompson, whom they fondly remember as a skilled and enthusiastic teacher.

The Stone sisters, Edith and Helen, joined the Grads in 1931 and remained until 1934. Evelyn Coulson and Jessie Innes came to the team in 1933, but each played only a year. Two other players joined in 1933: Mabel Munton, a stalwart player until the end; and Noel MacDonald, perhaps the most well-known of all the Grads. Helen Northup came in 1934, followed by Etta Dann and Sophie Brown in 1935, with Frances Gordon and Winnie Gallen in 1936. Betty Ross, Jean Williamson, and Muriel "Babe" Daniel joined in 1937, and the last two Grads, Betty Bawden and Kay MacRitchie, were brought onto the team in 1939. Some played for not much more than a year, and others competed for five or six years.

Attendance at games was slowly declining, and there were increasingly frequent rumours of the team's demise, but the Grads remained as active as ever during this period. There were frequent Underwood trophy challenge series; they attended the 1932 Olympics in Los Angeles to promote the game of basketball for women; they undertook several exhibition tours throughout Canada and the United States with a final goodwill tour in early 1939; and most exciting of all, they enjoyed a lengthy European trip in conjunction with the 1936 Berlin Olympics. Most players in this group were born in Edmonton or elsewhere in Alberta or the Prairies, and without exception, they attended McDougall Commercial High School. These women were the last members of the famous team, and when this book went to press, two of them were still alive.

Edith Stone Sutton and Helen Stone Stewart (1931–1934)

Two sets of sisters played for the Grads over the years. The first were Dorothy and Daisy Johnson in the 1920s, and identical twins Edith and Helen Stone in the 1930s. Born in Edmonton on April 9, 1910, the Stone sisters, along with older brother Frank, younger brother Walter, and a much younger sister Dorothy, were

Edith Stone Sutton.

[PAA A11430]

the children of Frank and Cecilia Stone. When Edith and Helen
were six years old, the family moved to England for a couple of
years because their father was with the military postal service.
They returned to Edmonton in 1918, where Mr. Stone continued
working for the postal service until his retirement thirty years
later. Both Helen and Edith went to Parkdale Public School, followed immediately by high school at McDougall Commercial.

As for basketball, the sisters had a lengthy apprenticeship with
the Gradettes, having been introduced to the game at Parkdale
and then playing with the school teams at Commercial. They were
good enough to play for the Gradettes in 1927 while they were still
students; Edith played centre and Helen was a forward. They continued to play for the Gradettes throughout 1928, 1929, and 1930,
but at the beginning of the 1931 season, they got their opportunity to play with the Grads. Early in January, Gladys Fry had an
appendix operation, and Coach Page knew he needed someone
to fill the centre position while she recuperated. Both Mae Brown

Helen Stone Stewart.

[PAA A11430]

and Margaret Kinney had left the team at the end of the previous season, and the Stone twins replaced them. They played their first games as Grads in March against the Calgary Centrals in the senior ladies' provincial championship, and they played their first international series in May when the Forest Park Cardinals of Chicago came to Edmonton. By this point, Gladys Fry had recovered and was back playing in her regular centre slot.

The sisters were used mostly as substitutes during the 1932 season, but they were thrilled to be with the team in the summer when it went to the Olympics in Los Angeles. Early in 1933, Helen became a regular when she took Elsie Bennie's place and was paired with Doris Neale on defence. Edith remained a relief player along with Evelyn Coulson and Jessie Innes, who had been recently brought up from the Gradettes. All were on the team that was defeated by the Durant Cardinals in the game that determined who would represent North America at the 1934 Women's World Games in London, England. Page carried a large team of eleven players in 1934; not all of them got to play in every series, but as a consolation for missing the trip to London, he took the entire team on an extended exhibition tour through Winnipeg, Fort William, Montreal, and Toronto. After eight years of playing with the Gradettes and the Grads, Edith and Helen decided it was enough and they both resigned from the team in the fall of 1934.

By 1929, the twins were employed as stenographers—Edith for Alberta Dairy Supplies and Helen for the *Edmonton Bulletin*. A few years later, both were working at the University of Alberta. Helen worked in the university library and Edith was typing manuscripts for Dr. W.G. Hardy in the Classics Department. While Helen stayed at the university until she was married, Edith found more permanent employment at Waterous Ltd., the manufacturers of large machinery. She worked there until she too was married.

Edith's husband was Elmer Sutton, a basketball player, coach, and manager whom she met in Winnipeg in the summer of 1934 when the Grads took a three-week exhibition tour to eastern Canada. He was the driving force behind the St. Andrew's Basketball Club in the 1930s, and he served for many years on the executive of the Manitoba Amateur Basketball Association. Edith likes to comment that "Mr. Page discouraged dating but this is one rule I broke. I'm not sorry. I married my date."[1] They married in 1940 and lived for a few years in Calgary, where their two children, Philip and Margaret were born in 1944 and 1947 respectively. Elmer, who constructed and inspected passenger and freight elevators for a living, was transferred to Edmonton in the early 1950s. Edith had a busy life bringing up her family, especially when they discovered that their daughter Margaret was developmentally disabled. In her spare time, Edith enjoyed badminton, curling, golf, and creative writing. She was also a long-time volunteer in the library at the University of Alberta Hospital. When Margaret attended Winnifred Stewart School for students with developmental disabilities, Edith also became a volunteer at the school. Sometime in the 1960s she went back to work as a secretary at various businesses in Edmonton, most notably the World Book Encyclopedia.

Helen married Charlie Todd of Edmonton just before he was leaving to serve overseas in a non-combat role when World War II was declared. Unfortunately, Charlie decided that he would rather be married to someone he met in England and asked his wife for a divorce. When the war ended, Helen married again, this time to William James "Jimmy" Stewart and the couple moved to Vancouver, where Helen worked as a steno in a law firm. Her second marriage was also short-lived. There were no children from either marriage, and Helen went on to a successful business career in Vancouver real estate. She and Edith enjoyed travelling together, especially to Hawaii and England.

Edith's husband passed away in 1981, and her daughter died of cancer in 1996. Now over 101 years old, she still lives in the same house in Edmonton that she and her husband purchased more than sixty years ago. At her 100th birthday party, one of her grandsons said that if he only had one word to describe his grandmother, it would be "independent," and if he had two, they would be "fiercely independent." Edith is the last remaining Grad living in Edmonton, and over the years she has given generously of her time to keep the Grads' memory alive by giving interviews and speaking to interested groups. Helen, unfortunately, suffered a stroke in her late nineties and spent the last years of her life in extended care. She died in Vancouver on June 24, 2011.

Evelyn Coulson Cameron (1933–1934)

Evelyn Coulson was born in Calgary on January 28, 1912, the youngest of four sisters, Helen (Buddy), Olive (Shorty), and Dorothy (Dodie). Their father, Frank, originally from Ontario and a good

athlete, was involved in hockey and baseball, and encouraged his
daughters to be active. Evelyn started school in Calgary, but the family moved to Edmonton in 1918, where she first attended Cromdale,
then Parkdale public schools and finally McDougall Commercial.
By 1928 she was a member of the Gradettes, where she served a five-
year apprenticeship before moving up to the Grads in the spring
of 1933. Along with Jessie Innes and Edith Stone, Evelyn was used
primarily for relief purposes. In 1934, she was among the eleven
players Page carried throughout the year. She was also a member of the team that travelled to eastern Canada and the United
States for an exhibition tour. At the end of the season, she left the
team having played for the Grads a little over a year. "She wasn't
outstanding," remembered Margaret MacBurney Vasheresse many
years later, "but she was a good calm player and a good shooter."[2]

After graduating from Commercial in 1930, Evelyn went to
work as a stenographer at the Swift meat packing plant, where
she was employed for the next fourteen years. On November 9,

1935, she married Alfred (Alf) Cameron, an employee of the Great Western Garment Company. She continued to work after her marriage, which was unusual in those days. In fact, Evelyn continued to work at Swift until the birth of their first child, James, in 1944. She gave birth to a daughter, Verna, in 1948. Although a keen bowler and churchgoer, Evelyn's life revolved mostly around her family and she took great pride in her children's athletic endeavours, especially in baseball and hockey. Widowed in 1986, Evelyn remained healthy and active for several years, but in her last years, suffering memory loss, she was cared for in a nursing home. She died on February 11, 2001 at eighty-nine years, survived by her two children and their spouses, nine grandchildren, and ten great-grandchildren.

Mabel Munton McCloy (1933–1940)

Like Gladys Fry Douglas before her, Mabel continued to play on the Grads after she was married, although at first Coach Page was completely unaware of her new status. When asked if he would have let her play anyway, he said he didn't know.[3] Both Mabel and Noel MacDonald decided not to take any chances about whether they would be allowed to continue playing, so they kept their marriages secret from Page and the rest of the team in 1939. As a Grad, Mabel had a wonderful run of seven years and she was still a member of the team in June 1940, when the Grads played their last game and were disbanded.

Born on March 30, 1914 to Charles and Alice Munton in a small community just west of Edmonton called Winterburn (now part of the city), Mabel was the youngest of four daughters. Raised on a farm, Elsie, Margaret, Rosie, and Mabel eventually moved with their parents into the city, where their father started his own business as an auctioneer. Mabel went to Norwood Public School, then to Victoria High School, and finally to McDougall Commercial. Solid

Mabel Munton McCloy.

[CEA 80-16-194]

and stocky, she was an outstanding guard on the Gradettes in 1931 and 1932 before being moved up to the Grads in June 1933 as a substitute player for the ill-fated series with the Durant Cardinals. By October the same year, it was announced that Mabel was officially a Grad, and in a series with the Chicago Red Devils, Page was pleased with her classy play on defence. Disaster struck in June 1934, just before an important series with the Tulsa Stenos, when Mabel and two Gradette players were hit by a careening truck while walking to basketball practice. She was the most seriously injured with fractured ribs, lacerations, and a concussion, requiring hospital care. To make matters worse, her mother was in lying ill in another city hospital after undergoing a major operation. Strong and tough, Mabel recovered sufficiently to accompany the team on their eastern exhibition tour a couple of months later, although she did not play much.

Harry Wilson, coach of the Chicago Taylor Trunks and also a great friend to the Grads, said of Mabel that she was the kind of guard every coach likes to have on their team: "While not as spectacular as many other guards who have been seen in the Arena, Mabel has always been one of the most dependable players on the Grad line-up. For a girl of her size, she is remarkably fast, and can pick a hole in the opposing defence at the slightest slip on the part of her opponents."[4] By 1935, Mabel was a regular on defence, and in 1936, she was a member of the team that travelled to Europe.

In September 1939, the Grads were scheduled to play two Underwood international challenge series—the first against a team representing the American Institute of Business in Des Moines, Iowa and the second against the Wichita Thurstons from Kansas. It was also rumoured that wedding bells were in the offing for Mabel as well as Noel MacDonald, and that these would be their last games as Grads. Mabel played in the first series against Des Moines, but on September 23, just before the start of the second series, she was secretly married in Edmonton to Jack McCloy, a local fireman. A few days later, she played in the games against the Wichita Thurstons. It was not until a party at the home of Mr. and Mrs. Page a couple of weeks later that Mabel announced her marriage, much to everyone's surprise. Obviously all was forgiven because she continued to play under her married name until the team's last series in June 1940 against the Chicago Queen Anne Aces. During fan balloting on this occasion, she was honoured as one of the Grads' all-time greats. Little is known about Mabel's life after the Grads except that she had two children, Patricia and Robert. She was very active in curling and a member of Edmonton's Thistle Club for many years; her rink won the Ladies' Northern Alberta championship in 1953 and the Alberta championship in 1957. She died in Edmonton on January 16, 1994 at seventy-nine years after a lengthy illness, survived by her husband Jack, her son and daughter and four grandchildren.

Jessie Innes Maloney.

[ASHFM 951.62.04]

Jessie Innes Maloney (1933–1934)

Jessie was another player brought forward from the Gradettes in the spring of 1933. She had been playing on the farm team since 1928 and was a former captain. Like Evelyn Coulson and Edith Stone, Jessie was used primarily in a relief role. Because the 1934 team had eleven players, and only eight could be used at one time, Jessie did not get an opportunity to play as a Grad until just before an important series with Tulsa, when she replaced Mabel Munton, who had been seriously injured in a truck accident. As a newspaper article pointed out, "Miss Innes will play under a decided handicap, having been out of training for several weeks."[5] Although she dressed for the series, she sat on the bench. However, she did get to play in exhibition games during the team's extended tour of eastern Canada later that summer. After their return, it was announced that Jessie was retiring from competition along with several other players.

Named after her mother, Jessie was born in Edmonton on January 16, 1911, a sister to older brother John. Her parents and brother had emigrated from Scotland in 1909, and her father worked in Edmonton as a motorman on the street railway. A good athlete, Jessie excelled at diving and was a member of the Toddies baseball team. As a youngster she attended Parkdale School. After graduating from McDougall Commercial, she worked as a stenographer for several Edmonton businesses before settling into a job at the Woodland Dairy company, where she worked until her marriage on June 30, 1938. Her husband was Edward Maloney, and she had one son, Bill. Jessie died at seventy-six years of age in August 1987, although I have not been able to find an obituary.

Noel MacDonald Robertson (1933–1939)

If there is one player among the Grads who stood out above the rest, it was Noel MacDonald. She is the Grads' all-time high scorer. Over a six-year career she appeared in 135 games and scored an average of 13.8 points a game. She is also the most decorated player, and the only one to be singled out in this way. Named Canada's female athlete of the year in 1938, she was also elected to Canada's Sports Hall of Fame in 1971 and to the Canadian Basketball Hall of Fame in 1978. Uncomfortable with these individual honours, Noel stressed she accepted them on behalf of the team; indeed, through skill, courage, and selfless team play, she exemplified the qualities that made the Grads great.

Noel Marguerite was born on January 23, 1915 in Mortlach, Saskatchewan to George and Jennie MacDonald. Like so many farmers in the drought-ridden 1920s, George was blown off his land and forced to move first to Estevan, then to Moose Jaw, and finally to Edmonton where he found work. Noel was an only child, and she attended several Edmonton public

Noel MacDonald Robertson.

[CEA 80-16-194]

schools—Cromdale, Alex Taylor, Calder, and Westmount High—
before completing grade twelve at Victoria High School and
then the two-year business course at McDougall Commercial.

Having played basketball throughout her school years, Noel was
already a skilled player when she was invited to join the Gradettes
in 1931, and, besides, she was tall. At just over 5'10", she was the
tallest player ever on the Grads' roster. Her natural position was at
centre, where she had the advantage of tipping the ball to her teammates and rebounding under the basket. Along with Mabel Munton,
Noel's first game in a Grads uniform was in June 1933 during a series
with the Durant Cardinals when they lost three straight games along
with their opportunity to represent North America at the Women's
World Games in London the following year. By October, she was
officially a Grad, giving "every promise of developing into a classy
centre player."[6] Although she began her career as a substitute forward, sometimes relieving the great Gladys Fry at centre, she soon
proved she was first-string material. In a particularly tight series

against Oklahoma's Tulsa Stenos in 1934, Noel shone, especially in the final game: "Throughout the encounter, Miss MacDonald was always in the limelight. She led all the scorers with 20 points, and besides being the sharpshooter deluxe of the night, put up a brand of checking and intercepting that left nothing to be desired."[7] Noel was most effective on the move and around the key, with a quick snap shot almost impossible to check. With Gladys Fry she also controlled the backboards and scored many points off rebounds. When Gladys left the team after the European summer tour of 1936, Noel replaced her as the first-string centre. She was so effective at controlling the tip during a centre-jump, which in those days occurred after every basket, the Grads developed a series of plays to further their advantage. Perhaps Noel's most outstanding individual performance, and one remembered for years afterwards, was in the second game of a five-game series against the El Dorado Lions from Arkansas in 1936. The Grads were in serious trouble; they had lost the first game and were behind 33–35 in the second as time was running out. Noel won the jump, received a pass, and tied it up. With the seconds ticking, she again tipped the ball to a teammate, broke clear again, got the pass, and just past centre looped in the winning shot as the timer's gun roared. After playing the entire game without substitution, Noel was exhausted and collapsed in the middle of the floor while delirious fans rushed out to congratulate the team. The Grads went on to win the series easily in two more games.

Made captain of the team in the fall of 1936, Noel went on to play for another three years, always a star and an effective leader. Like most of her teammates, she earned a living as a stenographer, working first in the Small Debts Court and then in the Muttart Library. By the fall of 1939, it was rumoured that Noel was to be married soon and that she would leave the team after playing in two international series with teams from Des Moines and Wichita. Noel played all right, but what nobody knew was that she and Harry Robertson had eloped in August to be married in Bonner's Ferry, Idaho. Like Mabel Munton, Noel was married secretly because she feared that Page would not let her play in those two last series if he knew she was married. Her husband was a former Edmonton amateur hockey star who helped the Kimberley Dynamiters win the world title in 1937. When her playing days ended, Noel turned her attention to coaching, especially at the high school level, and to the development of girls' basketball. She followed her husband, an oil company executive, to various communities in Alberta and Saskatchewan. They also lived for more than a decade in Tripoli, Libya. The couple had two children, Dale and Donald. Everywhere she went, Noel helped coach local basketball teams. The family's final stop was in Alaska before Noel and Harry retired to British Columbia and finally to Arizona. Predeceased by her husband in 1990, Noel died on May 13, 2008 at the age of ninety-three, having spent the last eight years of her life in an Edmonton nursing home struggling with Alzheimer's disease.

In June 1940, Noel MacDonald was named the greatest player in the Grads' history by fans—more than 4,000 of them—who voted for the all-time, all-star team when they played their last game. A few years later, she received the ultimate accolade from Coach Page when he named her the greatest all-round star in the twenty-five-year history of the Grads: "Noel had the height which nearly all basketball greats possess and she used it to advantage to control the tip-off much of the time as well as for grabbing rebounds off the backboard for telling shots. Add to this her competitive spirit and her phenomenal scoring feats and you have the answer to any coach's prayer."[8]

Helen Northup Alexander (1934–1940)

At barely 5'2" on tiptoes and weighing less than 110 pounds, Helen Northup was the smallest player ever to don a Grads uniform. Sportswriters called her a "speedball," but her teammates nicknamed

Helen Northup Alexander.

[PAA BL2638/2]

her "Pee Wee."[9] What she lacked in height, she made up for in speed and accuracy. A graceful athlete, she had a floor game equal to any of the great players of the day; she could handle the ball with either hand and was a deadly shot; and she was, as they said, "rank poison" when left unguarded.[10] Helen was born on March 16, 1916 in Arcadia, Florida, the youngest among brothers Clarence and Ralph and her sister Leila. When she was six months old, the family came north and settled on a wheat farm just outside of Vegreville. Eventually, they moved to Edmonton. Helen attended H.A. Gray and Highlands public schools and Eastwood, where one of her teachers was former Grads star Daisy Johnson—who, despite the size of her pupil, encouraged her to try basketball.

When it was time for Helen to start high school, her family thought it best that she continue at Eastwood High because it was right across the street from where they lived. Helen, however, had her own ideas and she chose to attend McDougall Commercial, much against the wishes of her parents and siblings. In the midst of an economic depression she reasoned that business training would get her a job faster after graduation than any academic program, and most importantly, she wanted to play basketball with the best. She entered McDougall in 1932 and immediately played on the senior team, which was still coached by Page. A year later, she started playing for the Gradettes.

Her big break to enter the ranks of the Grads came in August 1934, when the team was about to embark on a three-week exhibition tour to eastern Canada. Captain Margaret MacBurney was unable to go because she was recovering from an appendicitis operation, and Helen was invited to take her place. She practised with the Grads when they returned in the fall, and by early 1935, she was on the team for good. As a rookie forward, she was surprisingly brilliant and her apprenticeship as a substitute did not last long; by October, Margaret had retired from the team, leaving the spot open for Helen.

When I interviewed Helen in 2007, she was a spry ninety-one years old—tiny, white-haired, and totally forthcoming. When asked about the highlight of her career with the Grads, she immediately spoke of the 1936 summer trip to Europe and the Berlin Olympics. What she remembered best was attending the Olympics and seeing athletes like Jesse Owens, Helen Stephens, and Stella Walsh compete and then meeting them afterwards. "We were lucky to get out of Edmonton in those days," she observed, figuring that she had been across Canada about ten times during her playing days. In all, Helen played in 105 games, scored a total of 1,019 points with an average of 9.7 points per game, the sixth highest among the Grads.

After graduating from Commercial, and just as she had predicted, Helen found work. She was employed by Swift, the meat packing plant, but broke her arm playing basketball, so for a while she wasn't much use to either her team or employer. Most local employers were keen to have a member of the Grads working for them and were flexible about giving them time off for travel. When she returned from the long summer trip to Europe in 1936, Helen talked to the manager at the Metropolitan store, and being an enthusiastic Grads supporter, he hired her right away. She worked as a clerk on the floor, but when a secretarial job came up at Wilson's Stationery, she grabbed it. Helen was married in June 1940 to Harry Alexander, who at the time was in the Canadian Navy. After the war, Harry went into the restaurant business in Edmonton, where they raised Jim and Keith, their two boys. Helen became an avid golfer in summer and curler in winter. Her curling team won the provincial championship in 1952. Eventually, Helen and Harry retired to the west coast. Helen was living in Sidney on Vancouver Island when she died on May 15, 2009, at age ninety-three, survived by her two sons, four grandchildren, and six great-grandchildren.

Etta Dann Soderberg (1935–1940)

Called the "Little Irisher" in the newspapers, presumably because her father was Irish and because, at 5'4", she was small for a basketball player, Etta Dann never let her size hold her back. She was a highly mobile guard who could shut down the opposition while pumping in the baskets herself.[11] She was also one of the most popular players ever to play for the Grads, and she came second only to Noel MacDonald in the 1940 polling for the eight members on the all-time, all-star team. Ted Watt, a long-time Grads observer, summed her up this way: "She is one of the smallest, lightest players ever to have appeared in the Arena. Her field accuracy surpasses anything the club has ever seen. She is constantly appearing under the enemy basket with the ball poised for the shot that stands a fifty-fifty chance of scoring. This is very confusing, both to spectators and opponents, in view of the fact that a moment before she has been filling her post as guard at the opposite end of the court."[12] She was a scrappy little player, but very effective.

Etta Dann Soderberg.
[CEA 80-16-194]

Born in Edmonton on March 29, 1913, Etta came by her athletic
ability naturally; her father had been a standout lacrosse player.
She had two older brothers, William and Joe. After completing her
public school education at H.A. Gray, Etta attended McDougall
Commercial for high school. Like nearly all those before her, she
worked her way up through the junior and senior basketball teams
and then to the Gradettes. Her first opportunity in a Grad uniform came during a trip to the west coast in the spring of 1935,
where the Grads battled the Vancouver Province team for the western Canadian championships. Substituting for guard Doris Neale,
Etta turned in a brilliant performance. The press predicted that
she would become one of the finest guards ever developed by Coach
Page. Later that spring in a tussle with their arch rivals the Tulsa
Stenos, with the series tied up at one game apiece, Etta checked
the Tulsa star Frances "Sonny" Dunlap to a standstill, earning her
thunderous applause from an appreciative crowd. With the retirement of Margaret MacBurney at the end of the 1935 season, Etta

moved into her slot. For the rest of her career, Etta continued to play both offence and defence—wherever she was needed most.

Rarely in the long history of the Grads did Page ever single out a player for special praise, but in 1939 he singled out Etta at an Edmonton Sport Boosters' club reception for the team after their successful, goodwill tour through eastern Canada. "If I was to name an all-time, all-star team," declared the coach, "Etta Dann would be on that club. She gave the most remarkable exhibition of defensive basketball I have ever seen. She stopped the great Stella Walsh without permitting a single score. She was even better in that Toronto game than she has been in games here against Sonny Dunlap of Tulsa Stenos."[13] Page was referring to a game against the Toronto Ladies, which strangely included the famous Polish-American track star Stella Walsh at centre. Not only did Etta stop her cold, but she did so without committing a single foul. Still with the team when it disbanded in 1940, Etta had played in 118 games and earned 1,022 points with a game average of 8.6 points, which established her place among the top ten Grad players.

Etta was shy and unassuming, and we know little about her life after the Grads. After graduating from McDougall Commercial, it's not clear whether she worked, although, during the war, she had a job as a bookkeeper and stenographer at Hillas Electric in Edmonton. On March 1, 1953, Etta married Leland Soderberg with whom she had a son named Edward. At some point, the family moved to a farm near High River, Alberta. She lost her sight due to cataracts, but it was restored in one eye after an operation. After a long battle with cancer, Etta died in High River on August 22, 1978 at age sixty-five, survived by her husband, son, and two brothers.

Sophie Brown Drake.
[PAA A11429]

Sophie Brown Drake (1935–1940)

Another small player of this era was Sophie Brown, who stood just over 5'4". Like many of the earlier Grads, she was not born in Canada and her family emigrated when she was a young child. Her proper name was Sophia, and she was born in London, England to James and Florence Brown on September 21, 1916, the youngest of three children. The family arrived by ship in Saint John, New Brunswick, on April 21, 1921, and immediately headed for a farm in Egremont, Alberta, a small hamlet north of Edmonton. At some point, Mr. Brown decided to move his family to Edmonton, where he worked for many years at the Swift meat packing plant. Sophie attended North Edmonton Public School, followed by business training at McDougall Commercial.

Like so many of those who went before her, Sophie worked her way up the junior and senior basketball teams and then onto the Gradettes. Along with Etta Dann, she got her first opportunity to play as a Grad in the spring of 1935 when the team went to Vancouver for the western Canadian championships. In their first international series against a team from Des Moines in Iowa, Sophie and the other two young recruits—Helen Northup and Etta Dann—made a splendid showing. Even if they were small, they were mighty. All three also played softball and were members of the Muttart Lumber Pats, winners of the city championship later that year. In the winter of 1936, Sophie had knee problems and did not see much action, but she was fit enough to travel to Europe that summer for their exhibition tour. Originally a guard, she was switched to the forward position in 1937. Although she was often referred to as a "veteran relief star," she was a regular by the end of that year.[14] Still a member of the team when it disbanded in 1940, Sophie played in a total of 103 games, accumulating 551 points for an average of 5.1 points per game.

After graduating from Commercial, Sophie worked as a stenographer at the Provincial News Company, better known as Mike's. On November 15, 1941 she married Frank Drake, who was serving in the Canadian Navy, and by 1949, the couple had settled in Victoria, British Columbia, where they raised their daughter Barbara and son Bill. Little is known about Sophie's married life. She was an active member of the Victoria Lawn Bowling Club for many years. Widowed in 1979, she died suddenly at age sixty-nine on July 4, 1986, survived by her two children and their spouses, one grandson, several nieces and nephews, and her sister May.

Winnie Gallen Reid (1936–1937, 1939–1940)

Probably one of the most talented and versatile athletes to play with the Grads, Winnie excelled at track and field, softball, hockey, and curling, and of course basketball. She was inducted with the other Grads into the Alberta Sports Hall of Fame and Museum in 1974 and for her individual sports achievements in 1989. At the time of her

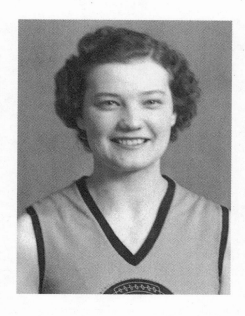

Winnie Gallen Reid.

[PAA A11429]

death in 1996, her son Ian commented, "she was a fanatic on sports to her dying day."[15]

Winnifred Phyllis Gallen was born on July 4, 1917 in Mawer, Saskatchewan. Her parents divorced when she was a young child and she came to live in Edmonton, but little is known about her childhood. Winnie attended Eastwood School, which in those days offered grades one through twelve. After high school, Winnie wanted to train as a nurse. As she recalled, "Eastwood didn't have a gym. While those kids at McDougall were practising every day with Mr. Page, I had to make a decision, nursing or the Grads. So I transferred to McDougall."[16] By 1934 she had joined the Gradettes, and after two years, she was given a trial as a guard with the Grads. At the time she was better known as a softball player, having been a pitcher for the Army and Navy Pats for some time. When the 1937 edition of the Grads was announced in the spring, one of the new faces was Winnie. Her first game in a Grad uniform was against a team from Cleveland. By October, when Coach Page was getting his team ready for the 1938 season, all of the players who had been called up in 1937—Winnie, Betty Ross, Jean Williamson, and Frances Gordon—were back with the Gradettes. Winnie captained the Gradettes throughout 1938 and in 1939 when they won the senior women's provincial championship for the first time. (The Grads had a bye into the Canadian finals.) Winnie was also playing top-level softball. She pitched her Army and Navy Pats to the senior women's provincial championship in the fall of 1939. Earlier in the year she was brought back up to the Grads to bolster the team for their international series against Chicago and Des Moines, and she remained with the team until they played their last game in June 1940. After the Grads disbanded, Winnie captained the Comets, a senior team sponsored by the former Grad organiz-ation and coached by long-time referee Bill Douglas. The Comets went on to win several provincial and western Canadian titles.

After graduating from Commercial, Winnie worked as a steno at the Muttart Library, and then settled into a job as a clerk at the Hudson's Bay Company store until she was married in April 1943. Her husband was Peter Reid, a commercial artist, and for many years she worked in his business. In 1946, Winnie was asked to play semi-professional softball with the Parichy Bloomer Girls of the National Girls Baseball League (NGBL). The NGBL was formed in 1944 among a half dozen semi-pro teams in the Chicago area. The league rivalled the more famous All-American Girls Professional Baseball League, which eventually led to salary wars, talent raid-ing, and a nasty lawsuit. Winnie played one season and then hightailed it home: "The money was all right but a year of it was enough. I had played too long for the love of the game. The finan-cial and political angles in professionalism and the jealousies that went with them got to me. So I came home again to play for fun."[17] After basketball and softball, Winnie turned to curling, where, throughout the 1950s and 1960s, she perennially led her rink to the Edmonton and northern Alberta finals and won the provincial crown in 1971. She continued curling well into her seventies.

Winnie died of heart disease on February 5, 1996 at seventy-eight years of age, survived by her husband, three children, Ian, Suellen, and Melanie, and eight grandchildren. She left us with these memorable words: "I loved playing and watching sports, and I liked team sports, but I enjoyed baseball the best. With baseball, everyone has a turn at bat and everyone gets to field the ball."[18]

Betty Ross Bellamy (1936–1939)

Along with Winnie Gallen, Betty was given her first trial with the Grads in the fall of 1936. At the time she was twenty-one years old and had played for the Gradettes for the past four years as both a forward and centre. She was too short at 5'5" to be an effective centre, but Coach Page used her on both offence and defence. When the 1937 team was announced in the spring, Betty was one of the new recruits and she saw her first action in a series against Cleveland. However, like the others, she returned to the Gradettes in the fall, and throughout 1938 was occasionally in a Grad uniform as a substitute if needed. By early 1939, she was a regular on the team. She enjoyed a goodwill tour of eastern Canada and she continued to play throughout the season until her marriage in August.

Mary Elizabeth, or more informally Betty, was born in Edmonton on April 3, 1914 to Thomas and Margaret Ross, a younger sister to Helen and Florence. Betty attended Oliver Public School and then went to high school at McDougall Commercial. After graduating, she worked as a cashier at the Hudson's Bay Company before marrying Jules Gardner (Bill) Chevalier on August 23, 1939. Bill managed a service station in Edmonton. The couple had two sons, Richard and Ross, but unfortunately their marriage fell apart. Betty's second

husband was Oscar (Ray) Bellamy, a heavy duty mechanic, and they lived most of their married life in Edmonton. Together they had three children. The oldest, Penny, was born in 1945, followed by Betty-Raye and Douglas. The couple moved to Summerland, British Columbia in 1985, and sadly Ray died of Parkinson's disease in 1998. Betty lived for some years in an extended care facility in Kelowna before dying on May 16, 2010, at the age of ninety-six, survived by her three children, eight grandchildren, and thirteen great-grandchildren from her second marriage, as well as two sons from her first marriage and their children and grandchildren.[19]

Frances Gordon Mills (1937–1938)

Frances Gordon, "Gordie" to her teammates and friends, had a relatively short career as a Grad but an extended one as a Gradette. By the end of 1936, Frances had played on the Gradettes' team for two years and was trying out for the eighth position on the Grad lineup.

Frances Gordon Mills.

[ASHFM 951.62.12C]

She was also playing stellar basketball, as evidenced by the press reports: "The one player who stood out head and shoulders above all the others for her scintillating shooting was Frances Gordon of the Gradettes. She outscored all others and generated most of the plays which brought points to the Edmonton squad."[20] Despite Frances's efforts, the Gradettes were beaten 37–34 by the Calgary Jimmies in that particular game.

Her first chance to play as a Grad came in an international series against Cleveland, and she was named to the 1937 edition of the team. Frances was over 5'9" and it was predicted that her height would make her a good candidate to relieve centre Noel MacDonald. But Coach Page had also brought Jean Williamson up from the Gradettes, and Jean proved to be a better replacement at centre, especially after Noel was injured later in the season. Frances played very little as a substitute, and by the fall, she was back with the Gradettes, again trying out for a regular position on the Grads. Similarly, in the 1938 season, Frances was brought up from the Gradettes for a couple of international series as a substitute player, but Page did not make her a regular. By 1939 she was back playing with the Gradettes, and she continued to play with them until they too were disbanded in 1940.

Frances was born on January 19, 1915 in Red Deer to Peter and Hilda Gordon, who were originally from Sweden and had immigrated to Canada before World War I. She had three brothers—Arthur, older by three years, and younger brothers, Philip and Wilf. After high school in Red Deer, Frances trained as a teacher at the Edmonton Normal School and then taught for two years in a one-room school. Teaching was difficult and did not pay well, so she decided a business education was more to her liking and she took her training at McDougall Commercial. After graduating she worked as a stenographer at the Gutta Percha and Rubber Company until 1946, when she returned to Red Deer to work for the city. There she met Oswin "Ossie" Mills. The two married on December 3, 1948 and later had two sons, Brian and Gerry. She loved to be active and her favourite activities included tennis, speed skating, downhill and cross-country skiing. Her husband died in 1980. In her later years, Frances became deaf but she still enjoyed watching sports on television and playing the piano. She died peacefully in a Red Deer nursing home on April 14, 2004 at the age of eighty-four, survived by her two sons and their spouses, four grandchildren, and her brother Wilf.

Jean Williamson Quilley (1937–1940)

Jean was another "south side girl," unlike most Grads whose families lived on the north side. She attended King Edward Public School followed by high school at Strathcona before completing her education at McDougall Commercial. Born in Edmonton on February 4, 1919 to Albert and Melinda Williamson, Jean had two brothers, Gordon and Marvin, and a sister, Mary. Her basketball career began early, presumably in public school, and by 1937, while a student at Commercial,

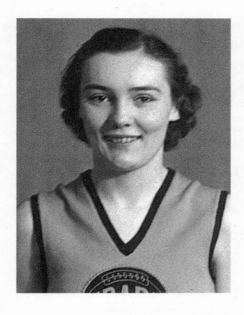

Jean Williamson Quilley.

[PAA A11429]

she had played on the Gradettes for two years and was now their captain. At 5'9", she was described as "tall, graceful, pretty, speedy and an accurate shot."[21]

Jean first donned a Grad uniform in April 1937 when she was brought up from the Gradettes to help the team in a series against Cleveland, which they won in three straight games. Along with the other new recruits, she was nervous but performed brilliantly when she got the chance. No one was more proud than her older brother Gordon, whose job it was to call the Grad games over the radio for CFRN. After a tight series later that spring with the Tulsa Stenos, a team that forced the Grads to play a fourth game, Jean came into her own with high praise from the Tulsa manager, who thought she looked like a second Noel MacDonald. Unfortunately for Jean this was true; to a certain extent she was forced to play in Noel's shadow until Noel retired at the end of the 1939 season, at which point the team was basically winding down. During the 1938 and 1939 seasons, Jean sharpened her shooting skills and took over at centre on the infrequent occasions when Noel was injured. In the opening game of a four-game series against the Wichita Thurstons in the fall of 1939, Jean had a very big night. *Edmonton Journal* sports editor George Mackintosh praised Jean: "This starry forward, whose development as a sniper in the last two seasons has been remarkable, led the scoring parade with a total of 16 points, made up of seven field goals and a pair of free throws."[22] In all, Jean played 71 games as a Grad and scored a total of 544 points, with an average of 7.6 points per game, placing her ninth among the all-time best shooting stars.

Following graduation from Commercial, Jean worked as a stenographer for the City of Edmonton until her marriage in June 1941 to Thomas Quilley. The couple had three children—Wendy, Ron, and Douglas. As lifetime members of the Canadian Kennel Club, Jean and her husband had a great interest in dog breeding and judging and they travelled extensively throughout North America to dog shows. She also loved watching her grandchildren play sports. Jean died on March 3, 2003 at eighty-four years of age, predeceased by her siblings, husband, and son Douglas, but survived by her other two children and four grandchildren. She just missed seeing a great-grandson, who was born on the same day she died.

Muriel "Babe" Daniel Loughlin (1937–1939)

Muriel Rosamond Daniel acquired the nickname "Babe" after fans watched her smash balls out of the baseball park, likening her to the more famous Babe Ruth. Playing for the Muttart Pats, she was a star pitcher and, by the time she became a Grad, her reputation as a talented athlete was without question. Born in Camrose on May 30, 1917, Babe grew up in the Bonnie Doon area of Edmonton, where she attended Victoria Composite High School before completing business training at McDougall Commercial. Like a couple of others before her, she was "south side girl."

Muriel "Babe" Daniel Loughlin.
[PAA A11426]

By 1937, she had played for the Gradettes for three years, and in December she got the call to replace the similarly named Babe Belanger, who had earlier retired. At 5'4", Muriel was also small and fast, but, more important, she could play either the forward or guard position. Used primarily as a substitute forward, she was unfortunately hampered by knee problems. After an operation to remove some cartilage early in the 1939 season, Babe hoped her knee would be better but she was injured again, and a few months later she was forced to give up basketball and softball. She instead turned to golf and bowling, becoming particularly adept at the latter.

Babe had a fair amount of bad luck throughout her life, especially when it came to marriage. When she was twenty-one, she became engaged to Ralph Morgan, who coached the Muttart Pats softball team, and they were married on January 22, 1940. Several years later they adopted two children, Marilyn and Susan, but Ralph's alcohol problem finally precipitated a divorce in 1969. For many years, Babe worked as a secretary at the University of Alberta Hospital. In

September 1972 she was married again, this time to Michael Lickoch, from whom she also divorced after just a few years. In the summer of 1977 she was married yet again, this time to George Lineham. Unfortunately, George died in February 1981. Her fourth and final marriage was in 1986 to Reginald Loughlin; the two had dated years ago in high school. Tragically, the couple were killed in a car accident on October 5, 1995 while travelling through British Columbia. She was survived by her two daughters, several grandchildren and step-grandchildren.

Kay MacRitchie MacBeth (1939–1940)

In 1935, when Kay was in grade ten at Westmount High School in Edmonton, Gradette coach Bill Tait, also the sports officer for the school board, visited the school and taught a basketball lesson on how to do a lay-up shot. This was the first time Kay had ever handled a basketball, and she was enthralled. Tait watched the thirteen-year-old, and although at 5'4" she was short, he saw immediately that she was athletic and could jump, so he suggested she come to McDougall Commercial and try out for one of their teams. Kay took his advice, and by 1936, she was playing on the Wasps, a junior team coached by Clare Hollingsworth, and then on the Cubs, coached by Arnold Henderson. Kay considered Henderson a fantastic coach, and he taught her to shoot one-handed. Coach Page later made her shoot with two hands, however, because he considered it more ladylike.

It was clear that Kay would move up to the Grads once she got more experience. She reflected, "I dribbled more than those girls and I was fast, although I don't think they paid much attention to me because I was too young."[23] By September of 1938, she was working out with the team but still playing on the Cubs. The following spring, she led the Cubs to victory over the Calgary Wittichens for the provincial intermediate championship: "Kay MacRitchie

Kay MacRitchie MacBeth.

[PAA A11429]

was the guiding factor that carried the Cubs to their smashing victory. She set up plays, back-checked hard and was in there all the time looking for openings."[24] It came as no surprise when Kay replaced the injured Babe Daniel, who was forced into retirement due to knee problems, and played in her first Underwood international series against a team from St. Louis. Just seventeen, Kay was the first and only player to jump from a junior team to the Grads without first playing on the Gradettes. She was given an ovation by the fans when she came on the floor and shortly after scored on a free throw, her first official point as a Grad. Kay was thrilled when Coach Page, who rarely complimented individual players, told her she reminded him of Frances (Sonny) Dunlap of the Tulsa Stenos. Kay remained a Grad until the team disbanded, and then, along with several others, joined the Comets.

Born in Saskatoon on January 22, 1922, Kay was brought up in a devout Christian home, and her parents firmly believed in helping those in need. Even during the "dirty thirties," her father, originally from Scotland, always had a good job in management and was transferred several times. In 1941 Kay moved with her family to Vancouver and immediately began playing basketball with the Vancouver Hedlunds, who, for the next several years, took over from the Grads as senior Canadian champions.[25] Also an excellent fastball player, Kay turned down an offer to play semi-pro with a team in Little Rock, Arkansas mainly because she was married on July 2, 1946 to D. Ross MacBeth, a pilot with the RCAF, who had been overseas for four years during the war. The couple had two children—son Donald and daughter Kerry. They first lived in Vancouver and then in Edmonton. Kay pursued her athletic career in softball and basketball until she retired for good in 1951. She then took up golf, playing in local tournaments and working on her handicap, which she got down to twelve. Her other passion was music; she played the piano and organ at her church and directed the youth choral group.

In 2011, Kay was eighty-nine years old and had been a widow since 1997. She was living in Comox, British Columbia and enjoying her four grandchildren and three great grandchildren.

Betty Bawden Bowen (1939–1940)

Betty was the final player to become a member of the team, and although she played only during their last season, her basketball career started long before. Born in Edmonton on December 22, 1917, she and her sister Pauline grew up near the city's Borden Park, where, as a young girl, she loved to swim and dive and take part in the local galas at the new swimming pool. Like several Grads before her, she was taught the fundamentals of basketball at Parkdale School. When she went to McDougall Commercial, she worked her way up through the junior and senior high school teams, playing with the Imps in the city league, and finally onto the Gradettes. Like many Grads of this era, she was

Betty Bawden Bowen.
[PAA A11429]

small at 5'4½". But she was also a fast and accurate shooter. In
December 1939, about the same time as her twenty-second birthday, it was announced that she was moving up to the Grads.

Her first opportunity to play in the Arena before the home
crowd was in May 1940 against the Vancouver Westerns, who the
Grads beat in two games to ensure their retirement as Canadian
champions. In the publicity leading up to an international series with Wichita, the Thurstons' Maxine Woodman, known as the
"blonde bombshell," was featured alongside Betty under the caption "How Would These Two Women Basketball Players Rate
in a Beauty Competition?"[26] With her golden curls, Betty was
thought to be the clear favourite, at least among Edmonton fans.
The team went on to beat the Wichita Thurstons and Chicago's
Queen Anne Aces in their last ever series; Betty played in both.

Betty had chosen McDougall Commercial to gain the skills needed
to work in business, one of the few ways a young woman could find
a job in the middle of a depression. In 1936, she started as a clerk at

Woodward's department store, and by 1942 she was the manager and buyer in the hosiery department. After childhood friend, Bob Bowen, an officer in the Royal Canadian Air Force, came home from overseas, they were married in June 1944. The couple settled in Edmonton, and Betty stayed at home to raise their two children, Rowena and Robert. She encouraged their sports activities and happily took them to figure skating, hockey, and little league baseball. Later she worked in the library at Victoria Composite High School. Betty's husband, who became the personnel director for the City of Edmonton, died in 1977.

She played a major role in helping to organize Grad reunions, answering correspondence and dealing with requests, making certain their memorabilia were preserved, and attending functions on behalf of the organization. She was able to do this until her health began to fail. In the late 1990s, she moved to be with her daughter in Oakville, Ontario. Betty died of heart failure on October 17, 2007 at the age of eighty-nine, survived by her daughter and son, two granddaughters, and a great-grandson.

GRADS BASKET BALL TEAM.

9 Papa Page and the Family

"YOU SEE," explained a spry ninety-one-year-old Helen Northup Alexander, who played with the Grads from 1934 until 1940, "we were sort of like a family and he was head of it. You didn't want to come up with something that would disturb him."[1] The notion of the Grads being a family comes up time and time again in articles about the Grads. Likewise, the players themselves repeatedly refer to the team as a family. Some of the Grads fondly called Coach Page "Papa Page," especially as he got older, but to most players he was "Mr. Page," an appellation those living today still use. Percy Page himself often compared the Grads to a family in interviews with sports journalists:

COMMERCIAL GRADS BASKET BALL TEAM — EDMONTON

Percy and Maude Page surrounded by the Grads, en route to Europe, June 1924.
[CEA EB-27-18]

*From the very commencement of the girls' associations with me as
supervisor of their school studies and their basketball activities, I
seek to win their respect. I accept them as members of my own family
and treat them as such, expecting them to give me that respect and
confidence and loyalty they would give in their own homes. We are
therefore a large family, all growing up together in an understanding,
loyalty, and friendship that completely does away with the necessity of any rigid form of discipline. The girls know exactly what I
expect of them. They know that to stay with the family they must
at all times conduct themselves as to reflect credit on the whole.*[2]

Just what did Page expect of his students and players, aside
from respect, confidence, and loyalty? Above all, he expected them
to be gracious young ladies in every aspect of their behaviour and

deportment. One girl using the banister at McDougall school as a quick way down the stairs received a stern reprimand from Page: "Young ladies in my school do not slide down banisters!"[3] In interviews, almost every Grad recalled his slogan: "Ladies first, basketball players second." Being a "lady" mostly meant dressing neatly and appropriately, not drinking or smoking, and keeping "reputable" company, especially with the opposite sex. The Grads trained and practised hard, sometimes with boys' teams, but away from the basketball floor, they were expected to dress and behave like the respectable young working women they were.

There was no deliberate effort on the part of Page or his wife Maude to "feminize" his players, and he did not need to lay down specific rules for conduct. In fact, no Grad remembers any specific rule, written or otherwise. They simply knew what was expected of them. Page himself once said, "I place no restrictions on the girls' movements. At home and abroad, in the matters of diet, conduct, recreational diversion and so forth, there have never been any misunderstandings....They are not treated as small children, but as sensible grown-up members of their own family."[4] Betty Bawden Bowen, who played on the last team before it disbanded, described Mr. Page as a "very quiet gentleman." She went on to say, "People thought that he was like a general—do this—do that—but he wasn't. He had these special thoughts— what he lived by. You did your best at everything you did."[5]

Page was a slightly built man, fit and trim his whole life, with what one observer described as a "perennial well-scrubbed look."[6] Even later in life, well into his seventies, Percy was slim, ramrod straight, and dignified, just as he had been in his coaching days. He was a solemn man with a crisp and precise manner and very blue piercing eyes. Quiet and reserved, he was not in any way impulsive; everything he did was detailed and executed with precision. He was not known for his loquaciousness, something his daughter Patricia

Percy Page, 1928. [GA NA-3578-1]

periodically complained about in her "Feminine Flashes" newspaper column. "Believe it or not," she wrote, "basketball is rarely
mentioned at home. We get very little encouragement if we try to
start an argument, and even the ordinary question having to do with
basketball is usually answered with a simple yes or no."[7] Perhaps
Robert Collins summed him up best: "Page was strait-laced, even for
those decorous times."[8] No doubt, but the coach and his wife also
enjoyed a fun-filled social life, whether it was an evening of music
with friends, with Percy playing the violin and Maude at the piano,

or weekly outings at the *Les Amies* Dance Club, which they founded. His other interests included bridge, gardening, golf, and curling.

Page's beliefs and philosophy were very much aligned with the Christian life as lived in fellowship with Christ and the Church. In his youth, the Page family belonged to the Methodist Church, which became the United Church of Canada when the Methodists, most Presbyterians, and other churches joined together in 1925. At Robertson-Wesley United Church in Edmonton, Page served as a steward for many years, and Maude was a member of the Women's Auxiliary.[9] He did not impose his religious beliefs on his players, but they infused everything he thought and did. Adhering to a strict code of personal behaviour, he is not known to have made a misstep at any time, especially where it concerned the Grads. He did not drink or smoke, and certainly never swore, thereby setting an example for his players to follow. Always proper, he would knock before entering the Grads' dressing room or send someone to tell them he was on his way.

Page's mild manner belied a will of iron. Everyone, especially his students and players, understood this. He was, as one journalist aptly stated, "as stern and unbending as the Sphinx."[10] It was simply not a wise idea to cross him. Maude Page once told an interviewer about a girl who played guard for one of the Commercial High School teams. On the night of the city finals the player informed Coach Page she would rather play centre, and when he requested that she play her regular position, she refused. She was immediately told to remove her uniform and was never allowed to wear it again.[11] On the other hand, no Grad ever had to turn in her uniform before she was ready to retire, although Coach Page sometimes made it clear when it was time for a player to go because he had another one waiting in the wings.

Coach Page's influence was not just confined to practices and the basketball court. As members of a "family," all players in the Grads' organization, whether they were on the junior or senior high school teams, the Gradettes, or the Grads themselves, were expected to behave in accordance with Page's expectations. Basketball talent was not in itself a passport to membership on any of these teams. Being well-behaved was not simply a manner of dress and deportment, it also meant the company the girls kept and the places they went, especially in Edmonton. It was unthinkable that a Grad be seen with a young man of questionable character or in a place of doubtful reputation. Concerned Edmonton citizens would sometimes phone Page if they saw any of the Grads out with someone, presumably male, who was less than highly respectable. What constituted "highly respectable" is unclear, but no doubt the offending Grad, embarrassed and remorseful, never saw the poor fellow again.[12] One time a party of boys invited the team on a well-chaperoned weekend canoe trip. Page vetoed the outing, not because it was improper but because outsiders might *think* it was.[13]

No dating was a very firm rule on trips away from Edmonton. Both Mr. and Mrs. Page felt strongly about this decree. Maude Page probably felt more strongly about this because she was usually along as the official chaperone. "Some writers refer to me as a strict disciplinarian and even criticize this," Page once commented. "Probably, if something happened on these trips, the same writers would be the first to crucify me."[14] Edith Stone once confided to an interviewer that she met her future husband, Elmer Sutton, then secretary of the Manitoba Basketball Association, while on a road trip with the Grads. "You weren't supposed to do that—go out with boys," she admitted proudly, "I did something I wasn't supposed to do."[15]

When one of the Grads was dating, everyone else knew about it. On a two-week road trip in April 1926, when the Grads went east to play teams in Ontario and the United States, they were entertained on the long journey by the "Commercial Chronicle," a typed bulletin as a "special dispatch to train No. 3, CPR." Surprisingly, it was written by Page himself, one of the few times he displayed a wicked sense of humour. As the "Chronicle" duly noted, "Kate Macrae is reported to be the only member of the Grads to spear a prospect up to the time of writing. Unfortunately he left the train at Saskatoon, and Kate can scarcely be consoled."[16] Of course, the prospect was hockey player Eddie Shore, who was then playing for the Edmonton Eskimos in the Western Canada Hockey League; the courtship continued, and Kate and Eddie were married three years later. Page even jested about sex in the "Commercial Chronicle" again at Kate's expense: "The lady in the hairdressing parlour who thought Kate's black and blue spots on her arm were a sure sign of a honeymoon probably spoke from experience. It's a tough life Kate."[17]

Even after individual Grads retired, were married and raising their own families, the long reach of Page's influence was still evident. Several times he was called upon to propose the toast to the bride when a Grad was married. He did so, for example, when Elsie Bennie, whose father had passed away, was married in 1937, and again when Winnie Gallen married Peter Reid in 1943. No doubt Page was an esteemed guest of honour at many more Grad weddings. The Pages also kept track of the growing number of offspring that the former Grads produced. Clearly, they were interested in their growing extended family, but the former Grads' successful reproductive lives also laid to rest earlier concerns among physical educators and the media that highly competitive basketball was harmful to a woman's reproductive system. By 1955, there were twenty-seven boys and twenty-five girls counted among the children of former Grads, and several former Grads were now also grandmothers.[18] One of the original Grads and their first captain, Winnie Martin Tait, was the proud mother of six children, all of whom were musicians and played in a string sextet together. Several years later, Helen Eckert, a researcher at the University of British Columbia published the results of a questionnaire she had distributed seeking information on the topic of fertility and competitive basketball. Of the thirty-one

Babe Belanger MacLean and her children Neil and Heather, 1947. [CEA EA-600-163B]

former Grads who had been contacted, twenty-five replied to the questionnaire, which suggests that they were as keen as anyone to assure the world that no reproductive damage had occurred through their participation in international basketball. The results were entirely predictable: an average of 2.13 children per married Grad.[19]

Maude and Papa Page took great pride in the accomplishments of former Grads, which for the most part, meant marriage and raising a family, although several Grads continued to work in the labour force after they were married. This was an era of traditional marriages, and as husbands pursued jobs or careers, their wives followed them. Only two of the thirty-eight Grads never married; one was Daisy Johnson, who had a long career as a schoolteacher. The other was Hattie Hopkins, a stenographer in the private sector, then an administrative clerk in the RCAF Women's Division during World War II, and, finally, for a short time, a handicraft instructor prior to her early death in 1953. The majority of marriages endured, and although a few ended in divorce, most Grads were widowed and outlived their husbands. Among the seven Grads who divorced, three remarried, including one who married four times. Ending a marriage was not as common or as easy in those days as it is today, and evidence of adultery was often the only way to obtain a divorce. When it was known that a Grad's marriage ended because of an affair on her part, her relationship with Mr. and Mrs. Page was affected; in fact, the Pages made it clear that those Grads were not welcome at the Grads reunions. After the Pages passed away, they were invited to return to the fold and attend reunions.

Despite evidence that certain behaviour on the part of individual Grads was unacceptable to the Pages, there are also stories about the Pages' generosity and goodwill. Page frequently intervened to help his students, most of whom were young women, obtain jobs in local businesses—something not always easy to accomplish in the middle of the Great Depression. It did not matter whether the students were Grads, although businesses were more than keen to employ members of the team, not just because of their superb stenographic skills, but because they also brought publicity and approval to the firm. As happens in large families, there were occasional problems and issues, especially when it came to marriages and children. The Pages' customary approach was to refrain from addressing these issues in public. Troubles were dealt with quietly, without fuss, and only those within the family were aware. One

1960 Grads reunion. Sitting: Babe Belanger MacLean, Winnie Gallen Reid, Percy Page, Maude Page, Mae Brown Webb, Nellie Perry McIntosh, and Gladys Fry Douglas; standing: Abbie Scott Kennedy, Connie Smith McIntyre, Mary Dunn Dickson, Elsie Bennie Robson, and Daisy Johnson. [PAA A11437]

story concerns a baby born out of wedlock to a young student at McDougall High School; the child was adopted by one of the Grads.

While the Grads resembled a large family, and certainly one in which Papa Page was the head, the team was not a substitute for Page's own family. Patricia, their daughter, arrived in 1915. While she was still a child, and obviously too young to travel on extended journeys throughout Europe, Maude Page would take her to Ontario, where she was cared for by relatives until her parents returned.

Until she was six years old, she was the Grads' mascot, wearing a special uniform with a zero on it. Before the start of a game, it was her job to bring their other well-travelled mascot, Spark Plug, out onto the middle of floor, where the team gathered in a circle to chant their famous yell.[20] As a student at McDougall Commercial High School, Patricia was a talented athlete. She preferred track and field to basketball, and she was good enough to succeed at the provincial level. As she grew up, she sometimes travelled with the Grads, including to the Berlin Olympics in 1936. She worked at the *Edmonton Journal* as a secretary, and in 1935, at the suggestion of the sports editor, she began writing her "Feminine Flashes" column to promote girls' high school sport in the city and to provide information about the Grads. In 1939, she married Clare Hollingsworth, a well-known figure in local sports circles and a teacher and basketball coach at McDougall. After the Grads disbanded in June 1940, she stopped writing her column to pursue other interests. She gave birth to a daughter Diane in 1943 and a son Donald in 1949.

Percy Page's life outside the Grads also included politics. Page's interest and involvement in Alberta politics stemmed from his opposition to William Aberhart and his Social Credit government, which came to power in 1935. The business communities in Edmonton and Calgary were hit hard by Aberhart's radical policies concerning monetary reform. Banks, mortgage companies, insurance agencies, bondholders, and other financial agencies were the most affected. Many of these were the same businesses and agencies that employed Page's McDougall graduates. Page became active in the movement to restore a business-friendly government to Alberta by defeating the Social Credit, which could only happen if the opposition parties were united under a non-partisan banner. As a member of the Unity Council of Alberta, Page became involved in developing its policies. In 1938, he was elected president of the Edmonton branch. In the 1940 provincial election, "Citizens'" slates, which combined Independent, Liberal, and Conservative candidates, were put forward in an attempt to unseat the Social Credit government. Page squeaked in as an Independent, along with nineteen other candidates who formed the Independent Citizens' Association of Alberta and set about drafting party policies for the next election. Page was re-elected to the Legislature in 1944 and recognized as Leader of the Official Opposition. He was unsuccessful in the 1948 provincial election, but ran as a Conservative in 1952. He was the only Conservative to be elected that year. He successfully ran again in 1955, and this time, he was one of three Conservatives elected. However, he was defeated in the next election in 1959.

Throughout Page's career in provincial politics he was interested in many issues, but education was always at the top of his list. He began teaching at Victoria High School in 1912, and in 1914 moved to McDougall Commercial High School, becoming its principal in 1921. He taught there until 1949 when the commercial program at McDougall was transferred to Victoria Composite High School, where Page continued as principal of the program until his retirement from teaching in June 1952. His textbook, *Practical Office Training*, first published in 1933, was so successful as a teaching tool, it was revised and enlarged through five editions. In his retirement, and still in the midst of his political career as a member of the Alberta Legislature, he was elected a trustee of the Edmonton Public School Board and served two terms.

In December 1959, at seventy-two years old, Page became the eighth Lieutenant Governor of Alberta. He and his wife continued to live in their own home located in Edmonton's Glenora neighbourhood, although official entertaining took place elsewhere. As the Vice-Regal representative in Alberta, it was a busy life for Page and his wife, performing official duties and attending ceremonial and social functions. Page's term as Lieutenant Governor was extended by a year, and he continued in this position until the

Hon. J. Percy Page, Lieutenant Governor of Alberta, 1959–1965. [CEA EB-27-134]

end of 1965. At a testimonial dinner to mark the end of Page's tenure as Lieutenant Governor, guest speaker Dick Rice, founder of Sunwapta Broadcasting and also a McDougall Commercial graduate, reflected on the contribution Page had made to the community over a period of fifty years. Rice noted that Page's four careers—educator, coach, politician, and Vice-Regal representative—had required wide talents and abilities, considerable agility, and great stamina.[21]

Page continued in good health until 1969 when he suffered a stroke, which resulted in partial paralysis to his right side. The Pages celebrated their sixtieth wedding anniversary early in 1970, and by then he had recovered sufficiently to walk about with a cane and crank out a regular five miles a day on his stationary bike. He enjoyed watching all manner of sports on television, and, with his left hand, he personally answered the many "Dear Papa" letters from his beloved Grads.[22] He was to live only a couple of more years, and on March 2, 1973, he died of complications from pneumonia at eighty-five years of age. Left to mourn were his wife Maude, his daughter Patricia and her husband Clare Hollingsworth, two grand-children, and a great-granddaughter. In the eulogy at his funeral, delivered by the Rev. Dr. Edworthy of Robertson-Wesley United Church, Percy Page was described as a man "standing as it were on tiptoe...the better to see what life is really all about."[23] The minis-ter summed up the man perhaps better than anyone had before:

> How warm and personable he was; how human and humane; how modest and unassuming. He was a gentle man. There was noth-ing officious or aggressive about him, and his influence was felt more by attraction than by assertion. But not only was he a gen-tle man, he was a gentleman. In victory and in defeat: at the curling rink, on the basketball court, on the floor of the Legislature, he was a gentleman...a true sportsman who never took unfair advantage of his opponents, and yet who, at the same time, expected of them the same high standards he had set for himself. It is indeed a remarkable tribute that in all his years of public service, his integrity and hon-esty and personal conduct were never once called into question.[24]

Maude Page died on June 27, 1978 at the age of ninety. As her daughter Patricia noted, "She could have written a book on her experiences with the team but she never got around to it."[25] So could have Patricia Page Hollingsworth herself because she grew up with the Grads, was their mascot as a child, went on many a journey with the team, and as a young woman was a part-time sports journalist covering their story. As this book goes to press, she is ninety-five years old and enjoying her own grandchildren.

10   Remembering the Grads

ON THE NIGHT OF JUNE 5, 1940, more than 6,000 devoted fans watched the Grads play their last game in the Arena against the Chicago Queen Anne Aces. It was the third game of an exhibition series, and having already won the first two games, the Grads finished the series with yet another solid win. The following night, some 250 guests crowded into the banquet room of the Corona Hotel to celebrate the achievements and passing of the Edmonton Commercial Graduates. Nearly all former Grads attended, as did their many supporters, including dignitaries, cheerleaders, media,

Former Grads and the last team at the final series, June 3, 1940. Back row: Helen Stone, Abbie Scott Kennedy, Edith Stone, Frances Gordon, Nellie Perry McIntosh, Elena Todd Downie, Ethel Anderson Lovatt, Evelyn Coulson Cameron, Daisy Johnson, Babe Daniel Morgan; third row: Babe Belanger MacLean, Doris Neale Chapman, Jessie Innes Maloney, Elizabeth Elrick Murray, Mildred McCormack Wilkie, Marguerite Bailey, Helen McIntosh Lees, Harriet Hopkins, Mae Brown Webb, Betty Ross Chevalier. Second row: Gladys Fry Douglas, Elsie Bennie Robson, Winnie Martin Tait, Etta Dann, Percy Page, Margaret MacBurney, Dorothy Johnson Sherlock, Connie Smith McIntyre; front row: Betty Bawden, Helen Northup, Kay MacRitchie, Mabel Munton McCloy, Jean Williamson, Winnie Gallen, Sophie Brown. Missing: Eleanor Mountifield Vogelsong, Noel MacDonald Robertson, Margaret Kinney, Mary Dunn Dickson, Joan Johnston, and Kate Macrae Shore.

[PAA KS35/1]

Gradettes, Cubs, and others involved in this extraordinary organization. Those who spoke touched upon the Grads' remarkable team spirit, developed from the beginning and untarnished for twenty-five years. As many concurred, Coach Page had been primarily responsible for instilling this spirit. Page responded by stressing the loyalty he had always received from his players. For him, disbanding the team was a "great personal wrench." The greatest contribution the Grads had made to the city and the country, observed Page, was as an incentive and example for hundreds of other girls who had hoped one day to play on the team.[1] The Grads were no longer, but their spirit would live on.

The reasons for disbanding the team were clear enough. The primary reason was that the federal government had taken over the Arena for use by the Air Commonwealth Training Force in wartime, which made it impossible to schedule any international series. Certainly, another factor was that attendance at games had fallen off considerably. The Grads were simply too good and there was a lack of top competition, even from the United States. The war was making travel difficult, and many competitions, especially Dominion tournaments, were routinely cancelled, as were all European and world championships, including the 1940 and 1944 Olympics. The radio broadcasting of the Grads' games had also affected attendance. Beginning in 1933, their games were heard regularly over CFRN, primarily for the benefit of fans outside of Edmonton, but more and more city dwellers chose to listen to the games rather than go to the Arena. Finally, even though Page had brought others into the organization to assist him, especially with coaching, he was still the mainstay of the team and their most valued mentor. He was a busy man in his main job as teacher and principal at McDougall Commercial High School, but also as a recently elected member of the Legislative Assembly of Alberta. He was about to embark on a lengthy political career and he could no longer give as much to the organization as he once did.

In August 1940, the team made one final trip together. Accompanied by Maude and Percy Page, Patricia and Clare Hollingsworth, and *Edmonton Journal* sports editor George Mackintosh and his wife, the team travelled through the Rockies and up the coastline of British Columbia to Alaska. It was purely a holiday and no games were arranged. Travelling in comfortable slacks and matching jackets adorned with the Grads' crest, eight team members—Winnie Gallen, Kay MacRitchie, Helen Northup Alexander, Sophie Brown, Etta Dann, Betty Bawden, Mabel Munton McCloy, and Jean Williamson—went on the vacation trip. They first motored in the Rockies, stopping in Calgary, Banff, Lake Louise, and Jasper to take in the sights and go for a horseback ride. From Jasper they took the train to Vancouver, where they spent a few days and then travelled by boat through the Inside Passage to Alert Bay, Ocean Falls, Prince Rupert, and as far north as Stewart, British Columbia. In Stewart, they went on a short hike into the bordering town of Hyder, Alaska. Back down the coast to Victoria, they enjoyed Butchart Gardens and some salmon fishing, and then went over to Vancouver for a bike ride around Stanley Park. Finally, they took the train back to Jasper to pick up their cars for the journey home. Patricia Hollingsworth wrote a series of articles for the *Edmonton Journal* describing their various adventures, the places they saw, and the fun they had. These were, according to her, the last pieces she wrote for any publication.[2] Remembering times past, when triumphal teams returned to Edmonton to an ecstatic and noisy welcome, she ended her last column with some sadness: "There were no brass bands, nor flags flying—the 'gang' had moved out and returned without more than a ripple of interest on the part of the public. Nevertheless it was a glorious trip—a fitting wind-up to an organization that has now passed out of existence."[3]

In October 1940 the Edmonton Commercial Basketball Club was officially dissolved and the account books closed for the last time. Financially, the club was in good shape, so much so that $100 was put aside to purchase a cup for international competition to be known as the J.J. Seitz Memorial Trophy, and another $100 was donated to the Edmonton "Spitfire" fund to help buy a wartime fighter airplane. The

Edmonton Comets, 1942. [PAA KS45/1]

considerable sum of $500 was also given to the City of Edmonton
"in appreciation of the cordial relations between the two organizations."[4] Most of the remaining funds were invested in government
war bonds, but some was allotted to help further the development
of girls' basketball in Edmonton. The club gave their official blessing
to the formation of two new girls' basketball teams, which they also
agreed to sponsor. One was a senior team named the Comets, which
competed for city, provincial, dominion, and international titles. The
Comets were coached by Bill Douglas, a Commercial graduate and
well-known basketball referee. The other team, called the Starlets,
competed at the intermediate level and was coached by Clare
Hollingsworth. Percy Page agreed to act as business manager for
both teams and be available for advice. Several former Grads—Helen
Northup, Winnie Gallen, Etta Dann, Kay MacRitchie, Betty Bawden,

Betty Bawden Bowen and Mayor Terry Cavanagh at the opening of Edmonton Grads Park, September 23, 1989. [CEA EB-27-301]

and Noel MacDonald—played initially for the Comets. Because only the Starlets were allowed to compete in the city league, the Comets were left without regular competition and they played primarily against men's teams like the Boy Grads. Regardless, Edmonton's domination of provincial, Western, and Canadian women's basketball titles was over, and the Grads' British Columbia counterparts, especially the Vancouver Hedlunds, took over as perpetual winners of the Canadian title.[5] When Kay MacRitchie moved to Vancouver in 1941, she joined the Hedlunds and played with them for several years.

The Grads suggested that the money they donated to the City of Edmonton should go toward creating a permanent memorial, such as a spray fountain in the city's centre, to honour their contributions to the city.[6] A three-man committee was appointed by city council to investigate the possibilities. It has been impossible to discover what happened to the original idea, but it took the City of Edmonton almost fifty years before it finally created a fitting memorial to the Grads. In 1989, a large strip of land in the Westmount community, spanning the distance from 107 to 111 Avenue and east of 122 Street, was designated as Edmonton Grads Park. Throughout the well-lit park are rolling hills, ample trees, and pathways for walkers and cyclists. In the middle is a small but paved area around a basketball hoop, large enough for a pick-up game. A well-equipped children's playground and picnic tables were added later near the main entrance to the park at the end of 109A Avenue. A plaque detailing the club's accomplishments and the names of the individual Grads, which sits on a huge boulder, is also located at the entrance, alongside a permanent, weatherproof historical display of team photos and players throughout the years. It originally cost the city $230,000 to build and landscape the park, and obviously much more over the years for upkeep.

The Grads began holding reunions some time before the team disbanded. The first reunion was in 1935 to celebrate the twentieth

1965 reunion during Klondike Days in Edmonton. [GA NA-3578-12]

anniversary of the club. Many former Grads were married by then, but most still lived in the city, which made it relatively easy to bring them together. It was also an ideal occasion to have everyone associated with the organization gather, including former players, the current team, the Gradettes and Cubs, as well as supporters and intimate friends. The windup of the team in 1940 was a memorable affair with almost all former players returning to take part in a reunion that lasted several days. Mr. and Mrs. Page began the custom of giving each Grad a silver souvenir spoon at each reunion to mark the occasion. Similarly, in 1947, the first reunion following the war, the Grads and others associated with the team returned to Edmonton for four days of luncheons, picnics, banquets, and a guest appearance at a fastball game. These events were always given good press in the local papers with photos and the inevitable recounting of the Grads' history and their accomplishments. After celebrating the thirty-fifth anniversary of the organization of the club in 1950, reunions were held every five years. The media focus was less on the former accomplishments of team, but on the ever-growing and large extended family represented by the Grads. "Boys Win, 27 to 25, in Family Score of Grads, Now Proud Wives, Mothers," announced an *Edmonton Journal* headline.[7] Some Grads were also now grand-mothers. These reunions were fairly formal affairs with a set schedule of events, characterized by the detail and precision for which Percy Page was noted. In 1965, for example, he sent out a "Papa Page" letter outlining the schedule for their fiftieth anniversary:

July 8	*Rotary Day; government has invited them to dinner*
July 9	*Picnic Day in Emily Murphy Park; children can come at 2:30 pm*
July 10	*Banquet Day sponsored by Gladys and Merrill Muttart (can bring one guest—husband or a friend)*
July 11	*Klondike preview; Page's residence for tea*
July 12	*Klondike exhibition parade in the morning; Grandstand at night; former captains introduced.*

The Grads still living in Edmonton were able to get together more frequently and they often did so whenever one of their mem-bers who resided somewhere else came to the city for a visit. These were far less formal occasions, and the many photographs in scrap-books attest to their fun and laughter. It was also an opportunity for women over several generations to meet and get to know each other better. In 1961, the Grads decided that they needed a more for-mal organization, especially a newsletter, to keep them informed about their collective lives. Percy and Maude Page were getting older, and the Grads realized that one day they would not be around to gather the family together. As time went on, more and more requests were being made for information about the Grads from stu-dents, researchers, and the media, and they needed to designate

(Top) Mary Dunn Dickson, Dot Johnson Sherlock, Eleanor Mountifield Vogelsong, Daisy Johnson, and Abbie Scott Kennedy at the June 1975 reunion. [CEA EB-27-191]
(Bottom) Last official gathering of the Grads, September 1987. [CEA EB-27-294]

someone responsible for answering these inquiries. They called their organization the "Edmonton Grads Club," set their annual dues at two dollars (eventually raised to five dollars), elected officers, issued a newsletter, and set policy. For example, "it was decided that only on the occasion of serious illness or bereavement in the immediate family of members should flowers be sent at a cost of 5 or 6 dollars—mums should be sent if at all possible."[8]

At the 1970 reunion held in Edmonton as usual, the Grads decided that their next gathering should move to the west coast to give the ten former players living in British Columbia a chance to play host. They met in Victoria in June 1975, for the first time without Papa Page, who had passed away two years earlier, and Mrs. Page, who decided against attending. *Edmonton Journal* writer Ted Watt also attended to assist the ACCESS television outlet make a half-hour documentary of the reunion.[9] The last official gathering of the Grads, their thirteenth reunion since 1935, was in Edmonton in September 1987 when the film *Shooting Stars*, a National Film Board and CBC documentary about the Grads, premiered. Twenty-one Grads, some in wheelchairs and others pushing walkers, were able to be there for the event.

As the Grads began to pass away, those remaining realized the importance of saving their scrapbooks, old uniforms, and other memorabilia so these items could be donated to an archives or museum. Daisy Johnson was the unofficial Grads historian, responsible for accumulating much of this material. When Daisy died in 1979, Betty Bawden Bowen took over the task. It is primarily through Betty's efforts that considerable archival material about the Grads is readily available to anyone interested, along with reams of correspondence related to the Edmonton Grads Club. Over the years, the Grads, and of course Percy Page, have received many honours (see Appendix 2). They have sought none of these accolades themselves and have left it to others to make certain their achievements have been properly recognized.

A lasting memorial to the Grads is the new GO Community Centre, which opened officially in September 2011 on the University of Alberta's South Campus. The centre was developed through the partnership of four established community sport organizations: the Edmonton Grads Basketball Centre, the Ortona Gymnastics Club, the Edmonton Volleyball Centre Society, and the University of Alberta. The purpose of the Edmonton Grads Basketball Centre is to preserve Edmonton's basketball roots while increasing the opportunity for growth and development of the sport. The GO Community Centre (the G stands for Grads and the O for Ortona) offers programming, facility rental space, and drop-in availability for the Edmonton and area basketball community. It will also preserve the memory of the Edmonton Grads through archiving and displaying historical artifacts. At over 200,000 square feet, the centre is huge. It contains several basketball and volleyball courts, almost 22,000 square feet of gymnastics space, a competition gymnasium with seating for 2,800 spectators, and other amenities, including fitness equipment, meeting rooms, offices, team rooms, referee rooms and a child care area.[10]

There is one honour that has eluded the Grads, an omission noted by long-time Edmonton sportswriter Terry Jones as far back as 1979. The team and Coach Page have yet to be inducted into the Naismith Memorial Basketball Hall of Fame in Springfield, Massachusetts, and their presence there is hardly noticeable. "Most likely, it's because of ignorance," wrote Jones, "but that's never much of an excuse." He went on: "The treatment the Grads get here—in the modern three-storey structure built on the very ground where Dr. James Naismith invented the game—is not only an insult to their greatness but would probably have Dr. Naismith turning in his grave if he had any idea."[11] It's too late now for the Grads because the Naismith Hall no longer inducts teams. The Grads have received slightly better treatment from the Women's Basketball Hall of Fame in Knoxville, Tennessee, where they were recognized in 2010, not by induction into the hall, but through a commemorative plaque. James A. Naismith, a Canadian and the founder of basketball, would likely not be pleased if he knew the Edmonton Grads are still seeking full recognition as one of the greatest teams ever to grace a basketball court. On the occasion of their twenty-first anniversary in 1936, Naismith paid a glowing tribute to the Grads and to Percy Page. Let us give him the last word:

> Your record is without parallel in the history of basketball. There is no team that I mention more frequently in talking about the game. My admiration is not only for your remarkable record of games won (which in itself would make you stand out in the history of basketball) but also for your record of clean play, versatility in meeting teams at their own style, and more especially for your unbroken record of good sportsmanship. It is the combination of all these things that make your record so wonderful....You are indeed fortunate in having a man like Mr. Page as your coach, for I regard him as the greatest coach and the most superb sportsman it ever has been my good fortune to meet.[12]

Appendix I
Edmonton Commercial Graduates Basketball Club Chronology (1915–1940)

1915

Players: Martin, Batson, Osborne, Reid, Anderson, and Bremner

MARCH

- Throughout this period, the team is referred to as the Commercials or Commercial High School and consists of the same six girls.
- Commercials win the Intercollegiate Basketball League title. League comprised of Varsity, Alberta College, Victoria, Strathcona, Commercial, and eventually Red Deer Ladies' College. This is the first year for the league.
- Commercials travel to Camrose and beat the Normal School students to win the first women's provincial basketball title in Alberta.

JUNE

- This first team graduated in the summer and unofficially formed the nucleus of what was to become the Commercial Graduates Basketball Club (see 1916 below).

OCTOBER

- Second year of competition for Commercials in the high school league. They lose in a playoff game.

1916

Players: Martin, Batson, Osborne, Reid, Anderson, and Bremner

FEBRUARY–MARCH

- Commercials win the Girls' City Basketball League in the senior division. There is also a junior league and girls from Commercial High School win it, too.
- Commercials again win the provincial championship against Camrose Normal School.

FALL

- Commercial High School had both junior and senior teams entered in the high school league. (The senior team is not the same one holding the provincial title because they had all graduated—see above.) This is the beginning of the informal feeder system for the Grads team.

DECEMBER

- Page explains the formation of the Commercial Athletic Society and that the Harold A. Wilson Company had donated a shield (trophy) for provincial competition on a challenge basis. This is the first formal acknowledgement of the Commercial Graduates Basketball Club.

1917

Players: Martin, Batson, Osborne, Reid, Anderson, and Todd

MARCH

- The team competes under their new name of Commercial Graduates for the first time. They play Alberta College in a warm up match, then beat Wetaskiwin for the provincial title (30–14). The players were the same as the 1916 team with one exception: Elena Todd, who replaced Mary Bremner.

1918

Players: Martin, Batson, Reid, Todd, Elrick, and Lamont

OCTOBER

- Grads are inactive until they defend their provincial title against a team from Stettler, which they win 17–7. This version of the Grads had three recent high school grads—Elena Todd, Elizabeth Elrick, and Connie Lamont—in addition to three of the old guard—Batson, Martin, and Reid. This is their fourth provincial title.

1919

Players: Martin, Reid, Todd, Elrick, Lamont, and Mountifield

APRIL

- Grads are challenged by the University of Alberta (U of A) for the provincial title. Batson and Martin cannot play and are replaced by Connie Smith and Mona Karran. They go down to defeat 14–16. The Grads want an immediate rematch but are refused because the rules require a two-month wait period until rematch.

NOVEMBER

- Grads challenge the U of A and beat them narrowly 21–18. The team consists of Elena Todd, Winnie Martin, Gerry Reid, Connie Lamont, Elizabeth Elrick, and rookie centre Eleanor Mountifield. Therefore, they regain the Wilson trophy and the provincial championship.

1920

Players: Martin, Elrick, Mountifield, Todd, Smith, Perry, Daisy Johnson, and Hall

APRIL

- Grads are not in a league, but are competing regularly.

- They successfully defend their provincial title against U of A in a rough game where a couple of players are knocked out for a moment or two (16–7).
- U of A protests the game because Grads had substituted Connie Smith in the second half. She was still a student at Commercial High School. Protest is upheld and the game is ordered replayed without Smith. The Grads lose the rematch and the provincial title (22–30). The U of A team also successfully defends the championship against the Commercial High School team just a few days later.

NOVEMBER
- Grads challenge U of A for Wilson shield again, which they regain 25–3.
- A letter appears in University of Alberta student newspaper *The Gateway* charging that the Grads had played dirty basketball and had influenced the referees to call the game in their favour. A second letter appears in *The Gateway* indicating that they would not publish a rebuttal by the Grads because it was too long. Charges are refuted by the executive committee of the Commercial Graduates' Club through a letter to the editor in both the *Edmonton Journal* and the *Edmonton Bulletin*. Grads offer to waive the time limit, choice of floors, and choice of referees for a rematch, but U of A rejects the offer.

DECEMBER
- Grads travel to Saskatchewan to play the YWCA and the University of Saskatchewan. Daisy Johnson is added to the team. They win both games, 50–8 and 47–15 respectively. This gives the Grads the interprovincial and western championship.

1921

Players: Martin, Mountifield, Smith, Daisy and Dot Johnson, Perry, and Elrick

There is no evidence the Grads played any official games in 1921. The 1921 Provincial loss in the Grads record books refers to a pair of games played between the Commercial High School team and Varsity.

- Edna Bakewell, President of the Women's Athletic Association at U of A, donates a cup, known as the Bakewell Cup, for the senior women's provincial basketball championship of Alberta.

1922

Players: Martin, Mountifield, Smith, Daisy and Dot Johnson, Perry, Elrick, and Dunn

---

JANUARY–MARCH

- First official provincial league and championship is played. The Edmonton district was comprised of Commercial Graduates, Varsity, Normal School and Victoria High. There was also a Calgary district and a Lethbridge district (eight teams in all) competing for the Bakewell cup. Grads win in sudden death against a team in Barons, 56–14.

MAY

- Grads go east to play London Shamrocks (eastern champions) for the Dominion championship. Elizabeth Elrick cannot get the time off work and doesn't go on the trip.
- Grads win the first game 41–8, played under Spalding ladies' rules, but lose the second game 8–21, played using men's rules; they nonetheless win series 49–29.
- First Dominion championship in any sport ever to come to Edmonton; Grads are greeted with a civic reception upon their return.

JUNE

- Grads play an exhibition game against a student team from Commercial High so fans can see the new Dominion champs.

OCTOBER

- Mary Dunn is added to the team in the fall, replacing Winnie Martin who went off to Queen's University.
- Grads play an exhibition game against an all-star team from the ladies' mercantile league.

1923

Players: Martin, Mountifield, Smith, Daisy and Dot Johnson, Dunn, Perry, Elrick, Scott, and McIntosh

---

FEBRUARY

- Grads beat the Mercantiles in a two out of three series, 50–16, to determine who enters provincial finals against the Calgary Barons.
- Grads play Barons; the Calgary team concedes the game at halftime.

MAY

- Wooden floor is constructed over the dirt oval in the Edmonton Arena.
- London Shamrocks come to Edmonton for Dominion championships; Grads win 17–6 and 34–22, for a total of 51–28.

JUNE

- Cleveland Favorite Knits come to Edmonton for the first Underwood trophy match—so-called "world" championship.
- Grads win 34–20 and 19–13; first world title ever for an Edmonton team.
- Elizabeth Elrick resigns from the team.

SEPTEMBER

- Toronto Maple Leafs challenge the Grads for the world championship; Grads win 41–11 and 26–13.

OCTOBER

- Helen McIntosh and Abbie Scott are added to the team.
- Chicago Uptown Brownies challenge the Grads for the world championship; Grads win 20–17 and 25–20. Nine thousand spectators watch the second game.
- Warren (Ohio) National Lamps challenge the Grads; Grads win 35–8 and 27–13.
- Percy Page is presented with an automobile by city businessmen as a token of their appreciation.

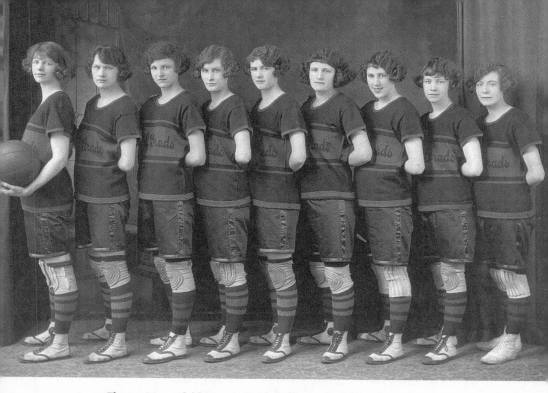

1924 team: Eleanor Mountifield, Connie Smith, Nellie Perry, Daisy Johnson, Dot Johnson, Abbie Scott, Winnie Martin, Mary Dunn, and Helen McIntosh. [LAC PA50440]

NOVEMBER

- At a meeting of the Alberta Basketball Association, the Grads are asked to accept a bye and not compete during the regular season, but to meet the winner of the senior league in home-and-home games for the provincial championship.

1924

Players: Martin, Mountifield, Smith, Daisy and Dot Johnson, Perry, Scott, McIntosh, and Dunn

FEBRUARY

- Grads play at Calgary winter carnival against Calgary All-Stars before largest crowd ever to witness a basketball game. They win 28–0.

- Grads beat U of A for Bakewell cup (28–13, 21–15) and the western championship. The only teams in contention are Calgary Buccaneers, U of A, and Grads.

- Grads beat Toronto Maple Leafs (26–6), who didn't score one basket (all points in free throws) for Canadian championship. Arena is filled to capacity. Score for second game is 23–14.

- Series with Chicago Lakeview Community; Grads win 44–11 and 42–10.

- Series with Cleveland Favorite Knits; Grads win 22–7 and 40–19.
- Grads leave on their first European trip. Eight players—Martin, Dunn, Smith, Scott, Dot and Daisy Johnson, Mountifield, and Perry—are accompanied by Percy and Maude Page.

- Grads play exhibition games coinciding with the 1924 Olympics in Paris. Games are arranged through the FSFI. Grads win all games. Scores and games:
    - Paris, practice game against a pick-up team: 64–16
    - Paris, pick-up team: 65–12
    - Paris, holders of the French championship: 69–17
    - Strasbourg, holders of the European championship: 37–8
    - Roubaix, local team: 65–4
    - Lille, local team: 61–1
- Grads are given undisputed right to the World's Basketball title by the International Basketball Federation. The title is to be played for again in 1926 at the Women's Olympiad.

- Winnie Martin (captain) leaves the team to marry; Connie Smith is appointed new captain.

- International series with Warren Elks of Ohio; Grads win 33–11 and 33–20.
- Grads enter a team in the provincial league under the name Gradettes; first official recognition of the feeder team.
- International series with Chicago Stars, formerly the Chicago Brownies; Grads win 26–13 and 39–8.

NOVEMBER

- Eleanor Mountifield, Nellie Perry, Abbie Scott, and Helen McIntosh resign from the team.

1925

Players: Smith, Daisy and Dot Johnson, Dunn, Bennie, Macrae, and Hopkins

JANUARY

- There is a significant change of players at the beginning of this season because of the number of players who had resigned during and at the end of 1924. Elsie Bennie and Harriett Hopkins are brought up from the Gradettes; Kate Macrae, who at the time was playing in the ladies' mercantile league, is also added.

FEBRUARY–MARCH

- Grads play an exhibition game against the Winnipeg All-Stars in Edmonton's Empire Theatre; Grads win 36–21.
- Grads lose a game in the Northern Alberta Ladies championship series against the Varsconas, but manage to hold onto the title for the tenth time; this counts as the provincial championship.

APRIL

- Grads travel to Vancouver and play a four-game exhibition series, winning all games:
  - Vancouver: 18–13
  - New Westminster: 25–12
  - Victoria: 30–6
  - Kamloops: 34–7

- Grads agree to play eastern winners if they came to Edmonton; Toronto YWHA, captained by Bobbie Rosenfeld, agrees; YWHA comes to Edmonton and loses both games with scores of 18–1 and 17–10.

JUNE

- International series with Chicago Lakeviews; Grads win 29–14 and 22–13. The crowds are small and there is some discussion in the media that Grads will have to disband.
- Second international series with Minneapolis Ascension Club; Grads win 51–9 and 33–3.
- Due to financial difficulties, Grads are forced to go on the road to defend their international title.

JULY

- Grads travel to Guthrie, Oklahoma to play champion Red Birds; Grads beat them 24–14 and 21–5.
- James Naismith is in the stands; he addresses crowd and later writes complimentary letter to Page.
- Grads play a series of exhibition games in the USA and win all but one:
  - Fort Worth, Texas: 47–6
  - Pasadena Athletic Club, California: 27–7
  - San Francisco Hoopers: 62–2
  - Pacific Coast 135-lb conference champions (boys' team): lost 42–15
  - Victoria (BC) All-Stars: 35–8
  - Kamloops boys' team: 24–20

AUGUST–NOVEMBER

- Grads do not play in Edmonton again throughout the fall.

DECEMBER

- International series with Chicago Tri-Chis; Grads win 35–12 and 34–8.

1926 team: Connie Smith, Dot Johnson, Daisy Johnson, Kate Macrae, Elsie Bennie, Hattie Hopkins, Mildred McCormack, Marguerite Bailey, and Margaret MacBurney.

[PAA A11418]

1926

Players: Smith, Daisy and Dot Johnson, Dunn (only briefly), Bennie, Macrae, Hopkins, Bailey, McCormack, and MacBurney

JANUARY–FEBRUARY

- Mary Dunn becomes engaged, gets married, and leaves the team immediately.
- Grads successfully defend provincial championship by defeating Varsity 49–16, then Gradettes 32–10, and again Varsity 52–21.

APRIL

- Marguerite Bailey, Mildred McCormack, and Margaret MacBurney are brought up from the Gradettes.
- Two-week road trip to eastern Canada and the USA:
  - Winnipeg All-Stars, exhibition: 44–9
  - Chicago Tri-Chis, exhibition: 19–17

- Warren Elks in Lincoln, Ohio, exhibition: 24–19.
- Four-game series for Underwood trophy against Newman-Sterns: 16–23 (lost), 26–21, 10–15, 8–13; Newman-Sterns win the series 72–60; these games are played in Cleveland and New York.
- Toronto Lakesides, two-game series for Dominion championship: Grads lose the first game 19–24.
- Travel to London to play Westervelt Grads in an exhibition game; Grads win 40–15.
- Return to Toronto for second game of series with Lakeside; Grads win 27–6 and win series 46–30.
- Grads had played ten games in seven cities in thirteen nights and won six of the games.
- Estimated crowd of 10,000 greet them on their return to Edmonton.

JUNE
- International series with St. Louis Curlees; Grads win 19–14 and 24–8.

SEPTEMBER
- Connie Smith resigns from the team and Dot Johnson succeeds her as captain.

OCTOBER
- International series with Guthrie Oklahoma Red Birds; Grads win 32–9 and 45–9.
- Second international series with Detroit Nationals. Game played in four ten-minute periods with girls' rules for first two quarters and men's rules for second two; Grads win 31–30 and 34–27.

1927

Players: Daisy and Dot Johnson, Macrae, Hopkins, Bailey, McCormack, MacBurney, Fry, Mae Brown, and Johnston

JANUARY
- Grads win city championship against Varsconas 70–7 and 61–6.

- Grads beat Calgary Centrals in provincial championship 58–3, 22–10, and 47–12. This is their sixth straight title. Gradettes win intermediate championship.

MARCH

- Grads defeat Vancouver Canucks for western Canadian championship 34–20 and 64–38.

APRIL

- International series with Peetz Undertakers from St. Louis; Grads win 33–13 and 33–14.
- Grads take a trip east:
  - Beat Toronto Lakesides for Canadian championship 34–24 and 19–14
  - Play exhibition games in the USA against:
    - in New York, Crofut-Knapp of Norwalk, Connecticut: 29–26
    - Detroit Nationals: 22–15
    - in Chicago, Taylor Trunks: 23–17

MAY

- International series with Cleveland Newman-Sterns; Grads win 25–10 and 28–22. There is a huge demand for tickets and there are very large crowds.

OCTOBER

- Daisy and Dot Johnson, Hattie Hopkins and Marguerite Bailey resign from team.
- Gladys Fry becomes the first "south side" player to be named to the team; she did not attend Commercial High School. Gladys is the new centre, taking over from Daisy Johnson.
- Margaret Nairn and Joan Johnston, both forwards playing on the Gradettes, are named to the team as substitutes, but after the series with the Chicago Taylor Trunks, it is announced that Margaret Nairn must give up all strenuous exercise.
- International series with Chicago Taylor Trunks; Grads win 27–19 and 39–8.

- Mae Brown, a forward, is brought onto the team. She is the only other player not to have gone to Commercial High School.
- Grads want to raise funds to go to 1928 Summer Olympics in Amsterdam, so they decide on another international series with an unknown team, Minnesota National Bankers, whom they completely outclass; Grads win the series 69–5 and 57–7. The weather is terrible and there are only 1,000 fans at the first game and 400 at the second. The Grads lose money.

1928

Players: Bennie, Macrae, McCormack, MacBurney, Fry, Mae Brown, and Johnston

---

MARCH

- International series with Chicago Uptown Brownies; Grads win 26–12 and 44–26.

APRIL

- Grads play Toronto Lakesides in Edmonton for Canadian championship; they win 29–27 and 33–22. However, after the series there is a controversy over Lakeside's right to represent the "east."

MAY

- Grads play Calgary Centrals for provincial championship in a sudden death match; Grads win 39–9.
- Grads play UBC for Western Canadian championship and win 40–24. Daisy Johnson returns to the team briefly because Kate Macrae is injured.
- Grads also play UBC for another Canadian championship and win 24–21 and 64–65.

JUNE

- Dalhousie University plays the Grads for yet another Canadian championship. The AAU of C threatened not to let the Grads go to Europe if they did not play Dalhousie. Grads win 64–6 and 83–12.

Grads of 1928. [PAA A11419]

- Joan Johnston does not accompany the team to Europe because they only
  have sufficient funds to carry six players.

JUNE–SEPTEMBER

- Grads leave for their European trip on June 21 and return on September 3.
  Teams played and scores:
  - Paris, French Racing Club: 65–18
  - Paris, Équipe de Paris: 109–20
  - Lyons: 81–9
  - Milan: 68–2

- Luxembourg: 67–6
- Strasbourg: 87–6
- Rheims: 88–11
- Paris, Linnets: 53–14
- Paris, All-Stars: 46–14
- Their wins over the Paris Linnets and the Paris All-Stars give them the French and World titles respectively.
- They did not play any further games this season after their return from Europe.

1929

Players: Bennie, McCormack, MacBurney, Fry, Macrae, Mae Brown, Johnston, Kinney, Belanger, and Neale

---

MARCH
- Grads beat the Calgary Centrals for provincial title, one game in Edmonton (43–13) and the other in Calgary (46–10).
- Grads pull out of Western playoffs. They would have had to travel to British Columbia, then Toronto.
- Vancouver Meralomas claim Western championship after defeating Calgary.
- Eastern winner refuses to bring Vancouver team to Toronto for championship. Canadian Amateur Basketball Association (CABA) rules that there will not be a Canadian championship this season.

APRIL
- Joan Johnston resigns from the team and Babe Belanger is added as a substitute.
- Series with Gerald's Café from Seattle in Edmonton; Grads win 56–24 and 37–16.
- Single exhibition game with the Vancouver Meralomas, who had beaten Calgary Centrals in Western finals; Grads win 49–15.

- Grads leave for the east. They are supposed to play in a Chicago series with the opening of new stadium but the game is cancelled just as they are leaving.
- Grads defeat Toronto Parkdales in an exhibition series 23–17 and 31–15.
- Chicago Uptown Brownies come to Edmonton for Underwood trophy challenge; Grads win 33–11 and 43–14.

JUNE

- Series with Detroit Centrals; Grads win 56–14 and 29–17.

SEPTEMBER

- Doris Neale is added to the team, replacing Kate Macrae, who was married in October.
- Gladys Fry is elected president of the Commercial Graduates Basketball Club, succeeding Kate Macrae. This is the first time the presidency has gone to anyone other than a graduate of Commercial High School.

OCTOBER

- Series with Cleveland Blepp-Knits in Edmonton; Grads win 50–31 and 27–13; James Naismith attended the second game.

NOVEMBER

- Margaret Kinney is added to the team as a substitute player.
- Grads play an exhibition game in Regina against Torrid Zones and win 50–12.
- McDougall High School is destroyed in a fire; many records are lost and equipment and trophies are damaged. Grads also lose a place to practise.

DECEMBER

- Exhibition game against Calgary Chinooks; Grads win 56–9.

1930

Players: Bennie, McCormack, MacBurney, Fry, Mae Brown, Kinney, Belanger, and Neale

---

JANUARY–FEBRUARY

- Controversy with U of A regarding Gladys Fry, specifically who would have her services for the provincial championships. The two teams play a game without Gladys to decide which team she'll play with for the championships. Grads win and Gladys plays for them.

MARCH

- Grads win provincial senior championship against Calgary Central Grads, 56–14 and 31–15.
- Gradettes win provincial intermediate championships against Calgary Follies.
- Noella "Babe" Belanger is brought up from the Gradettes.
- Underwood trophy challenge against Seattle Ferry Lines; Grads win 56–17 and 58–38.

APRIL

- Western Canadian championships in Vancouver; Grads beat UBC 37–20 and 26–14.
- Series with Toronto Lakesides in Edmonton for Canadian championship; Grads win 47–17 and 41–27.

MAY

- After 78 consecutive wins, Grads lose a game by 10 points (34–24) to Chicago Taylor Trunks. Nearly 7,000 spectators attend the second game, which the Grads win by a score of 40–13. They therefore win the series. The city telephone service is disrupted when 100,000 people call a special number to find out the results of the second game.

JULY

- Exhibition game in Wetaskiwin against Gradettes; Grads win 60–19.

- Summer tour in lieu of trip to Prague to play in Women's Olympics. The Grads travel to British Columbia and the west coast of the United States where they play games in Kelowna, Seattle, San Francisco, Prince Rupert, and Prince George, losing only once to the Pacific Coast 140-lb boy champions. Scores are very lopsided.
- No further games or series this season because changes had to be made to Grad lineup (Mae Brown and Margaret Kinney left the team) and because there were no challengers worthy of them.

1931

Players: Bennie, McCormack, MacBurney, Fry, Belanger, Neale, Helen and Edith Stone

MARCH

- Helen and Edith Stone move up from the Gradettes.
- Grads defeat Calgary Centrals for provincial title 104–24 and 38–27.

APRIL

- Controversy over national championships: the Grads did not wish to play Toronto on the dates suggested because they were having trouble getting financial backing; CABA awarded the championship to Toronto Lakesides; donor of the national championship trophy, Mr. J.J. Seitz, ruled that his trophy should only change hands through competition, but CABA did not accept his ruling.

MAY

- Series with Forest Park Cardinals from Chicago; Grads win 80–33 and 109–24.
- Series with Leavittsburg Aces from Ohio; Grads win 62–51 and 84–41.

SUMMER

- Grads play exhibition games in Westakiwin, Wainwright, Lloydminster, and Vegreville with the Gradettes as opposition. The purpose of the games was to promote basketball in the rural areas.

1931 team. Back row: Helen Stone, Gladys Fry, Percy Page, Elsie Bennie, Edith Stone; front row: Babe Belanger, Mildred McCormack, Margaret MacBurney, and Doris Neale. [PAA A11423]

OCTOBER

- Series with Pocatello Indians from Idaho; Grads win 82–20 and 113–22.

NOVEMBER

- Exhibition series with Toronto All-Stars, actually the Toronto Lakesides, with players added from Parkdales and one from Windsor; Grads win 129–19 and 100–18.
- Grads and Gradettes play exhibition game in Camrose at a school tournament; 900 fans come out to watch the game, which the Grads win 58–15.
- Alberta Basketball Association designate the Grads as Class "A" while all other teams in the province were Class "B." In future, all Class "B"

teams would play off against themselves, and if they felt they were strong enough, they could challenge the Grads for the actual provincial title.

1932

Players: Bennie, McCormack, MacBurney, Fry, Belanger, Neale, Helen and Edith Stone

MARCH

- Gradettes beat the Calgary Follies for the provincial senior "B" championship (15–28, 62–41) and therefore earn the right to play the Grads, who beat them 63–29 and 80–39.

APRIL

- Grads defeat Vancouver Witches in the Western final 100–45 and 98–56.
- Once again arrangements for the national final cause problems over money; Windsor-Walkerville Alumnae come to Edmonton and the Grads beat them 60–32 and 46–18; Grads earn their ninth national title.

MAY

- Grads complete their twenty-ninth defence of the Underwood trophy against the Chicago Red Devils. Over 8,000 fans watch the series. Scores were 44–34 and 49–25.
- Same teams play an exhibition game in Calgary before 3,000 appreciative fans. Grads flew in two small planes to Calgary. Grads win 27–18.

AUGUST

- Grads attend Los Angeles Olympics as spectators because there were no games played in and around Los Angeles. The team went to promote basketball for women and to draw interest from Europe.
- Grads play three exhibition games on the way home: San Francisco All-Stars (40–7); young men's team in Prince Rupert (32–26), and team in Victoria (72–24).

OCTOBER

- Exhibition game with Regina Smeeds in Edmonton; Grads win 84–23.

- Second annual tournament of exhibition games/display with Gradettes in Camrose.
- Elsie Bennie resigns from the team; Margaret MacBurney is named captain.

1933

Players: MacBurney, Belanger, Fry, Neale, Helen and Edith Stone, Coulson, Innes, MacDonald, and Munton

---

MARCH

- Evelyn Coulson and Jessie Innes are brought up from the Gradettes as substitutes.
- Gradettes beat Calgary Beavers in Senior "B" Alberta Ladies championship.
- Gradettes and Grads compete in Senior "A" Alberta Ladies championship; Grads win 78–35 and 87–43.

APRIL

- Western finals against Vancouver Province; Grads win 94–58 and 74–42.
- Dominion final with Toronto Ladies Athletic Club; Grads win 79–24 and 72–32. Attendance at games is poor.

MAY

- Underwood trophy series with Chicago Red Devils; Grads win 74–35, 60–48 and 67–53. The third game in the series was an exhibition.

JUNE

- Durant, Oklahoma Cardinals come to Edmonton for the first official North American championship; Cardinals win in three straight games, 59–52, 60–48, 67–53. Games used men's and women's rules alternately.
- Series was staged to determine the North American representative to the Women's Olympics scheduled for London, England in 1934.
- Huge controversy was sparked by Coach Babb of the Cardinals over how the U.S. team was treated and over the fact that the Grads would not relinquish the Underwood trophy.

- Noel MacDonald and Mabel Munton were brought up from the Gradettes for the series.

OCTOBER

- Another Underwood trophy series with the Chicago Red Devils; Grads win 75–35, 54–29, and 54–38.
- MacDonald and Munton officially become Grads.
- An AAU official comes from the States to investigate Coach Babb's complaints.
- Grads issue a challenge to Durant Cardinals or any other U.S. team who wishes to play them.

1934

Players: MacBurney, Belanger, Fry, Neale, Helen and Edith Stone, Coulson, Innes, Munton, MacDonald, Bennie, and Northup

MARCH

- Series with Calgary Beavers for provincial title; Grads win 35–22 and 99–21.
- Elsie Bennie rejoins team; she had retired two years previously.

APRIL

- Series for Western Canadian championship with Vancouver Province; Grads win 45–27 and 35–30.
- Grads are carrying eleven players but only eight are permitted to play in the semi-finals and finals.
- Grads play Canadian championships in Edmonton against Windsor Alumnae. Championship is now best three games out of five; Grads win 84–20, 47–30, and 57–30. Crowds are very small.

MAY

- Chicago Spencer Coals challenge Grads for Underwood trophy; Grads win two-game series 100–39 and 46–37. Crowds are much better.

- Grads meet Tulsa (Oklahoma) Stenos for 1934 North American championship in Edmonton; Grads take the title in three straight games 41–31, 35–28, and 48–41. There are capacity crowds at the Arena.

AUGUST–SEPTEMBER

- Three-week trip east; Grads play four exhibition games and win them all:
  - Fort William: 104–8
  - Montreal Stars: 63–6
  - Toronto All-Stars: 49–12
  - Winnipeg Eagles: 64–4
- Helen Northup is added to the team because Margaret MacBurney is recovering from appendicitis and cannot go on the trip.
- After the tour, Helen and Edith Stone, Elsie Bennie, Edith Coulson, and Jessie Innes resign from the team.

1935

Players: Fry, MacBurney, Belanger, Neale, MacDonald, Munton, Northup, Dann, and Sophie Brown

MARCH

- Grads beat Calgary Beavers 59–27 and 48–26 for provincial senior championship. Gradettes defeat Calgary Carsons with a total score of 84–73 for intermediate championship.
- Etta Dann and Sophie Brown are brought up from the Gradettes.
- Grads defeat Vancouver Province at Western finals in Vancouver 63–24, 64–42.

APRIL

- Grads play a team in Windsor for the Canadian championship; Grads win in three straight games: 34–30, 58–31, 44–31. On the way home, they play the Winnipeg Blue Eagles and the Saskatoon Grads in exhibition games and win both by scores of 51–17 and 116–15 respectively.

1935–1936 team: Noel MacDonald, Gladys Fry, Mabel Munton, Etta Dann, Sophie Brown, Margaret MacBurney (retired in October 1935), Doris Neale, Babe Belanger, and Helen Northup. [PAA BL2636/4]

MAY

- Routine international series with American Institute of Business Secretaries (AIB) from Des Moines, Iowa; Grads win 60–28, 49–41, and 56–28.

JUNE

- Tulsa Stenos are back in Edmonton for North American championship. Grads win by slight margin. Score in first game was 53–49; second game was 49–53; third game was 37–31; Grads win fourth game 43–40, taking the series.

SEPTEMBER

- Page announces he will step down as coach of the Grads at the end of the season and his assistant, Arnold Henderson, will take over. Page will remain as business manager.

- Series against Chicago Usherettes; only two games played. Grads win 54–36 and 42–27.
- Series against St. Louis Shaw Stephens; Grads win 55–20, 51–24, and 43–24.
- Interest drops off after the first game in each series with less than 1,000 fans at the second and third games.
- Patricia Page begins writing her "Feminine Flashes" column for the *Edmonton Journal*.
- Marg MacBurney announces retirement from the team; Gladys Fry is named captain.
- Grads play no further games this season.

1936

Players: Fry, Belanger, Neale, MacDonald, Munton, Northup, Sophie Brown, and Dann

---

MARCH

- Page is still coaching the Grads, although it is rumoured that he may turn the team over to Arnold Henderson in the fall. Page never does do this.
- Grads pass up the provincial playoffs. The Gradettes win the provincial playoff against the Calgary Wittichens. No Western or Canadian finals were held because the Grads were not available.

APRIL

- International series against the Des Moines A I B; Grads win 54–40 and 43–37.
- Grads play series for North American title against Tulsa Stenos, who took the Grads to four games by winning the third game; scores: 42–24, 34–24, 33–40, and 35–30.

MAY

- Gladys Fry gets married but remains with the team and goes on the European tour in June.

JUNE

- Grads compete against El Dorado Lion-Oilers of Arkansas, formerly the Durant Cardinals. It's a close best-out-of-five series: 40–44 (Grads lose), 37–35, 38–29, and 41–24. Fan attendance is not great.

JUNE–SEPTEMBER

- Trip to Europe and the Berlin Olympics. Grads sail from Quebec after playing exhibition games in Regina (90–16), Peterborough (107–6), Ottawa (99–11), and Montreal (90–20).
- Canadian Olympic Committee honours the team by allowing them to wear the official Canadian blazers and sit in the athletes' section. The Grads don't arrive in Berlin in time to march in the open ceremonies.
- During their two-month stay, Grads win nine straight games against various European opponents:
  - London Pioneers: 100–2
  - Nice: 85–9
  - Monte Carlo, European champions: 77–14
  - Rome: 67–8
  - Milan: 25–8
  - Strasbourg: 83–25
  - Douai: 87–15
  - Lens: 87–10
  - Paris: 86–14

OCTOBER

- Gladys Fry Douglas and Doris Neale resign from the team. Winnie Gallen and Betty Ross of the Gradettes are added to the team on a trial basis; Noel MacDonald becomes captain.

1937

Players: Belanger, Macdonald, Munton, Northup, Dann, Sophie Brown, Ross, Gallen, Gordon, Williamson, and Daniel

MARCH

- Grads defeat Calgary Beavers 74–27 and 58–31 to regain provincial title.

APRIL

- Grads win Western championship in Vancouver against Spencers: 43–15, 37–26.
- Canadian finals not held again this year.
- Four new players appear on Grads lineup for international competition: Betty Ross, Winnie Gallen, Frances Gordon, and Jean Williamson.
- Series against Cleveland Fisher Foods; Grads win in three straight games 50–24, 42–17, and 48–26.

MAY

- Series against Wichita Thurstons from Kansas; Grads win 58–18, 48–12, and 46–25.

JUNE

- Series against Tulsa Stenos, the only team in 1937 to take the Grads to four games. Scores: 31–23, 38–29, 35–46, and 27–19.
- Babe Belanger announces her retirement after the Tulsa series.

OCTOBER

- No international series played in the fall because arena was not available.
- Only five players were seen as "regulars": MacDonald, Dann, Munton, Northup, and Sophie Brown; all others were working with the Gradettes; it is uncertain who will be moved up to the Grads.

NOVEMBER

- Jean Williamson is brought up again to play with the Grads because Noel MacDonald was injured.

- Babe Daniel, who was playing with the Gradettes, is invited to join the Grads to replace Babe Belanger.

1938

Players: Macdonald, Munton, Northup, Dann, Sophie Brown, Williamson, Daniel, Gordon, and Ross

MARCH

- Although Betty Ross, Frances Gordon, and Winnie Gallen saw service with the Grads last year, they are back playing with the Gradettes at the beginning of the season.
- Grads defeat Calgary Buffaloes (52–32 and 56–13) and thus win the Alberta Senior "A" championship.

APRIL

- Grads handily beat Victoria Gainer-Superiors (80–34 and 78–19) for Western Canadian title.
- Grads beat Toronto British Consols (72–28, 66–29, and 58–13) for Canadian title.

MAY

- Underwood international series against Chicago All-Stars; Grads win 40–33, 42–26, and 40–31.
- Frances Gordon and Betty Ross are in Grad uniforms in case they are needed; they did get to play at the end of the second game.
- Underwood international series with Cleveland Fisher Foods; scores: 61–38, 53–24, 36–44 (Grads lose), 61–48.

JUNE

- Rochester Filarets ask that their Underwood series with the Grads be set back until next spring. They hope the Grads can accommodate them during their planned eastern tour in early 1939.

1938 team. Back row: Muriel Daniel, Jean Williamson, Percy Page, Noel MacDonald, Mabel Munton; front row: Sophie Brown, Etta Dann, Helen Northup. [PAA A11426]

AUGUST

- Grads go on two-week holiday trip to Yellowstone with Mr. and Mrs. Page. They don't play any games on the trip.

SEPTEMBER

- Underwood international series with Canton Engravers; Grads win 75–25, 79–52, and 68–32. Page is convinced that fans have lost interest; there are less than 500 in attendance throughout series games.

OCTOBER

- Underwood international series with Wichita Thurstons; Grads win 41–27, 43–22, and 33–29. Fan attendance is much higher.

- Frances Gordon and Betty Ross are working out again with the Grads.
- Noel MacDonald is named outstanding Canadian female athlete of 1938.
- Grads place second to Toronto Argonauts for Canadian team of the year.

DECEMBER

- Percy Page is named leader of the newly formed Edmonton Unity Association, which hopes to elect candidates in next provincial election.

1939

Players: Macdonald, Munton, Northup, Dann, Sophie Brown, Gallen, Williamson, Daniel, Ross, and MacRitchie

---

FEBRUARY–MARCH

- Grads leave on a two-week goodwill tour of eastern Canada; they play seven games and win them all:
  - Windsor: 39–20
  - McMaster University: 71–28
  - Niagara Falls Anglicans: 51–11
  - Toronto Ladies and Consols: 65–25
  - Montreal Olympics: 87–14
  - Queen's University: 91–25
  - Detroit Holzbaugh: 25–13

MARCH

- Babe Daniel is forced to retire because of knee problems.
- There is no Dominion championship held this year.

APRIL

- Kay MacRitchie is brought up from the Grad Cubs to replace Babe Daniel.
- Underwood international series with St. Louis Stockman Legion, who take the Grads to four games: 35–24, 27–28 (Grads lose), 50–34, and 37–25.
- Grads are riddled with injuries. Fan attendance is low.

- Underwood international series with Cleveland Nokolds, formerly Fisher Foods; Grads win 61-32, 39-26, and 43-34. This was their fiftieth consecutive defence of the Underwood trophy.

MAY–JUNE

- Underwood international series with Chicago Queen Anne Aces; Grads win 41-29, 46-34, and 33-35.

AUGUST

- Betty Ross marries in late August and leaves the team.

SEPTEMBER

- Underwood international series with Des Moines AIB: Grads win 61-20, 49-24, and 61-34. Attendance is disappointingly small, which prompts rumours that team would not continue after 1939.

SEPTEMBER–OCTOBER

- Underwood international series with Wichita Thurstons; Grads win 47-26, 45-30, and 44-24.
- Noel MacDonald retires after Wichita series; Noel and Mabel Munton announce that they have been married already (Noel in August, and Mabel in September).
- Etta Dann takes over as captain.

DECEMBER

- Controversy occurs when the Rochester Filarets claim the world championship because, they contend, the Grads avoided meeting them. In fact, the Grads were unable to arrange a series with Rochester during their eastern tour earlier in the year due to prior commitments.
- Page announces that a series could be arranged despite the fact that the Arena would be unavailable.
- Page also announces that Betty Bawden would be added to the team for 1940; also Mabel Munton McCloy will be the eighth member until a player from either the Gradettes or the Cubs can be brought up to the senior team.

1940 team. Back row: Mabel Munton McCloy, Jean Williamson, Percy Page, Winnie Gallen, Kay MacRitchie; front row: Betty Bawden, Helen Northup, Etta Dann, Sophie Brown. [PAA A11429]

1940

Players: Northup, Dann, Sophie Brown, Gallen, Williamson, MacRitchie, Bawden, and McCloy (Munton)

JANUARY

- Charges and countercharges continue with the Rochester Filarets; the coach demands that games be played in Toronto, Montreal, and Rochester even though the Underwood trophy rules stated that the defending team has the right to choose the floor.
- Grads return to city competition after an absence of twenty-four years in the Edmonton Basketball league, where the Gradettes, Grad Cubs, and Varsity squads provided the competition organized on a handicap system.

- Amateur status of Rochester Filarets in doubt and the series in question.

MARCH

- It is announced that the series with Rochester has been cancelled because they refused to meet the Grads.
- Page is elected as an Independent in the Alberta provincial general election.

APRIL

- Gradettes win senior women's provincial championship.
- The United States AAU investigates after Page charges that the Rochester team never intended to come to Edmonton. Therefore, they would never get another chance to play the Grads; as a result, the AAU will suspend any American teams who play the Grads in the future.
- Grads announce that they will withdraw from competition on their twenty-fifth anniversary in June.
- Gradettes win Western Canadian championship against Winnipeg Dominions. Scores are 48–27 and 45–26.
- Gradettes are defeated by the Vancouver Westerns in Canadian final series (26–40, 31–46), which meant that Vancouver could challenge Grads for title.

MAY

- Grads defeat Vancouver Westerns (48–47 and 59–36) to ensure their retirement as Canadian champions.
- A team from Wichita, Kansas defies the AAU and plays an exhibition series with the Grads; the Grads win 52–34, 50–33, and 37–38.

JUNE

- Grads play a final exhibition series against Chicago Queen Anne Aces, who also defied the AAU; Grads win 56–34, 45–38, and 62–52. They play their last game on June 5.

- Grads go on a holiday trip through the Rockies and up the British Columbia coastline by boat to Alaska, accompanied by Maude and Percy Page and others.

OCTOBER

- Edmonton Commercial Graduates Basketball Club are officially dissolved and account books are closed.

Appendix 2
Honours and Awards to the Edmonton Grads and
J. Percy Page

1950
- Edmonton Grads voted Canada's greatest basketball team of the first half century by sports editors and sportscasters in a Canadian Press poll.

1955
- J. Percy Page inducted into Canada's Sports Hall of Fame.

1961
- J. Percy Page inducted into the City of Edmonton Sports Hall of Fame.
- J. Percy Page received honorary degree from the University of Alberta.

1966
- J. Percy Page inducted into the Alberta Sports Hall of Fame and Museum.

1971
- Noel MacDonald Robertson inducted into Canada's Sports Hall of Fame.

1973
- Edmonton Grads inducted into the City of Edmonton Sports Hall of Fame.

Unveiling of Parks Canada plaque at Commonwealth Stadium with Muriel Daniel Lineham and Kay MacRitchie MacBeth, 1978. [CEA EB-27-274]

- Opening of the Percy Page Centre for Recreation Associations, located at the corner of Groat Road and 118 Avenue, Edmonton. The centre provides office and meeting room space for provincial amateur sport and recreation associations.

1978

- Unveiling of a plaque by Parks Canada "commemorating the national historic significance" of the Edmonton Grads, located at the southeast entrance to Commonwealth Stadium, Edmonton.
- J. Percy Page inducted into the Canadian Basketball Hall of Fame.

1981

- Edmonton Grads inducted into the Canadian Basketball Hall of Fame.

1983

- Edmonton Grads inducted into the Alberta Sports Hall of Fame and Museum.

1984

- J. Percy Page Composite High School officially opened in Mill Woods, Edmonton.

1985

- Edmonton Grads honoured by the Edmonton Oilers prior to the face off at a game with the Toronto Maple Leafs at Rexall Place. Following the game, Edmonton Northlands, who operate Rexall Place, hosted the Grads at a private reception.

1987

- Premiere of the National Film Board and CBC production of the film *Shooting Stars* in Edmonton.

1989

- Edmonton Grads receive a Tribute to Women (Edmonton YWCA) Special Award.
- Edmonton Grads Park (entrance at 122 Street and 109A Avenue) opened with the unveiling of a commemorative plaque.

1990

- Dedication of "Grad Hall" in McDougall High School.

1991

- Travelling exhibition about the Edmonton Grads organized by the Alberta Sports Hall of Fame and Museum.
- Presented with a Great Canadian Award (nominations received from the public to honour Albertans who deserved recognition because of world-renowned accomplishments).

1995

- Canadian Sport Awards Female Team of the Year is named the "Edmonton Grads Trophy." This award is presented annually to Canada's outstanding junior or senior female team.

2001

- Edmonton Grads named "Female Team of the Century" by the Alberta Sports Hall of Fame and Museum.

2002

- Edmonton Grads Youth Basketball Association founded to honour the legacy of the Edmonton Grads by supporting youth basketball in Edmonton and the surrounding region.

2004

- "Queens of the Court: The Edmonton Grads" exhibition opened in November at the Royal Alberta Museum in Edmonton and continued until January 2006.

2010

- Edmonton Grads honoured by the Women's Basketball Hall of Fame in Knoxville, Tennessee, with a plaque bearing the names of all the Grads and J. Percy Page.

2011

- Opening of the GO Community Centre, a multi-sport complex on the University of Alberta's South Campus, Edmonton. The "G" stands for Grads.

Notes

1 How It Began

1. "Dominion Title Holders Given Civic Greetings," *Edmonton Journal*, 23 May 1922, 13.

2. A photo of the 1908 Lacombe team appeared in the *Edmonton Journal* on June 1, 1934 with a brief article on how girls' school basketball in Alberta began with the formation of the province.

3. "Five Basketball Teams in League," *Edmonton Journal*, 11 January 1915, 2.

4. "Commercial High Beats Camrose," *Edmonton Journal*, 29 March 1915, 11.

5. The Richardson trophy was donated by W. L. Richardson, the director of technical education for Edmonton public schools.

6. "Commercial Girls Tie League Series by Defeating Strathcona," *Edmonton Journal*, 19 November 1915, 14.

7. Ethel Anderson Moore, "Origin of the Grads," n.d., Edmonton Grads, File No. 2, CEA.

8. J.P. Page, Letter to Sporting Editor, *Edmonton Journal*, 4 December 1916, 9. Since the Grads always celebrated their anniversary counting from 15 June 1915, it is likely the club was formed a year earlier. See also Iva Hunch, "Commercial Graduates All Former Students of McDougall School," *Edmonton Bulletin*, 26 May 1924, 4.

9. J.P. Page, Letter to Sporting Editor.

10. The thirty-eight players whose names comprise the "official" Edmonton Grads begin with the 1922 team that won the first Dominion

championship and include those who played until the team disbanded in 1940.

11. J.P. Page to W.G. Carpenter, 30 September 1916. Accession No. 84.1.1048, Edmonton Public Schools Archives and Museum.

12. "H.B.C. Girls Organize for Basketball," *The Beaver*, June 1924, 344–45.

13. "Wilson Shield Changes Hands," *The Gateway*, 11 November 1920, 8.

14. "Commercial Graduates Claim Unfair Criticism By Varsity Publication," *Edmonton Journal*, 8 December 1920, 23.

15. "Commercial Graduates Club Elects New Executive," *Edmonton Journal*, 10 January 1920, 10.

16. " Commercial High School Girls' Basketball Teams Have Enviable Record," *Edmonton Journal*, 20 November 1920, 20.

17. "Commercial Graduates Basketball Team Made Big Hit in Saskatoon," *Edmonton Journal*, 16 December 1920, 18.

18. "Edmonton Woman Donates Trophy for Basketball," *Edmonton Journal*, 24 October 1921, 15.

19. "Varsity and Commercial Graduates Are Winners In Basketball League," *Edmonton Journal*, 13 January 1922, 18.

20. "Lethbridge Handed An Artistic Trimming," *Edmonton Journal*, 13 March 1922, 12.

21. Patricia Page, "Feminine Flashes," *Edmonton Journal*, 30 May 1936, 9.

22. "Commercial Grads Will Leave Friday in Quest [sic] Ladies Basketball Title," *Edmonton Journal*, 8 May 1922, 17. See also "J. Percy Page Gives Glowing Description of Champions' Trip," *Edmonton Bulletin*, 29 May 1922, 4, 7.

23. M.A. Kostek, *A Century and Ten: The History of the Edmonton Public Schools* (Edmonton, AB: Edmonton Public Schools, 1992), 212–13.

24. "Edmonton Basketball Team Swamps Londoners in First Game For Dominion Title," *Edmonton Journal*, 17 May 1922, 18.

25. "Random Notes On Current Sports," *Toronto Daily Star*, 15 May 1922, 8.

26. The Page family history is well-researched and documented in "The Honourable John Percy Page," in Sandra E. Perry and Karen L. Powell, *On Behalf of the Crown: Lieutenant Governors of the North-West Territories*

and *Alberta 1869–2005* (Edmonton: Legislative Assembly of Alberta, 2006), 493–512.

27. Philip Brimacombe, *The Story of Bronte Harbour* (Oakville, ON: Oakville Historical Society, 1976), 16.

28. "Introducing Grad Gallery," *Edmonton Journal*, 17 June 1936, 17.

29. Terry Jones, "Percy Page, Grads Greatest Ever," *Edmonton Journal*, 3 March 1973, 21.

30. "Pages Wed 60 Years," *Edmonton Journal*, 25 March 1970, 22.

31. Kostek, *A Century and Ten*, 212.

32. Carl Betke, "Sports Promotion in the Western Canadian City: The Example of Early Edmonton," *Urban History Review* 12, no. 2 (1983): 47–56.

33. *The Beaver*, July 1924, 380–82.

34. Henry H. Roxborough, "Give the Girls a Hand," *MacLean's Magazine*, 15 February 1929, 16.

2   Unlikely Civic Boosters

1. Patrick Lamb, "Deacon White, Sportsman," *Alberta History* 37, no. 1 (1989): 23–27.

2. George Mackintosh, "The Sporting Periscope," *Edmonton Journal*, 9 November 1939, 10.

3. Deacon White, "Much Credit Due Mr. Page For Developing Players," *Edmonton Bulletin*, 14 April 1923, 15.

4. The "Opposing Players" and "Opposing Coaches" snapshots, each containing a photo and brief write-up, appeared in the *Edmonton Bulletin* from 17 May to 25 May 1923.

5. "Grads Secure Commanding Lead in First Game," *Edmonton Bulletin*, 25 May 1923, 5.

6. "Letters to the Editor," *Edmonton Bulletin*, 1 June 1923, 5.

7. Susan K. Cahn, *Coming on Strong: Gender and Sexuality in Twentieth-Century Women's Sport* (New York: The Free Press, 1994), 42–44.

8. "Letters to the Sports Editor," *Edmonton Bulletin*, 27 June 1923, 7.

9. "Letters to the Sports Editor," *Edmonton Bulletin*, 9 June 1923, 6.

10. "Defeat Visitors by Score of 41 to 11," *Edmonton Bulletin*, 26 September 1923, 5.

11. Advertisement for the series in *Edmonton Bulletin*, 29 September 1923, 6.

12. "Brownies Supply Fans With Thrills," *Edmonton Bulletin*, 12 October 1923, 5.

13. "Grads Spread City's Fame on Continent," *Edmonton Bulletin*, 4 February 1924, 9.

14. "Rotary Hears Grads' Coach," *Edmonton Bulletin*, 5 September 1924, 3.

15. Ken McConnell, "Calgary Wants Winner, Propose Grads Play Remaining Games in South!," *Edmonton Journal*, 23 May 1939, 8.

16. Unfortunately, Percy Page's correspondence, records, and financial statements relating to the Grads have never been found, and it is likely they were destroyed sometime after the team disbanded. Although some of the Grads' trophies and belongings suffered in a disastrous fire that completely gutted McDougall High School in 1929, all their financial records were saved. When the Grads formally disbanded in October 1940, Page presented an audited statement of the club's affairs and offered to open the books to anyone who wished to examine them, but these have never been found either.

17. "Free Tickets to Game If You Know Your Grads," *Edmonton Journal*, 16 April 1930, 10–11.

18. Ken McConnell, "Grads Face Greater Difficulties Each Year In Keeping Record Intact, Paying Their Way," *Edmonton Journal*, 20 April 1934, 18.

19. "'Father of Basketball' Praises the Graduates," *Edmonton Bulletin*, 19 October 1926, 9.

20. Dorothy G. Bell, "Edmonton Commercial Grads Have No Equal Amongst Girls' Basket Ball Teams," *MacLean's Magazine*, 1 December 1923, 70.

21. "Dr. Naismith's Tribute to the Grads," in *"Sitting on Top of the World" 1915–1940* (Edmonton, AB: Commercial Graduates' Basketball Club, 1940), 7.

22. Elaine Chalus, "The Edmonton Commercial Graduates: Women's History: An Integrationist Approach," in *Winter Sports in the West*, eds. E.A. Corbet and A.W. Rasporich (Calgary, AB: The Historical Society of Alberta, 1990), 81.

3 Taking On the World

1. Alice Milliat to Percy Page, 12 September 1923. Copy reproduced in an Edmonton newspaper and found in Winnie Martin's scrapbook, Accession No. A2000-152, CEA.

2. Deacon White, "Sport is My Subject," *Edmonton Bulletin*, 25 April 1924, 5.

3. Deacon White, "Sport is My Subject," *Edmonton Bulletin*, 16 May 1924, 4.

4. Abbie Scott, diary, 1924, ASHFM.

5. Official Report of the *Fédération sportive féminine internationale* Congress, 31 July 1924, reproduced on an international basketball series scorecard between the Warren Elks and the Commercial Grads, Edmonton, 30 September and 2 October 1924. Scorecard held by Peel's Prairie Provinces, UAL.

6. See letter from the Executive Committee of the Commercial Graduates' Club to the Sporting Editor of the *Edmonton Bulletin*, 10 November 1927, 11; see also "The Olympic Committee and Commercial Graduates," *Edmonton Bulletin*, 1 December 1927, 13.

7. Ken McConnell, "Review of Sport," *Edmonton Bulletin*, 7 June 1928, 10.

8. Ken McConnell, "Review of Sport," *Edmonton Bulletin*, 9 June 1928, 10.

9. "Log of a Travelling 'Grad,'" *Edmonton Journal*, 15 August 1928, 7.

10. "Log of a Travelling 'Grad,'" *Edmonton Journal*, 15 August 1928, 7.

11. Mary Campbell, interview by author, 8 September 2000, Vancouver, British Columbia.

12. Robert W. Ikard, *Just for Fun: The Story of AAU Women's Basketball* (Fayetteville, AR: University of Arkansas Press, 2005), 33–39.

13. National Basketball Association, "Sam F. Babb," accessed 21 August 2011, NBA *Hoopedia: The Basketball Wiki*, http://157.166.255.30/index.php?title=Sam_F._Babb.

14. Bruce Kidd, "Canada's Opposition to the 1936 Olympics in Germany," *Canadian Journal of History of Sport and Physical Education* 9, no. 2 (1978): 20–40.

15. Alexandrine Gibb, "No Man's Land of Sport," *Toronto Daily Star*, 2 November 1935, 12.

16. "Grads' Mission Honors Name of German Ace," *Edmonton Journal*, 17 June 1936, 1.

17. Patricia Page Hollingsworth, interview by author, 25 June 1996, Edmonton, Alberta.

18. Patricia Page, "Feminine Flashes," *Edmonton Journal*, 21 August 1936, 6.

19. Patricia Page, "Feminine Flashes," *Edmonton Journal*, 26 August 1936, 11.

20. Patricia Page, "Feminine Flashes," *Edmonton Journal*, 16 September 1936, 12.

21. André Drevon, *Alice Milliat: La Pasionaria du Sport Féminin* (Paris: Vuibert, 2005).

4   The Grads 1915–1924

1. Although her husband's legal name was Robert Miller-Tait, he preferred simply Tait as his last name. Some of Winnie's children, grandchildren, and great-grandchildren use Miller-Tait and some prefer to shorten it to Tait.

2. "Star Performer," *Edmonton Journal*, 19 November 1915, 14.

3. "Opposing Players: Elizabeth Elrick," *Edmonton Bulletin*, 18 May 1923, 5.

4. "Commercial Grads Lose Popular Player," *Edmonton Journal*, 21 September 1923, 10.

5. "Capt. Eleanor Mountifield," *Edmonton Bulletin*, 22 May 1922, 5.

6. "Two Grads to Give Up Game Permanently," newspaper clipping in Abbie Scott's scrapbook, Edmonton Public Schools Archives and Museum, Edmonton, Accession No. 96.37.1.

7. Dale Grummert, "Dream Team 1924," *Lewiston Morning Tribune*, 2 August 1992, 3B. Information also came from letters written by Eleanor Vogelsong to Kay Sanderson in 1980. Sanderson wrote a book, *200 Remarkable Alberta Women*, and donated her research materials to the Bert Sheppard Library and Archives of the Stockmen's Memorial Foundation in Cochrane, Alberta.

8. "Who's Who on the Grads: Connie Smith," *Edmonton Bulletin*, 9 May 1924, 5.

9. Frederick B. Watt, "Kaptain Konnie," in *The Story of the "Grads": Being a Short History of the Edmonton Commercial Graduates' Basketball Club, Including a brief account of their European tour* (Edmonton, AB: Western Veteran Publishing Co., 1924), 4.

10. Wedding announcement of Connie Smith and Lloyd McIntyre in Daisy Johnson's scrapbook, Accession No. A93-29, CEA.

11. Ted Watt, "Seeking the Secret of the Grads' Success," *Edmonton Journal*, 14 June 1975, 15.

12. Deacon White, "Commercial Grads are Real Championship Team," *Edmonton Bulletin*, 14 April 1923, 15.

13. "Who's Who on the Grads: Daisy Johnson," *Edmonton Bulletin*, 15 May 1923, 5.

14. D.A. McCannel, "Teaching World New Hoop Tricks," *Calgary Daily Herald*, Magazine Section, 3 December 1932, 21.

15. "Varsity and Commercial Graduates Are Winners in Basketball League," *Edmonton Journal*, 13 January 1922, 18.

16. Obituary for Nellie McIntosh, née Perry, *Edmonton Journal*, 20 April 1991, G17.

17. "Who's Who on the Grads," *Edmonton Bulletin*, 11 May 1923, 5.

18. Deacon White, "Sport is My Subject," *Edmonton Bulletin*, 16 May 1924, 4.

19. "Two Grads to Give Up Game Permanently."

20. Watt, "Seeking the Secret," 13, 15.

21. "Opposing Players: Mary Dunn," *Edmonton Bulletin*, 22 May 1923, 5.

22. Mary Dunn Dickson, interview by W.J. Wood, July 1983, Petroleum Oral History Project, Calgary, AB, Accession No. RCT-503-1, GA.

23. "Who's Who On the Grads," *Edmonton Bulletin*, 10 May 1923, 5.

24. Elsie Bennie Robson and Mary Dunn Dickson, interview by Phillip Allen, 8 April 1980, Calgary, AB, ASHFM.

25. Deacon White, "Sport is My Subject," *Edmonton Bulletin*, 23 April 1924, 3.

5   Keeping It Simple

1. Frederick B. Watt, "The Winners," *Collier's*, 2 March 1940, 34.

2. Harold F. Cruickshank, "Tops for Twenty-Five Years," *Star Weekly* (Toronto), 1 June 1940, 7.

3. Clarence M. Hollingsworth, interview by Gord Goodwin, 19 November 1981, Edmonton, AB, ASHFM.

4. D.A. McCannel, "Wizard Coach Has Trained Wonder Team," *Calgary Herald*, Magazine Section, 3 December 1932, 28.

5. Page qtd. in Harold F. Cruickshank, "You Can't Lose," *Chatelaine*, September 1936, 41.

6. "Arnold Henderson to Take Charge; Page Will Remain as Manager," *Edmonton Journal*, 21 September 1935, 10.

7. Joe Dwyer, "Practices of Grads Are Perfect Drills; No Waste Movements," *Edmonton Bulletin*, 29 October 1930, 17.

8. Nora Delahunt Randall, "Ladies of the Court: The Edmonton Grads 1915–1940." *Makara* 1, no. 5 (1976): 13.

9. McCannel, "Wizard Coach."

10. Historica Dominion Institute, "The Great Teams," *History by the Minute*, accessed August 22, 2011, http://www.histori.ca/minutes/lp.do?id=13113.

11. Carl Betke, "Sports Promotion in the Western Canadian City: The Example of Early Edmonton," *Urban History Review* 12, no. 2 (1983): 53.

12. Pat Page, "Feminine Flashes," *Edmonton Journal*, 19 April 1939, 11.

13. Edith Sutton, "Frying Onions," accessed August 22, 2011, http://www.edmontonhistory.ca/prelaunch/citycalledhome/remember/rwindow.php?ResourceKey=5285.

14. Cruickshank, "Tops for Twenty-Five Years," 7.

15. "Commercial Grads Defeated Calgary All-Stars 28 to 0," *Albertan* (Calgary), 18 February 1924, 9.

16. "Calgary Girls Swamped By Champion Grads and Fail to Score a Single Point," *Calgary Herald*, 18 February 1924, 12.

17. McCannel, "Wizard Coach."

18. Jean M. Leiper, "J. Percy Page: An Ordinary Coach With Extraordinary Results" (paper, North American Society for Sport History, McMaster University, Hamilton, Ontario, May 1981), 7.

19. McCannel, "Wizard Coach."

20. McCannel, "Wizard Coach."

21. Cruickshank, "Tops for Twenty-Five Years," 7.

22. Arnold Henderson, "Commercial Grads Play Clean Basketball; Refuse to Reconsider So-Called 'Smart' Plays," *Edmonton Journal*, 21 May 1936, 6.

23. "Commercial Graduates Claim Unfair Criticism By Varsity Publication," *Edmonton Journal*, 8 December 1920, 23.

24. Ron Nichol, "A History of the Edmonton Commercial Graduates" (unpublished paper, 24 March 1972), Accession No. MS604.1, A94-15, Box 1, CEA.

25. Leiper, "Percy Page," 5.

26. Leiper, "Percy Page," 6.

27. Elsie Bennie Robson and Mary Dunn Dickson, interview by Phillip Allen, 8 April 1980, Calgary, AB, ASHFM.

28. Deacon White, "Sport is My Subject," *Edmonton Bulletin*, 30 April 1924, 4.

29. Janice Tyrwhitt, "The Grads Weren't Just a Team, They Were Virtually Invincible," in *Alberta in the 20th Century, vol. 5, Brownlee and the Triumph of Populism* (Edmonton, AB: United Western Communications, 1996), 267.

30. Stan Moher, "Noel MacDonald Named as Greatest All-Time," *Edmonton Journal*, 11 April 1944, 7.

6 The Grads 1925–1930

1. *The Beaver*, May 1924, 310.

2. Kate Macrae, scrapbook, Accession No. PR1970.27/6, PAA.

3. "World's Champions Defeat Varsconas By Score 12–11," *Edmonton Bulletin*, 23 February 1924, 2.

4. "Grads Given Real Battle By Detroit Team; Final Score Last Night 29–17," *Edmonton Journal*, 11 June 1929, 9.

5. Stan Moher, "See Here, Sportsman!," *Edmonton Journal*, 18 September 1945, 6.

6. Elsie Bennie Robson and Mary Dunn Dickson, interview by Phillip Allen, 8 April 1980, Calgary, AB, ASHFM.

7. Ken McConnell, "Sport Review," *Edmonton Bulletin*, 16 March 1928, 16.

8. Obituary for Elsie Norrie Robson, née Bennie, *Edmonton Journal*, 24 June 1999, E10.

9. A thorough search of online passenger lists (available through Ancestry.com) prior to 1920 from the United Kingdom to North America as well as border crossings from the United States into Canada has not turned up anything matching the Hopkins family.

10. "Hattie Hopkins," *Edmonton Bulletin*, 23 April 1925, 5.

11. Harriett McCleave Hopkins, W-300573, military service record 1942–1947, Privacy and Personnel Records Division, LAC.

12. "For Honour and Valour: Commonwealth Orders, Decorations and Medals awarded to RCAF Personnel during the Second World War (British Empire Medal)," Air Force Association of Canada, accessed 23 August 2011, http://airforce.ca/uploads/airforce/2009/07/ALPHA-HO.HR.html.

13. Several photos of Hattie Hopkins at the Camsell hospital can be found in *The Camsell Mosaic: The Charles Camsell Hospital 1945–1985* (Edmonton, AB: Charles Camsell History Committee, 1985), 171–72.

14. *The Camsell Arrow*, vol. VII, ed. I, May–June 1953, n.p.

15. Although an obituary for Hattie (*Vancouver Sun*, 16 August 1954, 22) states her middle name as McKeeve, her death certificate clearly indicates that it is McCleave (Registration No. 1954-59-008273, Vital Statistics Agency, Province of British Columbia) as does her military service record.

16. "Marguerite Bailey," *Edmonton Bulletin*, 6 October 1926, 9.

17. Adrian J. Brennan, "The Girls Take the Floor," *Converse Basketball Year Book 1930* (Malden, MA: Converse Rubber Company, 1930), 40. See also *Edmonton Journal*, 11 May 1929, 8.

18. "She'll Be Missed: Miss Mildred McCormack," *Edmonton Journal*, 10 May 1932, 13.

19. See, for example, Brian Bergman, "When Girls Ruled," *Maclean's*, 9 July 2001, 28–29.

20. Caster basketball team at Lacombe, Alberta, 1923, Accession No. NA-3876-31, GA.

21. "They Will 'Sub' With Grads," *Edmonton Bulletin*, 15 October 1927, 16.

22. "Grads Outscored Calgary Centrals 43–13 in First Clash of Title Series," *Edmonton Journal*, 18 March 1929, 20.

23. "Grads 'Little Sisters,'" *Edmonton Bulletin*, 24 March 1928, 21; "The 1928 Model of the 'Page Eight,'" *Edmonton Journal*, 24 March 1928, 33.

24. "The Sporting Periscope," *Edmonton Journal*, 15 October 1930,16.

25. *Retrospect: The Edmonton YWCA 1957–1991* (Edmonton, AB: YWCA of Edmonton History Project Group, 1993), 109.

26. "Edmonton Grad Dies," *Edmonton Journal*, 12 April 2000, B7.

27. Gladys Fry Douglas, interview by Kristin Chandler and Kerry Kadylo, 1 March 1991, Calgary, AB, ASHFM.

28. Harold F. Cruickshank, "These Girls Fight to Win," *Liberty*, 29 December 1934, 17.

29. "Ethel Catherwood Gives Exhibition of High Jumping," *Edmonton Journal*, 19 July 1929, 8.

30. Cruickshank, "These Girls Fight to Win," 17.

31. Pat Page, "Feminine Flashes," *Edmonton Journal*, 12 June 1937, 13.

32. Jim Farrell, "'Babe' Belanger MacLean Shunned Spotlight after Career with Grads," *Edmonton Journal*, 11 January 1999, B2.

33. "Grads Take 19-Point Lead Over Cleveland Basketball Team," *Edmonton Journal*, 28 October 1929, 8.

34. Interview with Judy Sivertsen, by telephone, 15 March 2010.

35. Jean Bruce, "Women in CBC Radio Talks and Public Affairs," *Canadian Oral History Association Journal* 5, no. 1 (1981–1982): 7–18.

36. Obituary for Margaret Kinney Howes, *Montreal Gazette*, 13 September 1995, F7.

7 Rhythm of the Years

1. James Naismith, *Basketball: Its Origin and Development* (New York: Association Press, 1941), 62.

2. Ralph Melnick, *Senda Berenson: The Unlikely Founder of Women's Basketball* (Amherst, MA: University of Massachusetts Press, 2007), 63–64.

3. J. Anna Norris, "Basketball—Girls' Rules," *Child Health Magazine*, December 1924. Reprinted in Helen Gurney, *Girls' Sports: A Century of Progress in Ontario High Schools* (Don Mills, ON: OFSAA, 1982), 37.

4. For more information concerning this philosophy, see M. Ann Hall, *The Girl and the Game: A History of Women's Sport In Canada* (Peterborough, ON: Broadview Press, 2002), 73–79.

5. "Random Notes on Current Sports," *Toronto Daily Star*, 2 April 1925, 12.

6. Canadian Women's Intercollegiate Basketball League, meeting minutes, 27 February 1925, University of Toronto Archives, cited in Anne Warner,

"Women's Intercollegiate Sport within a Patriarchal Institution" (MA thesis, Queen's University, 2005), 79.

7. "Expect Grads to Defend Championship Title Next Year," *Edmonton Bulletin*, 6 June 1925, 5.

8. Mary E. Keyes, "The History of the Women's Athletics Committee of the Canadian Association for Health, Physical Education and Recreation, 1940–1973" (PHD diss., Ohio State University, 1980), 48.

9. Alexandrine Gibb, "No Man's Land of Sport," *Toronto Daily Star*, 6 May 1939, 14.

10. "Mentor of Grads Denies Basketball is Injurious," *Edmonton Journal*, 17 May 1937, 13.

11. D.A. McCannel, "Teaching World New Hoop Tricks," *Calgary Herald*, Magazine Section, 3 December 1932, 28.

12. McCannel, "Teaching World," 28.

13. "University of Alberta Ladies' Basketball Five Defeated Calgary 'Bucks,'" *Edmonton Bulletin*, 10 March 1924, 5. "Cow Town" refers to Calgary.

14. "Remember the Last Time Chicago's Brownies Played Against the Grads Here?" *Edmonton Journal*, 11 May 1929, 8.

15. "Women's Basketball Teams Play Different Rules in the U.S. but Stenos Real Champions," *Edmonton Journal*, 29 May 1934, 10.

16. Robert W. Ikard, *Just for Fun: The Story of AAU Women's Basketball* (Fayetteville, AR: University of Arkansas Press), 40–41.

17. George Mackintosh, "Through the Sporting Periscope," *Edmonton Journal*, 4 June 1935, 8.

18. George Mackintosh, "Close to 13,000 Customers See Edmonton Girls Triumph in Great Basketball Series," *Edmonton Journal*, 8 June 1937, 8.

19. "Edmonton's Basketball Champions Win Series From Red Birds 45–19," *Edmonton Journal*, 6 July 1925, 15.

20. "Grads Overwhelm San Francisco Hoopers 62–2," *Edmonton Journal*, 16 July 1925, 15.

21. There is a wonderful scrapbook about this trip. It contains articles by George Mackintosh of the *Edmonton Journal*, who accompanied the Grads, as well as clippings from newspapers throughout the United

States and Canada. See Arthur Reid Lawrence, "The 'Grads' American Trip April 1926," Accession No. MS 421 A91-122, CEA.

22. Don Maxwell, "Girls War Like Amazons on Basket Floor," newspaper clipping found in scrapbook (see this chap., n. 21).

23. Maxwell, "Girls War Like."

24. From the *Edmonton Bulletin* (see this chap., n. 21).

25. J.P. Page, "What Coach Page Says," *Edmonton Journal*, 14 April 1926, 20.

26. J.P. Page, "Gamest Girls in History," *Edmonton Journal*, 16 April 1926, 29.

27. "Here's the 'Inside Dope' on Tour of the Grads," *Edmonton Journal*, 19 April 1926, 11.

28. There were four booklets in all (see details in Sources, p. 328).

29. The original statistical records accumulated by Gerald Whitley and Jake Buisman are in a loose-leaf binder preserved in the PAA, Edmonton, Accession No. 70.27, Box 1, Item 13.

30. Cathy Macdonald, "The Edmonton Grads: Canada's Most Successful Team, A History and Analysis of Their Success" (MHK thesis, University of Windsor, 1976), 23–24.

8 The Grads 1931–1940

1. Ted Watt, "Seeking the Secret of the Grads Success," *Edmonton Journal*, 14 June 1975, 15.

2. Jim Farrell, "Grads Player, Evelyn Cameron Dead at 89," *Edmonton Journal*, 13 February 2001, B2.

3. "Ex-Grad Greats Are Married," *Edmonton Journal*, 9 October 1939, 6.

4. "This Starry Pair Will Be Greatly Missed," *Edmonton Journal*, 28 September 1939, 10.

5. "Grads 'Blue' When Notified Guard's Injury," *Edmonton Journal*, 8 June 1934, 10.

6. "Page Machine Comes Back With Convincing Display," *Edmonton Journal*, 27 October 1933, 18.

7. "Game in Doubt to Last, But Champions Fight Back To Win in Great Finish," *Edmonton Journal*, 14 June 1934, 16.

8. Stan Moher, "Noel MacDonald Named as Greatest All-Time Grad," *Edmonton Journal*, 11 April 1944, 7.

9. "Introducing Grad Gallery: Helen Northup," *Edmonton Journal*, 13 June 1936, 9.

10. "Introducing Grad Gallery," 9.

11. "A Legend Lives On," *Edmonton Journal*, 24 August 1978, A1.

12. Frederick B. Watt, "The Winners," *Collier's*, 2 March 1940, 34.

13. Ken McConnell, "Present Rose Bowl, Gong as 400 Citizens Approve," *Edmonton Journal*, March 9, 1939, 6.

14. "Subs Performed Nobly for Grad Team," *Edmonton Journal*, 23 April 1937, 10.

15. "Teamwork Was the Joy, But Grad Winnie Reid Played to Win," *Edmonton Journal*, 8 February 1996, B3.

16. Nora Delahunt Randall, "Ladies of the Court: The Edmonton Grads 1915–1940" *Makara* 1, no. 5 (1976): 13.

17. Watt, "Seeking the Secret," 13.

18. Source unknown.

19. Obituary for Mary E. (Betty) Bellamy, *Edmonton Journal*, 28 May 2010, B10; Obituary for Jules Gardner (Bill) Chevalier, *Edmonton Journal*, 16 September 2000, B16.

20. "Gradette 'B' Team Beaten By Jimmies," *Edmonton Journal*, 28 December 1936, 7.

21. Harold F. Cruickshank, "Tops for Twenty-Five Years," *Star Weekly* (Toronto), 1 June 1940, 7.

22. George Mackintosh, "Champions Never in Danger Throughout Splendid Game," *Edmonton Journal*, 2 October 1939, 12.

23. Kay MacRitchie MacBeth, interview by author, 6 June 2007, Comox, British Columbia.

24. "Grad Clubs Sweep Hoop Title Play," *Edmonton Journal*, 27 March 1939, 6.

25. Barbara Schrodt, "Vancouver's Dynastic Domination of Canadian Senior Women's Basketball: 1942 to 1967," *Canadian Journal of History of Sport* 26, no. 2 (1995): 19–32.

26. "How Would These Two Women Basketball Players Rate in a Beauty Competition?," *Edmonton Journal*, 11 May 1940, 10.

9 Papa Page and the Family

1. Helen Northup Alexander, interview by the author, 8 June 2007, Sidney, British Columbia.

2. Harold F. Cruickshank, "These Girls Fight to Win," *Liberty*, 29 December 1934, 17.

3. Ken Bolton et al., "J. Percy Page," in *The Albertans* (Edmonton, AB: Lone Pine, 1981), 52.

4. Cruickshank, "These Girls Fight to Win," 17.

5. Betty Bawden Bowen, interview by the author, 11 July 2007, Oakville, Ontario.

6. Robert Collins, "The Deadliest Dipsy Doodlers in the World," *Reader's Digest*, May 1977, 52.

7. Patricia Page, "Feminine Flashes," *Edmonton Journal*, 25 April 1936, 11.

8. Collins, "The Deadliest," 54.

9. Sandra E. Perry and Karen L. Powell, "The Honourable John Percy Page," in *On Behalf of the Crown: Lieutenant Governors of the North-West Territories and Alberta 1869–2005* (Edmonton: Legislative Assembly of Alberta, 2006), 493; Edith Sutton Stone, "The Hon. Dr. J. Percy Page: Lieutenant Governor of Alberta," *Alberta Community Life* 5, no. 3 (1964): 11.

10. Harold F. Cruickshank, "You Can't Lose," *Chatelaine*, September 1936, 41.

11. Ron Nichol, "A History of the Edmonton Commercial Graduates" (unpublished paper, March 1972), Edmonton Grads File No. 2, CEA. Nichol interviewed Percy and Maude for what was likely a university assignment.

12. Nichol, "A History."

13. Robert Collins, "The Ferocious Young Ladies From Edmonton," *MacLean's Magazine*, 10 December 1955, 68.

14. Ken McConnell, "Present Rose Bowl, Gong As 400 Citizens Approve" *Edmonton Journal*, 9 March 1939, 9.

15. Brian Bergman, "When Girls Ruled," *Maclean's*, 9 July 2001, 29.

16. Daisy Johnson, scrapbook, Accession No. MS 604, A93-29, CEA.

17. Johnson, scrapbook.

18. "Boys Win, 27 to 25, in Family Score of Grads, Now Proud Wives, Mothers," *Edmonton Journal*, 6 September 1955, 18.

19. Helen Eckert, "Women and Competitive Basketball," *Journal of* CAHPER 26, no. 6 (1960): 5–8. Taking all thirty-eight Grads into account, they produced a total of seventy-one children. Seven Grads had no children and one Grad adopted two, but had none of her own.

20. Patricia Page Hollingsworth, interview by author, 25 June 1996, Edmonton, Alberta.

21. Dr. G.R.A. Rice, speech, 25 May 1965, Accession No. 604.1, A93-29, CEA.

22. Shawn Waddell, "Percy Page Still Lives at a Gallop," *Edmonton Journal*, 1 October 1971, 49.

23. "Funeral for J. Percy Page," *Edmonton Journal*, 6 March 1973, 3.

24. Service for Dr. Percy Page, 5 March 1973, cited in Perry and Powell, *On Behalf of the Crown*, 504.

25. "Mrs. J. Percy Page Dead," *Edmonton Journal*, 29 June 1978, B1.

10 Remembering the Grads

1. George Mackintosh, "The Sporting Periscope," *Edmonton Journal*, 7 June 1940, 10.

2. Patricia Page Hollingsworth, interview by the author, 25 June 1996, Edmonton, Alberta.

3. Patricia Page Hollingsworth, "With the Grads to Alaska," *Edmonton Journal*, 5 October 1940, 11.

4. "Famous Grads Officially Disbanded," *Edmonton Journal*, 16 October 1940, 9.

5. Barbara Schrodt, "Vancouver's Dynastic Domination of Canadian Senior Women's Basketball: 1942 to 1967," *Canadian Journal of History of Sport* 26, no. 2 (1995): 19–32.

6. "Grads Lauded by Aldermen," *Edmonton Journal*, 29 October 1940, 7.

7. "Boys Win, 27 to 25, in Family Score of Grads, Now Proud Wives, Mothers," *Edmonton Journal*, 6 September 1955, 18.

8. Edmonton Grads Club Newsletter, 2 March 1964, Accession No. A98-85, CEA.

9. Ted Watt, "Seeking the Secret of the Grads' Success," *Edmonton Journal*, 14 June 1975, 13, 15. The documentary filmed by ACCESS, and broadcast on television on September 5, 1975, has not survived.

10. Information about the GO Community Centre can be found online at http://www.gocentre.com/.
11. Terry Jones, *Edmonton Journal*, 15 February 1979, F1.
12. Full text in *"Sitting on Top of the World"* 1915–1940 (Edmonton, AB: Commercial Graduates' Basketball Club, 1940), 7.

Sources

Archival Material

The majority of archival material relating to the Edmonton Grads is located in the City of Edmonton Archives, the Provincial Archives of Alberta, the Glenbow Archives in Calgary, and the Alberta Sports Hall of Fame and Museum in Red Deer. Preserved in these archives are mainly scrapbooks, newspaper clippings, souvenir booklets, game programs, photos, and films. The items listed below are specific archival items cited in the text.

Dickson, Mary Dunn. Mary Dunn Dickson fonds, Accession No. M329, GA.

Lawrence, Arthur Reid. "The 'Grads' American Trip April 1926," Arthur Reid Lawrence fonds, Accession No. MS 421 A91-122, CEA.

Moore, Ethel Anderson. "Origin of the Grads." Unpublished paper, n.d., Edmonton Grads File No. 2, CEA.

Nichol, Ron. "A History of the Edmonton Commercial Graduates." Unpublished paper, 24 March 1972, Edmonton Grads File No. 2, Accession No. MS604.1, A94-15, Box 1, CEA.

Rice, Dr. G.R.A. Speech given at the testimonial dinner to the Honourable Dr. J. Percy Page, Lieutenant Governor of Alberta, May 25, 1965, Accession No. 604.1, A93-29, CEA.

Robson, Elsie Bennie. Elsie Bennie Robson fonds, Accession No. M7925, GA.

Scott, Abbie. Diary of the 1924 European tour undertaken by the Commercial Graduates, ASHFM.

——. Abbie Scott fonds, Accession No. 96.37.1, Edmonton Public Schools
Archives and Museum.

Smith, Janice, ed. *Edmonton Commercial Graduates Research Bibliography.*
Calgary, AB: Alberta Sports Hall of Fame and Museum, 1992.

Vogelson, Eleanor Mountifield. Information donated by Kay Sanderson.
Bert Sheppard Library and Archives. Stockmen's Memorial Foundation,
Cochrane, Alberta.

Articles

Bell, Dorothy G. "Edmonton Commercial Grads Have No Equal Amongst
Girls' Basket Ball Teams." *MacLean's Magazine,* 1 December 1923, 68–70.

Bergman, Brian. "When Girls Ruled." *Maclean's,* 9 July 2001, 28–29.

Betke, Carl. "Sports Promotion in the Western Canadian City: The Example
of Early Edmonton," *Urban History Review* 12, no. 2 (1983): 47–56.

Bishop, Elizabeth. "Percy Page and His Amazing Grads." *The ATA Magazine*
31, no. 6 (1951): 6–9, 36.

Bruce, Jean. "Women in CBC Radio Talks and Public Affairs," *Canadian Oral
History Association Journal* 5, no. 1 (1981–82): 7–18.

Collins, Robert. "The Ferocious Young Ladies From Edmonton." *MacLean's
Magazine,* 10 December 1955, 36–37, 66–73.

——. "The Deadliest Dipsy Doodlers in the World." *Reader's Digest,* May 1977,
51–55.

Cruickshank, Harold F. "These Girls Fight to Win." *Liberty,* 29 December
1934, 15–17.

——. "You Can't Lose." *Chatelaine,* September 1936, 21, 41–42.

Eckert, Helen. "Women and Competitive Basketball," *Journal of* CAHPER 26,
no. 6 (1960): 5–8.

Holmgren, Eric. "Percy's Girls." *Edmonton,* May 1981, 73–74, 76, 78.

Kidd, Bruce. "Canada's Opposition to the 1936 Olympics in Germany,"
Canadian Journal of History of Sport and Physical Education 9, no. 2 (1978):
20–40.

Lamb, Patrick. "Deacon White, Sportsman," *Alberta History* 37, no. 1 (1989):
23–27.

Leigh, Mary H., and Thérèse M. Bonin. "The Pioneering Role of Madame Alice Milliat and the FSFI in Establishing International Track and Field Competition for Women," *Journal of Sport History* 4, no. 1 (1977): 72–83.

Randall, Nora Delahunt. "Ladies of the Court: The Edmonton Grads 1915–1940." *Makara* 1, no. 5 (1976): 12–17.

——. "The Full-Court Flappers." *womenSports* 4, no. 11 (1977): 4–17.

Roxborough, Henry H. "Give the Girls a Hand," *MacLean's Magazine*, 15 February 1929, 16.

——. "The Illusion of Masculine Supremacy," *The Canadian Magazine*, May 1935, 15, 55.

Schrodt, Barbara. "Vancouver's Dynastic Domination of Canadian Senior Women's Basketball: 1942 to 1967," *Canadian Journal of History of Sport* 26, no. 2 (1995): 19–32.

Serfaty, Meir. "The Unity Movement in Alberta," *Alberta Historical Review* 21, no. 2 (1973): 1–9.

Sirrs, Tricia. "The Grads." *Amateur Sport*, Spring 1974: 10–12, 24.

Stone, Edith Sutton. "The Hon. Dr. J. Percy Page: Lieutenant Governor of Alberta," *Alberta Community Life* 5, no. 3 (1964): 9–13.

Toohey, Eileen Kell. "The Man Behind the Girl Behind the Ball." *Western Producer Magazine*, 27 May 1965, 21.

Wamsley, Kevin B. "Power and Privilege in Historiography: Constructing Percy Page," *Sport History Review* 28, no. 2 (1997): 146–55.

Watt, Frederick B. "They're World Champions." *Maclean's Magazine*, 15 January 1929, 8, 43–44.

——. "The Winners." *Collier's*, 2 March 1940, 18, 34–35.

Books and Book Chapters

Bolton, Ken et al. "J. Percy Page," In *The Albertans*, 52–53. Edmonton, AB: Lone Pine, 1981.

Brimacombe, Philip. *The Story of Bronte Harbour*. Oakville, ON: Oakville Historical Society, 1976.

Cahn, Susan. *Coming on Strong: Gender and Sexuality in Twentieth-Century Women's Sport*. New York: The Free Press, 1994.

Chalus, Elaine. "The Edmonton Commercial Graduates: Women's History: An Integrationist Approach." In *Winter Sports in the West*, edited by E.A. Corbet and A.W. Rasporich, 69–86. Calgary, AB: The Historical Society of Alberta, 1990.

Cosentino, Frank. "The Greatest." In *Not Bad, Eh?: Great Moments in Canadian Sports History*, 79–101. Burnstown, ON: General Store Publishing House, 1990.

Dewar, John. "The Edmonton Grads: The Team and Its Social Significance from 1915–1940." In *Her Story in Sport: A Historical Anthology of Women in Sports*, edited by Reet Howell, 541–47. Westport, NY: Leisure Press, 1982.

Drevon, André. *Alice Milliat: La Pasionaria du Sport Féminin*. Paris: Vuibert, 2005.

Ducey, Brant E. *The Rajah of Renfrew*. Edmonton: University of Alberta Press, 1998.

Frayne, Trent. "The Edmonton Grads: A Quarter-Century of Utter Destruction." In *Great Canadian Sports Stories: A Century of Competition*, edited by Trent Frayne and Peter Gzowski, 53–56. Toronto: Canadian Centennial Publishing Company, 1965.

Gilpin, John F. *Edmonton: Gateway to the North*. Woodland Hills, CA: Windsor Publications, 1984.

Grundy, Pamela, and Susan Shackelford. *Shattering the Glass: The Remarkable History of Women's Basketball*. New York and London: New Press, 2005.

Guttmann, Allen. *Women's Sports: A History*. New York: Columbia University Press, 1991.

Hall, M. Ann. *The Girl and the Game: A History of Women's Sport in Canada*. Peterborough, ON: Broadview Press, 2002.

Hult, Joan S., and Marianna Trekell, eds. *A Century of Women's Basketball: From Frailty to Final Hour*. Reston, VA: American Alliance for Health, Physical Education, Recreation and Dance, 1991.

Ikard, Robert W. *Just for Fun: The Story of AAU Women's Basketball*. Fayetteville, AR: University of Arkansas Press, 2005.

Kostek, M.A. *A Century and Ten: The History of the Edmonton Public Schools*. Edmonton, AB: Edmonton Public Schools, 1992.

Long, Wendy. "Basketball: The Edmonton Grads." In *Celebrating Excellence: Canadian Women Athletes*, 182–83. Vancouver, BC: Polestar, 1995.

McDonald, David. "Noel MacDonald, Basketball." In *For the Record: Canada's Greatest Women Athletes*, 53–60. Rexdale, ON: John Wiley & Sons, 1981.

McElwain, Max. *The Only Dance in Iowa: A History of Six-Player Girls' Basketball*. Lincoln, NE: University of Nebraska Press, 2004.

Melnick, Ralph. *Senda Berenson: The Unlikely Founder of Women's Basketball*. Amherst, MA: University of Massachusetts Press, 2007.

Naismith, James. *Basketball: Its Origin and Development*. New York: Association Press, 1941.

Norris, J. Anna. "Basketball—Girls' Rules." In *Girls' Sports: A Century of Progress in Ontario High Schools*, by Helen Gurney. Don Mills, ON: OFSAA, 1982.

Perry, Sandra E., and Karen L. Powell. "The Honourable John Percy Page." In *On Behalf of the Crown: Lieutenant Governors of the North-West Territories and Alberta 1869–2005*, 493–512. Edmonton: Legislative Assembly of Alberta, 2006.

Sutton, Edith Stone. "The Grads in Flight." In *Edmonton In Our Own Words*, Linda Goyette and Carolina Jakeway Roemmich, 291–94. Edmonton: University of Alberta Press, 2004.

Tyrwhitt, Janice. "The Grads Weren't Just a Team, They Were Virtually Invincible." In *Brownlee and the Triumph of Populism, 1920–1930*. Vol. 5 of *Alberta in the 20th Century*, 264–83. Edmonton, AB: United Western Communications, 1996.

Wise, S.F., and Douglas Fisher. "Noel MacDonald." In *Canada's Sporting Heroes*, 72–74. Don Mills, ON: General Publishing, 1974.

———. "John Percy Page." In *Canada's Sporting Heroes*, 76–78. Don Mills, ON: General Publishing, 1974.

YWCA History Project Group. *Retrospect: The Edmonton YWCA 1957–1991*. Edmonton, AB: YWCA of Edmonton History Project Group, 1993.

Taped Interviews

Alexander, Helen Northup. Taped interview by author, 8 June 2007, Sidney, British Columbia.

Bowen, Betty Bawden. Taped interview by author, 11 July 2007, Oakville, Ontario.

Bowen, Betty Bawden, Edith Stone Sutton, and Evelyn Coulson Cameron. Taped interview by Karen Larson, 29 March 1981, Edmonton, Alberta, ASHFM.

Campbell, Mary. Taped interview by author, 8 September 2000, Vancouver, British Columbia.

Cox, June Causgrove. Taped interview by author, 8 June 2009, Qualicum Beach, British Columbia.

Dickson, Mary Dunn. Taped interview by W.J. Wood for the Petroleum Oral History Project, July 1983, Calgary, Alberta, Accession No. RCT-503-1, GA.

Douglas, Gladys Fry. Taped interview by Kristin Chandler and Kerry Kadylo, 1 March 1991, Calgary, Alberta, ASHFM.

Hollingsworth, Clarence M. Taped interview by Gord Goodwin, 19 November 1981, Edmonton, Alberta, ASHFM.

Hollingsworth, Patricia Page. Taped interview by author, 25 June 1996, Edmonton, Alberta.

MacBeth, Kay MacRitchie. Taped interview by author, 6 June 2007, Comox, British Columbia.

Robson, Elsie Bennie, and Mary Dunn Dickson. Taped interview by Phillip Allen, April 8, 1980, Calgary, Alberta, ASHFM.

Newspapers and Newspaper Articles

Newspapers consulted were primarily the *Edmonton Journal* and *Edmonton Bulletin* between 1915 and 1940. Many newspaper articles about the Grads are itemized in Janice Smith, ed., *Edmonton Commercial Graduates Research Bibliography* (Calgary, AB: Alberta Sports Hall of Fame and Museum, 1992). However, many are also missing and it took an almost daily read of the sports pages in one or both papers, beginning in 1915 and ending in 1940, to fill in the gaps. Other Canadian newspapers were consulted for reports of games played away from Edmonton. Below are the few substantial articles published in newspapers about the Grads.

Cruickshank, Harold F. "Tops for Twenty-Five Years." *Star Weekly* (Toronto), 1 June 1940, 7.

McCannel, D.A. "Teaching World New Hoop Tricks." *Calgary Herald* (Magazine Section), 3 December 1932, 21, 28.

Watt, Ted. "Seeking the Secret of the Grads' Success." *Edmonton Journal*, 14 June 1975, 13, 15.

Whitehead, Eric. "Only 13 Years Ago." *Vancouver Daily Province* (Magazine Section), 27 June 1953, 16–17.

Unpublished and Internet Sources

Canadian Broadcasting Corporation (Radio). "Grads star centre Noel MacDonald recalls the team's glory days." CBC Digital Archives. Broadcast 13 June 1947. http://archives.cbc.ca/sports/more_sports/clips/4241/.

Canadian Broadcasting Corporation (Television). "The reigning queens of basketball." CBC Digital Archives. Broadcast 21 October 1991. http://archives.cbc.ca/sports/more_sports/clips/4214/.

Historica Dominion Institute, "The Great Teams," History by the Minute. Accessed 22 August 2011. http://www.histori.ca/minutes/lp.do?id=13113.

Keyes, Mary E. "The History of the Women's Athletics Committee of the Canadian Association for Health, Physical Education and Recreation, 1940–1973." PHD diss., Ohio State University, 1980.

Leiper, Jean M. "J. Percy Page: An Ordinary Coach With Extraordinary Results." Paper presented at the North American Society for Sport History, McMaster University, Hamilton, May 1981.

Library and Archives Canada. "The Edmonton Grads (1915–1940)." Last modified 16 September 2010. Celebrating Women's Achievements. http://www.collectionscanada.gc.ca/women/030001-1507-e.html.

Macdonald, Cathy. "The Edmonton Grads: Canada's Most Successful Team, A History and Analysis of Their Success." MHK thesis, University of Windsor, 1976.

National Basketball Association, "Sam F. Babb," NBA Hoopedia: The Basketball Wiki. Accessed 21 August 2011. http://157.166.255.30/index.php?title=Sam_F._Babb.

Russell, William. "The Edmonton Grads (1915–1940)." Miscellaneous Research Papers by William Russell, 1975–77. Manuscript Report Number 216, Parks Canada, Department of Indian and Northern Affairs.

Sutton, Edith Stone. "Frying Onions." Accessed 22 August 2011. http://www.edmontonhistory.ca/prelaunch/citycalledhome/remember/rwindow.php?ResourceKey=5285.

——. "Edmonton Grads Basketball Team on the Road." Accessed 22 August 2011. http://www.edmontonhistory.ca/prelaunch/citycalledhome/remember/rwindow.php?ResourceKey=5284.

Warner, Anne. "Women's Intercollegiate Sport within a Patriarchal Institution." MA thesis, Queen's University, 2005.

Official Records of the Edmonton Commercial Grads

Edmonton Commercial Grads. *The Story of the "Grads": Being a Short History of the Edmonton Commercial Graduates' Basketball Club, Including a brief account of their recent European tour.* Edmonton, AB: Western Veteran Publishing Co., 1924. http://peel.library.ualberta.ca/bibliography/4910.html

——. *Official Record of the Edmonton "Grads," World Champions: Covering 466 Games, 23 years of Play and over 100,000 Miles of Travel.* Edmonton, AB: Commercial Graduates' Basketball Club, 1938.

——. *"Sitting on Top of the World" 1915–1940: The Amazing Record of the Edmonton "Grads," official World's Basketball Champions, covering 25 years of play, 522 official games and over 125,000 miles of travel!* Edmonton, AB: Commercial Graduates' Basketball Club, 1940. http://peel.library.ualberta.ca/bibliography/6357.html.

——. *Edmonton Grads: 25 Years of Basketball Championships 1915–1940.* Montreal: Royal Bank of Canada, 1975. http://www.archive.org/details/edmontongrads25yo0cana.

Audiovisual Material

The Provincial Archives of Alberta houses several short, silent films pertaining to the Grads. Most of these are colour home movies filmed either by J. Percy Page or his daughter Patricia during the 1936 European tour and the holiday trips to Yellowstone and the Rockies. There is also a short black and white film showing part of their last game in June 1940. The most important audiovisual record is the documentary film *Shooting Stars*, directed and produced by Allan Stein (National Film Board of Canada, 1987, 50 minutes, VHS).

Index

McIntyre, Connie Smith, 94–96, *95*, 242. *See also* Smith, Connie

McIntyre, Lloyd, 96

McNeil, Isobel, *113*

Meagher, Aileen, 79

Mercantiles, 267, 268

Mets, Kay, 112

Michaels, John, 38, 42

Mike's News Stand, 38

Milliat, Alice, 50, 62–63, 76, 81–83

Mills, Frances Gordon, 220–22, *221*. *See also* Gordon, Frances

Mills, Oswin (Ossie), 222

Minneapolis Ascension Club, 272

Minnesota National Bankers, 153, 276

Mitchell, Iola, 4–5, *6*

Moir, Joe, 38, 42

Monaco, women's sports events, 50–51

Morgan, Ralph, 225

Mountifield, Eleanor
European tour (1924), 54, *54*, 55, *56*, 59–60, 270
as Grad, 2, 12, *13*, 14, *16*, 29–31, 33, 37, 40, *179*, 265–71, *269*
as Grad captain, *16*, 29–30, 92
life of, 92–93, *93*, *258*

Munton, Mabel
European tour (1936), 75, 77, *78*, *80*
first North American championship (1933), 72
as Grad, *250*, 284–97, *287*, 292, 295

as Gradette, 203, 285

life of, 77, 202–04, *203*, 252

as most reliable guard, 132

Murray, Elizabeth Elrick, *90*, 90–92. *See also* Elrick, Elizabeth

Murray, Richard (Rex), 90–91

Muttart, Gladys and Merrill, 257

Muttart Lumber Pats, 216, 224, 225

Nairn, Margaret, 154–55, 275

Naismith, James A.
basketball principles, 170–71
on the Grads, x, xii, 45, 46, 188, 261
the Grads and, 79, 162, 272, 279

Naismith Memorial Basketball Hall of Fame, 260–61

National Girls Baseball League, 218

Neale, Doris
European tour (1936), 75, 77, *78*, *80*
as Grad, 71–72, 74, 141, *250*, 278–89, *282*, 287
as Gradette, 112, 162
life of, 77, 162–64, *163*
Olympics (1932, Los Angeles), 69, *69*

Newman-Sterns (Cleveland), 189, 274

NFB documentary on Grads. See *Shooting Stars* (film)

NGBL. *See* National Girls Baseball League